LIFE IN THE SPIRIT

ROBERTSON MCQUILKIN

To. Virginia

Robertson McQuilkin

11-16-03

LifeWay Press
Nashville, Tennessee

Unless otherwise noted, Scripture quotations are from the Holy Bible, *New International Version,* © 1973, 1978, 1984 by International Bible Society. Other versions used: *New King James Version* (NKJV), © 1982, Thomas Nelson Inc., Publishers. Used by permission. *The Living Bible* (TLB), © 1971 Tyndale House Publishers, Wheaton, Illinois. Used by permission. *Good News Bible,* the Bible in Today's English Version (GNB), Old Testament: © American Bible Society 1976; New Testament: © American Bible Society 1966, 1971, 1976. Used by permission. *New American Standard Bible* (NASB), © The Lockman Foundation, 1960, 1962, 1963, 1968, 1971, 1972, 1973, 1975, 1977. Used by permission. *Revised Standard Version of the Bible* (RSV), © 1946, 1952, 1971, 1973. *New Revised Standard Version of the Bible* (NRSV), © 1989 by the Division of Christian Education of the National Council of Churches of Christ in the United States of America. Used by permission. All rights reserved. *The Holy Bible in the Language of Today* by William F. Beck (Beck), © Mrs. William F. Beck, 1976. Published by Holman Bible Publishers. Used by permission. *Holy Bible, New Living Translation,* (NLT), copyright © 1996. Used by permission of Tyndale House Publishers, Inc., Wheaton, Illinois 60189. All rights reserved. *King James Version* (KJV).

Order additional copies of this book by writing to Customer Service Center, MSN 113; 127 Ninth Avenue, North; Nashville, Tennessee 37234-0113; by calling toll free (800) 458-2772; by faxing (615) 251-5933; by ordering online at *www.lifeway.com;* by emailing *customerservice@lifeway.com;* or by visiting a LifeWay Christian Store.

For more information about adult discipleship and family resources, training, and events, visit our Web site at *www.lifewa.com/discipleplus.*

Cover Design: Edward Crawford
Cover Photography: FPG/Color Box

Printed in the United States of America

LifeWay Press
127 Ninth Avenue, North
Nashville, Tennessee 37234-0151

*As God works through us, we will help people and churches
know Jesus Christ and seek His kingdom by providing biblical solutions
that spiritually transform individuals and cultures.*

CONTENTS

About the Author 4

Foreword by Philip Yancey 5

Unit 1 THE SPIRIT AND THE SPIRAL 6
Life in the Spirit will examine 10 activities of the Holy Spirit and how they
impact your life as a disciple of Jesus.

Unit 2 DESIGNER MODEL 26
Activity 1: Creating

Unit 3 THE GREAT UNVEILING 42
Activity 2: Revealing

Unit 4 A NEW CREATION 60
Activity 3: Redeeming

Unit 5 INDWELLING: FAITH AND OBEDIENCE 78
Activity 4: Indwelling

Unit 6 SPIRALING UP 94
Activity 5: Transforming

Unit 7 EXPECTATIONS: 115
What can you expect from your life in the Spirit? Is the Spirit-filled life a matter of
resting or wrestling? perfection or failure? Can you really experience a life of victory over sin?

Unit 8 FILLED FULL 135
Activity 6: Filling

Unit 9 BATTLE PLAN 151
Activity 7: Overcoming

Unit 10 THE SPIRIT'S GIFTS 169
Activity 8: Gifting

Unit 11 POWER TO CHANGE THE WORLD 189
Activity 9: Sending

UNIT 12 A MARRIAGE MADE IN HEAVEN 206
Activity 10: Glorifying

Covenant 222

Christian Growth Study Plan 223

THE AUTHOR

Robertson McQuilkin

ROBERTSON MCQUILKIN is a homemaker, conference speaker, and writer.

Robertson served as president of Columbia International University, Columbia, South Carolina, for 22 years. In 1990 he stepped down to care full time for his wife Muriel, who had reached the stage of Alzheimer's disease in which she needed the care of her husband 24 hours a day. To his astonishment, that decision which he considered easy and unremarkable continues to reverberate throughout the evangelical world. Two articles about Muriel, "Living Vows" and "Muriel's Blessing," have been published in dozens of magazines and books in many languages.

Robertson and Muriel served in full partnership as missionaries in Japan for 12 years prior to his tenure at Columbia. In Columbia, Muriel spawned a host of ministries: a TV puppet show for children, a morning radio talk show, ministries among students' wives, along with constant counseling, entertaining, and various art projects.

The McQuilkins have six children. Mardi is an artist, living with her husband in Myrtle Beach, South Carolina; Bob is in heaven, having died in a diving accident in 1988; David is an executive with Xerox in Japan and father of two; Jan is a pastor's wife in Wisconsin and mother of three; Amy serves with her husband as missionaries to Japan and has three children; Kent ministers among the slum dwellers of Calcutta, India.

Robertson has written scores of articles for journals or as chapters in books and has published several books, three of which continue to exert wide influence: *An Introduction to Biblical Ethics* (Tyndale, rev. ed. 1995), *The Great Omission* (Baker, 1984), and *Understanding and Applying the Bible* (Moody, rev. ed. 1992).

FOREWORD

Dorothy Sayers tells of a Japanese convert struggling to grasp Christian theology. "Honorable Father, very good," he said to his missionary teacher. "Honorable son, very good. But Honorable Bird, I do not understand at all." Misunderstanding swirls around the third member of the Trinity, which is a great irony, for the Holy Spirit is the most personally intimate of the three. The Spirit lives inside us and prays on our behalf when we know not what to pray.

I readily admit to my own problems in understanding the Holy Spirit. I grew up in churches that used—and misused—the Spirit like some kind of magic genie. "The Spirit told me …" the pastor would say to justify some of his bizarre schemes. Members of the congregation talked about being "filled with the Spirit" and living the "victorious Christian life" even as they manifested glaring faults. In a denomination down the street, other churchgoers fell down in a trance after being "slain in the Spirit." As an adolescent, I developed a hard-shell resistance to talk about the Holy Spirit.

To break through this resistance, I needed a very wise guide: one who was down-to-earth practical and lived out the Spirit-filled life in a consistent, attractive way. I found such a guide in Robertson McQuilkin.

Robertson McQuilkin was reared in a home that hosted many of the leaders of the victorious Christian life movement. Growing into a mature faith, he always managed to keep his feet on the ground and his head in the clouds. He never lowered the lofty standards of the Christian life as described in the New Testament, yet neither did he deny his very real struggles with temptation and doubt. Twelve years in Japan, as a missionary in one of the cultures most resistant to Christianity, increased that sense of realism and forced a daily dependence on the Holy Spirit.

I got to know Robertson McQuilkin after he returned from Japan and became president of Columbia Bible College, where I was attending. There, I had the opportunity to observe his life at close range. As a teacher, he genuinely listened to students and their point of view. He never acted as if he were dispensing propaganda from on high; rather he gently and persuasively presented his own beliefs and perspectives. From that example, I learned that the Holy Spirit does not coerce, but rather coaxes and prompts.

Serving as president for more than two decades, McQuilkin led the school to a new plateau. For the first time the school attained fully accredited status from regional associations. New buildings were constructed, board members squabbled, faculty members came and went. I watched McQuilkin manage each of these challenges with a rare combination of humility and strength.

More important than these accomplishments, though—and I'm sure he would agree—I also observed McQuilkin in the role of father and husband. His oldest son, Bob, was my close friend until he died tragically at the age of 36 while scuba diving. Through Bob's eyes, I saw a long-suffering father who would let his children choose their own paths while praying earnestly for their spiritual welfare. Then in 1990, at the peak of his career, Robertson McQuilkin shocked the Bible College community by announcing his resignation. His beloved wife Muriel had developed an advanced case of Alzheimer's disease, and he resigned in order to become a homemaker and care for her.

McQuilkin has written two articles about his experience caring for Muriel, which have been reprinted around the world. The Christian life is put to the ultimate test when a man feels called by God to leave a position of prestige and influence in order to clean, change diapers, and care for the shell of a person who has been his partner and lover for 40 years. To students at Columbia Bible College, McQuilkin's decision offered a profound close-up example of sacrificial love. "Husbands, love your wives, just as Christ loved the Church and gave himself up for her," Paul urges (Eph. 5:25). I know of no more poignant illustration of Christ's love for us His church. The daily ministrations of Robertson McQuilkin for a wife whose mind is nearly vacant, who is in need of his constant attention is a picture of this love.

McQuilkin himself seems genuinely shocked that anyone would view his actions as exceptional. "I took marriage vows, didn't I?" he protests. In his own mind, he is merely living out in quiet faithfulness the promises he made nearly half a century ago. In the end, it is that kind of faithfulness that defines life in the Spirit—and you will learn from a master as you work through this course of intense practicality.

Philip Yancey

UNIT 1
THE SPIRIT AND THE SPIRAL

*Something happened to me in preparing this study, something I never expected.
When asked to write I was excited—hadn't I spent my whole life teaching
about life in the Spirit? And yet ...*

During World War I a powerful movement was born that emphasized a victorious Christian life. My father was a leading spokesman in the movement, so I drank the teaching in, along with my mother's milk. Such experience left me with high expectations for the Christian life. All my life I've been exposed to the teachings of spirit-filled living, and for several years I even taught theology at the college and seminary level. I knew all about pneumatology—the study of the person and work of the Spirit. As I look back, however, I see times that I allowed the busy-ness of life and knowing *about* the Spirit to crowd out actual time spent *with* the Spirit. Sometimes He was more like a friendly stranger than an intimate companion.

As I began again to focus on the person and work of the Spirit in preparing this study, I quickly rediscovered how His activity appears everywhere in Scripture—and in my life! I became more and more excited about our relationship. Every morning I awoke with high anticipation of what would happen between us that day. Often I'd awake early—at 3:00 or 4:00 in the morning—and couldn't sleep again, so consuming was the desire to see what new treasure the Spirit would uncover in Scripture that day. To my surprise, I found myself developing a closer relationship with Him—something we will call "spiraling up." As a consequence, I began to notice His working in me to make me what He created me to be—like Jesus.

Perhaps the Holy Spirit has been no more than a friendly stranger to you, a name you knew from the Apostles' Creed, "I believe in the Holy Ghost." Wherever you are today, you can experience a wonderful new relationship with a dear, personal friend—the Spirit of God. As a result you can anticipate a powerful transformation of life, becoming more and more what you were created to be.

This first unit is a road map—an overview of what you can expect in the rest of the study. Our theme verse for *Life in the Spirit* is also a kind of outline of the course. It's "my" verse, chosen early as a life theme, but it began to take on fresh meaning as I prepared this course. We'll study it in detail in unit 6, but it will be our memory verse for this unit.

Unit Memory Verse
*We all, with unveiled face, beholding as in a mirror the glory of the Lord, are being transformed
into the same image from glory to glory, just as by the Spirit of the Lord.*
–2 Corinthians 3:18, NKJV

> **What will I be studying in *Life in the Spirit*? What can I expect
> to learn? How will this study affect my life?**

DAY 1

GOD'S STANDARD

"Blessed are those who aim at nothing for verily they shall hit it!" states a popular proverb. We need to know what we're aiming at—in our jobs, marriages, responsibilities, and our relationship with God.

In this first unit, I will ask you to think about some very important issues. You may not have an answer to some of the questions and that's OK. We'll study the issues together. The point of the questions is to help you focus your thoughts as we begin this journey together.

    Here's the first question: What is your goal in life? What do you want to accomplish? I want to... Let God fully control my life
    ☑ survive with sanity
    ☑ build a good marriage with successful children
    ❑ make a bundle (= $_____?)
    ☒ become like Jesus
    ☑ maintain good health and happiness
    ☒ be filled with the Spirit

None of those objectives are bad, though some are more worthy than others. Since this course is called *Life in the Spirit*, you may have chosen "be filled with the Spirit." Whatever you checked, it's important to be honest about it.

If we want our goals in life to fit together and not compete, we've got to set an ultimate purpose that brings all the others together. Paul gives us a good goal: "We all ... are being transformed into the same image" (2 Cor. 3:18, NKJV). To be like Jesus! Now there's an objective that will purify and focus all our other goals. But why did God choose such a lofty plan for us?

God created us based on His design. So that's where we will begin in this study, with the Spirit's action of creating us. In unit 2, "Designer Model," we'll be thinking about what it means to be created in God's likeness. We're designed in some mysterious sense as models of the God who created us.

    Look at the course map for *Life in the Spirit*. The course map is the drawing on the inside front cover. It pictures 10 activities of the Spirit and our journey of living in the Spirit. The map begins with the first activity of the Spirit: creating.

God created us, but we rebelled against His purpose. On the course map you see the word we use to describe that event. We call it the *fall*. We became a fallen or broken model of God.

Because of the fall, we can't always act like Jesus. We fail to have His attitude about people or His kind of relationship with the Father. But God has a reconstruction program to take us—broken models of Himself—and re-make us into His likeness.

Before we come to know Jesus, we are all on the downward spiral away from God. His purpose is to turn us around and spiral us up toward ever greater likeness to Jesus: "We all ... are being transformed into the same image."

Before God could transform us, He had to get our attention and reveal Himself to us. So in unit 3 we will examine the Spirit's role in revealing God to humanity.

God created man in his own image,
in the image of God he created him;
male and female he created them.
—Genesis 1:27

All Scripture is God-breathed and is useful for teaching, rebuking, correcting and training in righteousness, so that the man of God may be thoroughly equipped for every good work.
—2 Timothy 3:16-17

"Do not think that I have come to abolish the Law or the Prophets; I have not come to abolish them but to fulfill them. I tell you the truth, until heaven and earth disappear, not the smallest letter, not the least stroke of a pen, will by any means disappear from the Law until everything is accomplished."
—Matthew 5:17-18

◎ **If you wanted to know what God expects of you or plans for you, how would you find out?**

❑ look at Jesus
❑ let your conscience be your guide
❑ watch other Christians carefully, especially the pastor
❑ try out the options and choose what works
☑ use the Bible as a road map
❑ make choices and, if it feels right, it probably is

Jesus is our model of what God is like. He is our standard. He is our goal. So the first answer would be good, except we don't know a thing about Jesus apart from the Bible. Besides, the Bible teaches us not only about Jesus but also about God and what He expects of us. The Bible is God's revelation of His will for us; it's our only sure road map for life. In unit 3 we'll ask some questions about the Bible and look at evidences of the trustworthiness of Scripture.

How can I know the Bible is reliable? (See 2 Tim. 3:16-17; Matt. 5:17-18 in margin.) Some folks say, "Try it and see for yourself." That's good common-sense advice, but the "what works is true" test won't do to prove the validity of the Bible.

What if my attempts to follow the Bible don't seem to work all that well? I try to do what I think the Bible teaches and everything comes unglued. Does that mean the instruction manual is unreliable, that it led me astray? Or does it mean I misread it and must study it more carefully? The bottom line is this: Jesus fully trusted the Scriptures. And I'm not smarter than He!

We have to lay a solid foundation. Some folks are impatient with foundation laying. They want to get on with the exciting truths about how to experience life in the Spirit—like the home builder who's so excited about the Jacuzzi for the second floor master bedroom that he neglects laying a solid foundation. Too bad for the Jacuzzi! We need to be sure of our foundation.

◎ **By way of review, mark the statements below with a T if they are wholly true and F if they are even partly in error.**

_T_ 1. God's standard for Christian living is His own character.
_F_ 2. The example of Jesus is the only way we know for sure what God wants of us.
_T_ 3. Humankind was originally designed on God's own pattern.
_T_ 4. None of us can measure up fully to God's standard in this life.
_T_ 5. The Holy Spirit is in the business of remaking us into something we are not naturally at birth.
_T_ 6. The Holy Spirit gave us the Bible to show us the way to experience life in the Spirit.
_T_ 7. The Bible is trustworthy because Jesus said so.
_T_ 8. God's plan is not to change us instantaneously into Christ's likeness, but to gradually remake us.
_F_ 9. The greatest evidence of the reliability of Scripture is that it works.

I marked all of them true except numbers 2 and 9. I don't think 2 is true because the Holy Spirit gave the whole Bible—not just the Gospels—to instruct us. As number 9 suggests, Scripture does work and that's reassuring. It strengthens our confidence, but the greatest evidence of the reliability of Scripture is that Jesus trusted it, not that it works.

Scripture is true whether it seems to work for me or not. If you don't understand why I answered any question the way I did or if you don't agree with my answer, that might be a good topic to discuss at your group meeting.

In summary, we must settle two questions. First, what is our objective? If we experience life in the Spirit, what will we be like? Second, who says so? How can we be sure that the people we listen to know what they're talking about? Units 2 and 3 will lay a foundation for our journey and help us understand the road map for getting there.

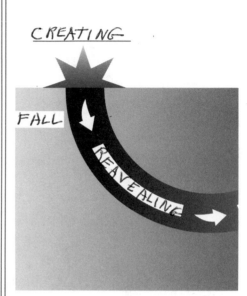

🌀 **A portion of the course map appears in the margin. Write on it the activities of the Spirit described in units 2 and 3. We use the word *fall* to speak of the entry of sin into the human race. Write *fall* in the appropriate place on the map.**

STUDYING *LIFE IN THE SPIRIT*

Life in the Spirit is a course in the Lay Institute for Equipping or LIFE. LIFE is an educational system designed to provide quality education in the areas of discipleship, leadership, and ministry. All LIFE courses have some common characteristics. These also apply to *Life in the Spirit.*

- Participants interact with a self-paced workbook (this is your workbook) for 30-60 minutes each day and do life-related learning activities.
- Participants meet for a one- and one-half to two-hour small-group learning session each week.
- The course leader (or facilitator) guides group members to reflect on and discuss what they have studied during the week and then make practical application of the study to everyday life. This small group becomes a support group for participants as they help each other come to understand and apply the Scriptures to life.
- An optional videotape provides additional content and learning experiences. The *Life in the Spirit* videotape assists the group to experience a relationship with the Spirit through learning, sharing, and worship.
- An attractive diploma from the Christian Growth Study plan is awarded for those who complete a LIFE course in a small-group study. (See p. 223 for complete details.)

This book is different from most books with which you may be familiar. Its design is not for you to sit down and read it from cover to cover. I want you to study, understand, and apply biblical principles to your life. This challenging goal takes time. To get the most out of this course, you must take your time by studying only one day's lesson at a time.

Do not try to study through several lessons in a single day. You need time to let these thoughts "sink in" to your understanding and practice. You are wanting to experience a Person—the Holy Spirit. Time and meditation are necessary to allow the Holy Spirit to work in your life.

Do not skip any of the learning activities. The assignments are designed to help you learn and apply the truths to life. They will help you establish a personal daily walk with God through the power of the Holy Spirit. Many of the activities are designed to lead you to interaction with the Spirit through prayer, meditation, and Bible study. If you leave out these activities, you may miss an encounter with the most important part of living life in the Spirit. Without an intimate relationship with Him, you will miss what He wants to do in and through your life.

◎ **The activities will begin with a symbol like this:** ◎ **pointing you to indented type. Follow the instructions given. After you have completed the activity you will return to the content.**

Normally you will be given answers following the activity, so you can check your own work. Write your own answer before reading mine. Sometimes your response to the activity will be your own response or opinion, and no right or wrong answer exists. If you have difficulty with an activity or you question the answers given, write a note about your concern in the margin. Discuss it with your leader or small group.

IMPORTANT ASSIGNMENTS

Spirit-led Christians through the ages have found great benefit in "journaling," keeping a record of what is going on each day in one's spiritual journey. What has God taught me today? What pain have I felt? What joy? What bewilderment? Journaling helps clarify thoughts, reinforce lessons learned, and keep a record for later review. Since during the next few weeks your life and your journey with God will focus especially on your interaction with this course, each day make your final assignment to visit with your spiritual diary or journal.

To fully experience life in the Spirit, we must not make it a solo journey. God intended us to live our lives in community. That's why He planned church—a local community of God's family to make the journey together, helping one another along the way. Part of church is the group with whom you may be working through this study. Sharing at the end of each unit is essential. In your weekly meeting you will discuss the content you studied the previous week, share insights and testimonies, encourage one another, and pray together.

To maximize the benefit you need a sharing partner, someone you can freely tell what is going on in your life as you work through the biblical truths about life in the Spirit. Just as a swimmer does well to have a buddy, in our spiritual lives the "buddy system" will keep us from many a tragedy and greatly enhance the potential for success in the Christian life.

These two spiritual disciplines—journaling and an accountability partner—would be a wonderful pattern for the rest of your life. But at least give it a try for the next few weeks as part of this course and see if you might not get hooked!

PRAYER AND THE SPIRIT

As we conclude each lesson in our study, we want to talk with God about what we've studied. We aren't trying merely to amass information about the Spirit, but to get acquainted with Him personally. I am going to suggest something that may be new to you. Most of our prayers, like most prayers in Scripture, aren't consciously addressed to one person of the Trinity. Sometimes we follow Jesus' example and pray specifically to the Father; sometimes we cry out to the Lord Jesus Himself, like many New Testament prayers. But usually we pray to "the Lord" or to "God," and we really are addressing the one God—Father, Son, and Holy Spirit.

In this course, because we focus on life in the Spirit, often we'll turn directly to the Spirit who lives inside to comfort us—that's what the Bible calls the "fellowship of the Holy Spirit" (2 Cor. 13:14; Phil. 2:1). That kind of prayer has enriched the church through the ages. Many of our great hymns are prayers directed to the Spirit: "Come, Holy Spirit, Heavenly Dove," "Breathe on Me Breath of God," and "Spirit of the Living God" are examples of such hymn-prayers. If that kind of communication hasn't been a vital part of your companionship with God, you can anticipate a wonderful enrichment in the weeks to come.

May the grace of the Lord Jesus Christ, and the love of God, and the fellowship of the Holy Spirit be with you all.
–2 Corinthians 13:14

If you have any encouragement from being united with Christ, if any comfort from his love, if any fellowship with the Spirit, if any tenderness and compassion.
–Philippians 2:1

Sometimes I'll suggest a prayer. If you feel the same way, don't hesitate to pray that prayer along with me. Or you might use it as a suggestion on how you want to formulate your own prayer. At other times I'll just suggest something you may want to pray about. Be sure to close each lesson by talking with God about the truths we've been studying. Here's my prayer for day 1 about God's standard for Christian living.

> Heavenly Father, thank You for Your incredible plan of creating me in Your likeness so that I can companion with You as best friends. When I broke covenant with You, sinning against Your loving purposes for me, still You loved me and planned a way for me to be restored to Your image. Thank You for showing me what I'll be like when I'm like You. Holy Spirit, thank You for the wonderful book You gave to show me the way. I want to study diligently to understand that plan and, more importantly, to experience it to the full. In Jesus' name I pray, amen.

DAY 2

GOD'S PROVISION

The 20th century could be called the century of the Holy Spirit. In 1901 the modern Pentecostal movement was born, and for the first time some identified speaking in tongues as the necessary evidence of being filled with the Spirit. The Pentecostal movement had phenomenal growth world-wide. Then in mid-century it broke out into mainstream denominations in what came to be called the *charismatic movement*. Finally, toward the end of the century, the missionary enterprise was inundated with an emphasis on *power encounter*, emphasizing the need for visible demonstrations of supernatural power to accomplish world evangelism. Many in that movement seemed to focus more on the enemy, the unholy spirits, than on the Holy Spirit. Still *power encounter* has grown directly out of the Pentecostal and charismatic context.

In reaction to this, many Christians have rejected all demonstrations of the Spirit's activity and have been afraid to emphasize the ministry of the Spirit at all. This attitude is a tragic loss since the Holy Spirit is the source of all spiritual blessing. We humans find it easier to take one side of biblical truth to one extreme or the other, neglecting the balancing truths of Scripture, rather than find the center of biblical balance. In this study we'll try to discover the core biblical teachings about the person and activity of the Holy Spirit. We'll explore the glorious truths on which we can all agree.

DIFFERENT WAYS OF UNDERSTANDING THE SPIRIT
Sincere believers differ greatly about how we relate to the Holy Spirit. All of the following attitudes can be found in the Christian community. You may find one or more of them express your thoughts.
- I've been baptized by the Spirit and the evidence was speaking in tongues.
- I've never spoken in tongues, but I would like to do so.
- I've never spoken in tongues, and I have no desire to do so.

- I'm not sure. I feel ambivalent about the experience some seem to have.
- I think the whole 20th century Holy Spirit movement is a grand self-deception or a delusion of the devil. Many are just plain fakes.
- I haven't spoken in tongues, but I have been baptized by the Holy Spirit.
- I don't know much about the Holy Spirit.
- I want to know more about the Holy Spirit. I want to experience all there is to experience of Him.
- I'm satisfied with my present understanding and experience of the Spirit.

Whatever your present knowledge or experience of the Holy Spirit, I hope you'll want to tap into His resources for living the Christian life. He has made full provision for you to do just that. Apart from Him there's no way you can experience a close friendship with God or become the person He intends you to be. We'll see how the Spirit works in our lives in unit 4, "A New Creation," unit 5, "Indwelling: Faith and Obedience," and unit 6, "Spiraling Up."

UNIT 4: REDEEMING

In unit 4 we will examine the operation of the Spirit in the process of redeeming fallen humanity. He brought about the birth, ministry, death, and resurrection of Jesus. The unit title is "A New Creation." The activity of the Spirit is redeeming.

Since the mid-eighties I've been computer-dependent in my writing. I was satisfied with the way my old computer worked–after all, it used to be state-of-the-art. But increasingly I experienced difficulties. Gradually I found my computer could "talk" with fewer and fewer other computers. It couldn't read what other people sent me. I began to use electronic mail, but the Internet was designed for speedy new models, not for my Noah's ark. I upgraded, but it wasn't enough. I needed a new model altogether. Dressing up the old one wasn't good enough.

Our experience with the Spirit resembles my situation with the computer. We humans were originally created God-compatible–we could communicate with Him. At least our first ancestor, Adam, could. But a breakdown occurred. I tried self-improvement–reprogramming my mind to think more like God so I could understand what He was saying in His Word–but it didn't work. I needed to be an altogether new model, a new creation (1 Cor. 2:14). That's exactly what the Holy Spirit provides–a new creation. My body and brain is the same, but when He re-created me He put a new spirit within me.

The inner workings of the new me are different from the old me. The new me is made God-compatible. Theologians call this change *regeneration*. It represents so radical a transformation, the Bible calls it "a new birth" (1 Pet. 1:3). Most of us, however, underestimate the potential in the new model. We don't tap into the resources the Holy Spirit has provided by making us new (2 Cor. 5:17).

In the list below, check the statements which sound like a person who has been re-created and cross through those that sound like a person who has not been re-created.

1. The Bible doesn't make a lot of sense to me.
2. I can sin, but I don't have to continue on deliberately choosing to sin.
3. I can't help sinning, and I enjoy sinful things.
4. I pray sometimes, but I'm not sure God is listening.
5. I feel uneasy around Christians who live out their faith.
6. I love to be around Christians who talk about God working in their lives.
7. I am growing in my understanding of spiritual truths.
8. I like reading the Bible, talking to my Heavenly Father, and associating with Christians.

The man without the Spirit does not accept the things that come from the Spirit of God, for they are foolishness to him, and he cannot understand them, because they are spiritually discerned.
—1 Corinthians 2:14

If anyone is in Christ, he is a new creation; the old has gone, the new has come!
—2 Corinthians 5:17

Numbers 2, 6, 7, and 8 are a few of the signs of someone who's been re-made by the Holy Spirit. What if you're feeling more like a 1, 3, 4, or 5 sort of person right now? Don't worry. If you've been born again the Spirit has already made you into something altogether new, so hang in there—we'll be studying all about how to experience the "new you." If you have never experienced re-creation or if you are uncertain, I encourage you to turn to pages 75-77 in unit 4 for an explanation about becoming a Christian.

UNIT 5: INDWELLING

Not only does the Spirit re-make us into new models, He begins a new personal relationship with us. His names hint at the personal aspect of our relationship. He is called Comforter and Counselor. Descriptions of His activity, such as convicting of sin and teaching us all things also point to His personal ministry in our lives.

> Can you think of any other names or activities of the Spirit that focus on your personal relationship with Him? List them in the margin.

Perhaps you responded with names or activities such as *the indwelling Spirit, Guide, Helper, walking with the Spirit, or being filled with the Spirit.* Actually the list is very long. We'll be studying about who He is and what He does throughout our time together. The Holy Spirit is God's provision for Christian living.

You might associate *indwelling* with the moment of salvation when the Spirit enters the new believer's life. In unit 5 we'll consider much more than that initial presence of the Spirit. We'll study how to tap into His infinite resources. We'll discover that His ultimate goal is not merely to make us like Jesus in attitude and behavior. The Spirit is making us like Jesus so we can have a love relationship with the Father—a relationship like the one Jesus has. The new relation is the beginning of an eternity of growing intimacy in our companionship with God.

> We can relate to God in several ways. Which of these phrases best pictures how you would like to experience your relationship with God.
>
> ❏ as Adam and Eve walked with God in the garden before the fall
> ❏ as Jesus related to His disciples in Palestine
> ☒ as the Christian may companion with the indwelling Holy Spirit
> ❏ as we all shall relate to God in our eternal home
> ☒ as the Father relates to His Son Jesus

People often speak of how wonderful joining the apostolic band and walking the roads of Galilee with Jesus would have been. But Jesus said another relationship is better: having the Holy Spirit living inside (John 16:7). Our relationship of immediate companionship with God in heaven will be something like Adam and Eve knew in the garden of Eden. Of course, the ultimate objective is to have the relationship Jesus described in His request of the Father: "That they all may be one, as You, Father, are in Me, and I in You, that they also may be one in Us" (John 17:21, NKJV).

"But I tell you the truth: It is for your good that I am going away. Unless I go away, the Counselor will not come to you; but if I go, I will send him to you."
—John 16:7

UNIT 6: TRANSFORMING

If you examine the course map you will see that it divides into two sections. The activities you have considered up till now appear on the lower half of the diagram. They are the activities of the Spirit in history and in bringing you into a love relationship with God. These activities take us from the moment of creation to our return to fellowship. The Spirit immediately begins to transform us into likeness to

Jesus. So unit 6 is called "Spiraling Up." It is about beginning the sanctification process, being made holy. The activity of the Spirit is transforming.

> On the course-map portion below, fill in the <u>first five activities of the Spirit</u>. Check your work with the inside front cover.

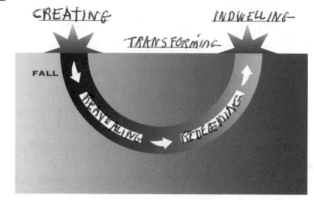

The second feature of the map is the spiral. The spiral represents the more individual and personal ministry of the Spirit. It pictures our growth into Christlikeness. The theological word for this process is sanctification. The five activities on the spiral are all part of the sanctification process. They all grow out of the basic unit called "Spiraling Up."

UNIT 7: EXPECTATIONS

As you examine the course map you will see that two units don't appear because they don't deal with a specific activity of the Spirit. Unit 1 is an overview of the course so it does not appear. Unit 7 deals with a critical issue to consider before approaching the remainder of the spiral: What can a believer expect from life in the Spirit? Can we be sinlessly perfect? Must we settle for a life of bondage to sin?

Take a moment to examine the outline on page 3. You can now see that the 12 units of *Life in the Spirit* will fall into a pattern. You are now overviewing the course. Next you will examine five activities of the Spirit from creation to the beginning of the Christian life. In unit 7 you will consider expectations, and then you will examine five more activities taking you from being filled with the Spirit to presence with God in glory.

UNIT 8: FILLING

So much controversy rages around being filled with the Spirit that I'm tempted to skip the subject altogether. But we can't do that! The New Testament contains far too much about fullness to pretend it's not there. So in unit 8, we'll examine the meaning of being filled with the Spirit. We don't want to skip the fullness theme for another reason; the truth is so glorious about our potential relationship to the Spirit. The only way to hint at the depth and height and breadth of the meaning is to say, "full"!

> What does the word *full* bring to your mind? Underline the first two or three terms triggered in your thinking when you hear the word.

total   all-absorbing   comprehensive   dominant   unlimited

unrestrained   extending to all parts   suffused   satisfying

<u>comple</u>te   <u>bountiful</u>   <u>abundan</u>t   other:_____

Now imagine any of those words describing your relationship with God! That kind of glorious relationship can be yours, not as a one-time event, but as a daily experience. Full!

When movies or fairy tales transform one creature into another, some secret formula or potion may work the magic. But God doesn't do it that way. When God reconstructs us in His likeness, He doesn't stay at a distance and send us a do-it-yourself kit. God's provision for changing us is very personal: He gives us Himself. The Holy Spirit comes and personally works the miracle. He makes new people out of us (unit 4), and then comes inside as a constant companion (unit 5). Better than that—He fills us up with Himself (unit 8)!

🌀 **Have you ever prayed to the Holy Spirit, addressing Him rather than the Father or the Lord Jesus? Why not close this lesson by thanking Him for all He has done, is doing, and will do? In your journal, write out your thanks to the Spirit.**

🌀 **Practice memorizing 2 Corinthians 3:18.**

We ... are being transformed into the same image from glory to glory, just as by the Spirit of the Lord.
—2 Corinthians 3:18, NKJV

DAY 3

MY RESPONSIBILITY

We've seen how God Himself, by the Spirit, has made full provision for us to spiral up into His very likeness and into intimate companionship with Him. But maybe that isn't happening. Maybe you're sort of plateaued out in your Christian life. Perhaps you are even starting to spiral down away from God. What's wrong? Why doesn't the Spirit-filled life seem to work?

🌀 **In the following list, check the response that best describes you at this time.**

❑ This is all new to me—I really don't know how to make it happen.
❑ It's too good to be true. It might happen for some people, but I can't see it working for me. Maybe I'm too difficult a case for God.
❑ I know exactly what's wrong. I won't let go of something.
❑ I seem to have drifted out of reach. Things aren't like they used to be. I need to come back into that first relationship I had with God.
☑ I'm growing, but my slow growth rate concerns me.

This list just about exhausts the possible reasons Christians fail to grow:
 1) I may be ignorant of God's provision or of my responsibility;
 2) I may have unbelief, lack of confidence in God;
 3) I may be practicing disobedience.
If disobedience is the problem, it can occur in two different ways:
 • conscious rejection of God's known will or
 • unconscious drift out of a close relationship.

A BIBLICAL EXAMPLE
Jacob wrestled all night with the angel, holding out for God's full blessing (Gen. 32:22-32). I guess he thought he could force God's hand, which was futile; but he

knew what he was after. Because he was so sincere, so determined in his quest for spiritual blessing, he finally won out. God gave Jacob the blessing he sought. Of course Jacob took a heavy hit—the angel gave him a permanent limp to remind him that God is in charge after all, and He alone is the source of all good.

> **When we get so desperate in our wrestlings with God that we are prepared to obey no matter the cost, the promised power will flow. The turning point for the sinner is called *repentance*. In the life of a wayward saint it's sometimes called *reconsecration* or *recommitment*. How would you define or describe repentance?**

Admitting my own powerlessness and asking God to take control of my life and give me His strength to turn my life around.

Christians through the ages have described this turning point in a number of ways. Like Jacob, some say they wrestled with God. Some say the love of Jesus overwhelmed them. They realized that rebellion against God is an affront to His love. Others have seen their arrogance and been humbled by the example of Jesus as the suffering servant.

Other words for repentance include: *yield, surrender, commit, abandon self, change management, get off the throne of my life and let God take His rightful place,* or *acknowledge Christ's lordship.* No matter how the Spirit breaks through to us, we must finally come to the place where we give in unconditionally. We say "I quit, you win!" That's the turning point.

> **Have you had such a turning point since your initial turning to God, your salvation repentance? If you have, write out your story in a paragraph, either here or in your journal.**

_____

_____

_____

_____

Here's a simple summary of how disobedience worked in my life. At first I knew I was saved and I thought that was enough. I didn't worry much about what salvation was supposed to produce in my life. Both the goal and the way to the goal were blurry in my thinking, but I sensed something was lacking. Surely Christianity was more than a fire-insurance policy! The Holy Spirit convicted me of my sin. As a result I turned my life over to Him unconditionally.

Unfortunately, I was still in the passive mode. My motto was: "God, You shove and I'll move." I wasn't eager to find out how to make Him happy. I wasn't trusting Him for any miracle change in my life, but a longing for a more genuine Christian experience began to grow in me. Finally, I had a moment of enlightenment—I realized that He has made full provision to do in me what I can't do on my own, and He will do it if I only trust Him.

I accepted that moment of enlightenment as God's word to me. I began to trust Him to keep the promises in His Word. I began to grow. I began to understand more about God's ways and experience the Spirit in my life.

🌀 **Carefully read "Holy Spirit, Light Divine," appearing in the margin. Circle the descriptions of the Spirit. Then read it again. This time underline the benefits the Spirit works in the believer.**

Trust is central to our Christian experience. Trusting comes before yielding. We won't surrender to God until we trust Him. But trust follows commitment as well. Sometimes "simply trusting" turns out to be not so simple! Since faith is a combination of yielding and trusting, we'll also consider what we can do to increase our faith. Trust, whether in human beings or in God, must grow.

We know that an electric appliance must be plugged in to operate. The plug-in that got me moving had two prongs: *trust* and *yield*. We'll study how to plug in to Holy Spirit power.

Of course we cannot trust someone we do not know. Faith implies knowledge. To have faith you have to know the Holy Spirit. You must know how He acts, whether or not He is dependable, and how to connect with Him. Ignorance can keep you disconnected. Thus the three elements of knowing, yielding, and trusting go together. They build upon each other. Stated negatively, three roots can result in failure in the Christian life: ignorance, unbelief, and unyieldedness.

🌀 **For each of the following spiritual ailments diagnose the problem using the following key:**
K – Knowledge deficiency. Put a K by those whose basic problem seems to be ignorance of what God wants or how to get there.
Y – Will distortion. Put a Y (Yield) by those whose basic problem seems to be a spirit of unyieldedness.
T – Trust deficiency. Put a T by those who seem to have a lack of confidence in God. Some may need both Y and T!

Y ___ Jim believes he has to practice a little deception to make his business succeed. He refuses to change his practices.

K ___ Mary is amazed at the way some of the Christians she's recently gotten acquainted with seem to be so full of joy and strength. They remind her of Jesus, in a way, and she'd like to be that way but doesn't know how.

T ___ Janet keeps stumbling around in her Christian life, trying first one thing and then another. She wants desperately to please God, but the strength just isn't there.

T~Y ___ Terry can't seem to break his bondage to alcohol.

T ___ Bill struggles with a bad temper, and try as he might he can't overcome it.

K-Y ___ Helen was only 12 when she was baptized. Still, she was elated with her new friend, Jesus, and her hope of heaven. But she was a busy girl and did not attend church faithfully. On Sundays she feels a little uneasy like something is wrong.

Y-T ___ Derrick finally gave in and admitted God wanted him to teach that Sunday School class, but he was afraid and put it off. His failure to follow-through seems to be affecting other parts of his life.

Y ___ Susan knows she shouldn't marry an unbeliever, but this may be her last chance and besides, she loves Harry. She's going ahead with wedding plans.

Who is obviously in need of knowledge? Mary certainly is. Mary's problem is ignorance—she never learned what the Christian life is all about. Helen's problem

---

Holy Spirit, Light Divine

Holy Spirit, Light divine,
Shine upon this heart of mine;
Chase the shades of night away,
Turn my darkness into day.

Holy Spirit, Power divine,
Cleanse this guilty heart of mine;
Long has sin without control
Held dominion o'er my soul.

Holy spirit, Joy divine,
Cheer this saddened heart of mine;
Bid my many woes depart,
Heal my wounded, bleeding heart.

Holy Spirit, all divine,
Dwell within this heart of mine;
Cast down every idol throne,
Reign supreme, and reign alone,'
—Andrew Reed

may be partly ignorance, too, but she definitely has a "yield" problem as well. She needs to do at least what she knows to be right. If she went to church she just might discover there's more to the Christian life. Jim and Susan also have clear-cut yield problems: they'll get nowhere till they decide to choose obedience to God over their selfish desires. Janet and Bill have a common need: to grow in trusting the Holy Spirit to do what they can't. Terry has one of the toughest problems. As with most people with addiction, he needs both a new surrender and a new level of confidence in the Spirit's power. Derrick needs to yield and trust, too.

PROACTIVE FAITH

We tend to go to one of two unbiblical extremes regarding faith:
• We disregard faith and seek to live on our own power, or
• We take a spectator role and wait for God to work.

The Bible does not teach either extreme. We need to participate *with* the Spirit in His activity in our lives. This Christian life is a hot war. We need a battle strategy that works. In unit 9 we'll develop an effective battle strategy—one custom designed just for you. The title for the unit is Battle Plan, and on the course map the activity of the Spirit is *overcoming*.

List below the ways the Spirit strengthens you as you join Him in confronting the enemy and winning your spiritual battles.

SUFFERING – PRAYER – BIBLE – CHURCH

You may have mentioned prayer, the Bible, and the church. Did you also mention suffering? We'll learn that the Spirit uses circumstances and gifts we may never have imagined as weapons in our war against sin.

In this lesson we've overviewed some of the basic truths about our responsibility and God's provision for Christian living. One of the first steps toward living *Life in the Spirit* is to understand God's provision. Then we must move from understanding to obeying.

Failure to respond obediently to the Holy Spirit damages our relationship with Him because disobedience distorts our belief system. Our beliefs ought to determine our behavior, but unfortunately, the opposite is often the case. Unless we become people who live very purposefully, we will follow the pattern below.
1. We experience temptation.
2. Rather than examine our value system and choose right, we give in to temptation.
3. We feel guilty because we have violated our value system.
4. So we twist our beliefs and values to relieve our guilt.

When we live in disobedience, we automatically twist our understanding to rationalize our behavior. Thus we blind ourselves to an accurate understanding of the Spirit and of the Christian life. Therefore, as you study *Life in the Spirit*, I will challenge you often at the point of obedience. I will challenge you to make the decision to trust and yield yourself to God. Then I will challenge you to carry out that decision by committing each area of your life to Him.

Have you linked up with the Spirit by yielding to His will and trusting in His power? The trust will grow, but the yield part you can settle right now. Tell Him you're not able on your own to live life as He intended but that you want to live a life of obedience. Commit yourself to God, through Jesus Christ, by the power of the Spirit. Ask Him to make you into Christ's likeness. Don't write conditional clauses in the contract, just respond to the Spirit with a simple, straightforward, complete, "Yes!"

Perhaps you have already yielded completely to the Spirit of God. This would be a good time to reaffirm that and ask Him to increase your faith through these studies and spiral you up into ever greater likeness to the Son. Thank Him, too, for the intimate companionship He offers.

🌀 **If the heart-cry of Charles Wesley matches your own, you may wish to use his hymn that appears in the margin as a prayer.**

🌀 **Below write the memory verse for this unit.**

We are being transformed into the same image from glory to glory, just as By the Spirit of the Lord.
II Cor. 3:18 (NKJV)

D A Y   4

RESULTS

God Himself is both the standard for the Christian life and the provision for reaching that standard. Our responsibility to connect with that provision is faith, with its two parts—yield and trust. When we yield and trust what can we expect as a result? Here again, sadly, we're tempted to go to one extreme or the other, either expecting too little of our lives in the Spirit, or having unbiblically high expectations.

🌀 **To see how our expectations influence life in the Spirit, discriminate among the following examples by marking + for those that seem to expect too much, - by those that expect too little, and a check (✓) by those that seem about right.**

- _+_ 1. Since I've been filled with the Spirit I need never struggle with temptation again.
- _✓_ 2. I sin often every day, knowing it's wrong but doing it anyway.
- _+_ 3. Since I was baptized in the Spirit, I haven't sinned in thought, word, or deed.
- _✓_ 4. I've been growing more like Jesus; I'm not at all what I used to be.
- _✓_ 5. The same temptation zaps me almost every day.
- ___ 6. The Holy Spirit is sort of like a friendly stranger to me.
- ___ 7. The Bible seems so dry, reading it is like eating sawdust and it's mostly irrelevant anyway.
- ___ 8. Prayer is a formal routine even when I get around to serious praying.
- ___ 9. I'm far from perfect, but friends and family say I've changed a lot.
- _✓_ 10. I love church and working for the Lord.

One reason we tend to go to an extreme is that the Bible itself emphasizes both sides of the truth about our Christian experience. For example, John says some puzzling things:

Depth of Mercy

Depth of mercy! can there be
Mercy still reserved for me?
Can my God His wrath forbear,
And the chief of sinners spare?

I my Master have denied;
I afresh have crucified,
Oft profaned His hallowed name,
Put Him to an open shame.

Now incline me to repent;
Let me now my sins lament;
Now my foul revolt deplore,
Weep, believe, and sin no more.

There for me the Savior stands,
Holding forth His wounded hands;
God is love! I know, I feel,
Jesus weeps and loves me still.
—Charles Wesley

"If we claim to be without sin, we deceive ourselves and the truth is not in us" (1 John 1:8).

"He who does what is sinful is of the devil.... No one who is born of God will continue to sin" (1 John 3:8-9).

The two passages seem contradictory, don't they? We'll study these puzzling passages in detail in unit 7, Expectations. However, two truths, are clear:

If you think you can have an experience that will remove all possibility of failure, and eliminate spiritual combat, you're badly deceived.

If you think you can live as you please, continuing in deliberate sin and still be OK with God, you're even more deceived.

In the last exercise I marked + by 1 and 3, – by 2, 5, 6, 7, 8, and ✓ by 4, 9, 10.

Terry was way out of alignment with God. He'd gotten into drugs and partying quite naturally—his parents were alcoholics. When he came to Christ the change was dramatic. But he had a long way to go. Although he was fun to be with, outgoing and smart, he didn't sound much like Jesus and he sure didn't act like Him!

Terry did, however, have one characteristic I've never quite seen in anyone else. Like many, he found admitting he was wrong or seeing what God expected of him difficult; but once he saw it, he changed. Period.

When he finally saw, for example, that he shouldn't spend all his time out talking to everyone else, but needed to spend some of his time at home with his wife and children, he just changed. I'm glad he did, because my daughter is his wife! He rearranged his entire life pattern to do right. In one area after another, Terry would finally see the truth, accept it, and spiral up a notch into greater likeness to Jesus. The Bible calls it the fruit of the Spirit.

Here's how it works. We all start out at a distance from God, some further away, less like Him than others:

The fruit of the Spirit is love, joy, peace, patience, kindness, goodness, faithfulness, gentleness and self-control. Against such things there is no law.
—Galatians 5:22-23

Terry
"Terry was about here—not perfect, like Christ, to be sure, but not nearly as bad as he might have been."

As a starting point, mark with an X on the spiral above some arbitrary point you might have been when you were saved. You weren't as bad as you might have been. But you were alienated from God, so don't put that starting point too high, either! Now put an asterisk (*) at the stage you think you are now, indicating how much you've grown and how far you have to go. Finally mark an up arrow or a down arrow to indicate the direction your life has been going the past year.

When we make the big turnaround, yielding to God's will and trusting Him to work, the Holy Spirit begins to change us. We become more like Jesus in our attitudes, in our view of things, in our goals and ambitions, in our responses and behavior. Consequently, we get closer and closer to Him in daily companionship (2 Cor. 3:18). The more we know Him, the more we love Him; the more we love Him, the more we want to be with Him; the more we're with Him the more we want to be like Him; the more we change to be like Him, the better we know Him, the more we love Him—the spiral continues toward likeness to Christ and a greater love relationship with God.

BEST FRIENDS

The ultimate goal God has in mind for you isn't merely a change in character to resemble Jesus. God intends for you to be like Jesus in another way, in your intimate love relationship with the Father. That's not only the grand climax of your existence as a redeemed human being, it's also the finale of our study. In unit 12 we'll deal with what it means to be best friends here and now, and how to experience that intimacy.

For starters, write here the name of one of your best (human) friends:

_____

How did you get to be such good friends? In other words, what helped the friendship grow? Name a few of the factors that come to mind.

_____

_____

_____

Here are some possibilities I thought of: spend time together; give/receive special gifts; make some sacrifice for each other, do something your friend wants to do that you don't; go through tough times—weep together; do fun things—laugh together; decide to focus on your friend's good points and not the weaknesses; choose to accept differences.

In the paragraph above and the list you wrote, number the five most important factors which bonded you with the person you named above.

God wants to be your best friend. Go back to your list, and circle those factors that bond you to Him. Pause now and ask God to make this much more than a study; ask Him to bond you to Himself as you think for 12 weeks about the wonderful Holy Spirit.

In this lesson we've looked at the results we can expect—and can't expect—from the activity of the Spirit, results we'll look at closely in units 6-9 and 12. To summarize: you can expect to spiral up into ever greater likeness to Jesus Christ and ever more intimate companionship with Him.

Practice repeating 2 Corinthians 3:18 from memory. Make it a habit to end every day's lesson with a time of Scripture memory.

We all, with unveiled face, beholding as in a mirror the glory of the Lord, are being transformed into the same image from glory to glory, just as by the Spirit of the Lord.
—2 Corinthians 3:18, NKJV

REACHING OUT

In studying the activity of the Spirit in our lives, we could become very introspective, even self-oriented. We live in an age of radical individualism and some people might see "spiraling up" as a very exclusive relationship between God and me. But the Holy Spirit won't let that happen! We were born in community and we were designed to live in community. Furthermore, the more like God we become the more we'll be oriented outward, preoccupied with others, not with self. And the startling thing is this: God has chosen to do His work in the world through us! So a major activity of the Holy Spirit is to get God's purposes on planet earth accomplished through His people reaching out.

SPIRIT-INFUSED CAPABILITIES

"People reaching out," however, does not mean individuals doing God's work independently of one another. God's method is called the church. The Spirit of God works primarily through and in relation to the church.

☺ **List tasks that are done or need to be done in your local church:**

_____

_____

_____

Did you name preaching, teaching, serving meals, counseling, ushering, singing, leading, managing money, helping those with physical or material needs, playing a musical instrument, evangelizing, starting new churches? Now underscore every activity that only the Spirit can make happen.

Actually, if we expect spiritual impact from any activity, the Spirit has to be involved! If you want those tasks in the church to have spiritual results, you should have marked all of them. When the Spirit supplies you with some ability to serve, it's called a gift. Spiritual gifts are not just natural abilities, though such talents are also gifts from God and used by Him to accomplish His purposes. A Spirit-gift points to something beyond our natural abilities.

Think of two jobs in the church. How could we tell if the person doing them has the touch of the Spirit on his or her work? For example, what might result from a naturally gifted person's teaching in Sunday School and what might happen if the Spirit worked through the teacher?

☺ **The phrases appearing in the margin describe what people do as the result of a teacher with either natural ability or spiritual giftedness. Below write each number under either natural or spiritual giftedness.**

Natural gift of teaching   Spirit gift of teaching

_____   _____

Under natural ability you may have put things like: people listen, it's interesting; people learn. Under the Spirit's gift you may have put things such as: people

People:
1. listen
2. understand spiritual truth
3. begin to act on spiritual truth
4. are interested
5. learn
6. experience the Bible coming to life
7. experience changed lives
8. grow spiritually

understand spiritual truth and begin to act on it; the Bible seems to come alive; lives are changed—people grow spiritually.

◎ **Try the same exercise with a different issue. Imagine on your church's finance committee a person with the natural ability to manage money being Spirit-led in exercising that gift, as opposed to the same person operating on natural ability alone. Seek to describe what might be the results of each person's management.**

Natural ability to manage money   Spirit-led ability to manage money

_____   _____

_____   _____

_____   _____

This one is tougher. Perhaps you put under natural ability things like we don't have to worry about finances—everything is honest, above board, and accounted for; we never get in a jam because our finance committee can project income and expenses and hold us to our budget. The Spirit's touch might be seen in the following ways: our finance committee members are people of faith, they encourage us to give generously and trust God for miracle provision; they are people of vision, making sure that the church invests in what is most important from God's perspective; they are compassionate, seeing needs both in the church and outside as well, and leading us to meet those needs.

We'll study about Spirit-given abilities in unit 10. In fact, we'll deal with how to identify, develop, and effectively use our spiritual gifts. Among all the gifts, two need special emphasis because of the way the Holy Spirit emphasizes them in the Book of Acts: evangelism and pioneer church-starting evangelism.

REPRODUCTION

◎ **Name several gifted evangelists you know or know about:**

_____

_____

I named Billy Graham, but I also listed Iijima and Ruth. They are very different from Billy Graham and from one another. Iijima is old; Ruth, young; Iijima is very timid, Ruth is bold; Iijima doesn't say much, Ruth talks a lot. Iijima is a widow who has won several to faith in Christ just by being their friends. Ruth has won many to Christ also by deliberately becoming friends but also through explaining Bible truth to them. She writes them letters, gives them pamphlets and books, provides transportation, throws birthday parties and plans special times for them. Billy Graham, Iijima, Ruth—all with the ability to win people to faith in Christ. That's the Spirit-gift of evangelism. We'll study about that in unit 11.

Not everyone is gifted in evangelism and even those who are have greater and lesser effectiveness. Who can compare with Billy Graham, for example? But all of us are responsible to share our faith. Some call that witnessing. We witness by the way we live a magnet life—drawing others to Jesus by the quality of our life. We witness by our talk—explaining how we got where we are. Thus every one of us is called to show and tell. If the church is witnessing, people will come to Christ. We could call it body-life reproduction. How that happens will be another theme of unit 11.

GOD SO LOVED THE WORLD

🌀 **I'm so glad He does, aren't you? But we tend to love our own more than others. Below write the names of people in each category who you believe need to know Jesus:**

in your immediate family: _____

_____

among acquaintances of another culture or race: _____

_____

people you haven't seen such as people you've heard mentioned in prayer meeting or people in distant mission fields for whom you pray (this might be groups, rather than individuals):

_____

_____

_____

friends for whom you are praying:

_____

_____

🌀 **Now go back and number from 1 to 4 those categories of lost people in order of how concerned you are for each group.**

Let me see if I can guess your order: family, friends, acquaintances, unknown people. That's natural and not necessarily wrong. But maybe you had few or none in the acquaintance-of-another-kind-of-people category or in the personally-unknown-but-prayer-request category. I think the more we have God's heart, the more we'll care about people at a distance, too, because God loves the whole world. In unit 11 we'll try to feel God's heartbeat, see the world with God's eyes, and discover how the Spirit will help us reach out to those who are presently out of reach.

🌀 **I hope you're half as excited as I am about what is going to happen in the next 11 weeks! As a final review of the road map before us, identify which of the following seem true T and which false F:**

____ 1. The first activity of the Holy Spirit in our behalf was to create us originally on the design of God Himself.
____ 2. The last activity of the Holy Spirit we'll study will be His role in uniting us in a completed love relationship with God.
____ 3. Everyone is gifted as an evangelist to a greater or lesser degree.

___ 4. Though it may not be easy, it is possible to reach God's standard of sinless perfection in this life.

___ 5. All Christians live at relatively the same level of intimacy with God.

___ 6. The "new me" is programmed by the Spirit with potentialities the "old me" never had.

___ 7. Biblical faith is a synonym for trust and doesn't always include yielding to God's will.

___ 8. No one can be expected to love or try to work for the salvation of people they've never even seen.

___ 9. Thinking like Jesus thinks and behaving like Him are the ultimate goals of life in the Spirit.

__ 10. The Christian life isn't passive—there is a battle to be won against temptation and we are expected to fight to win.

__ 11. Christians are given a gift of the Spirit to serve God in the church.

__ 12. Without confidence in the trustworthiness and authority of the Bible, it's unlikely a person could live a Spirit-filled life.

My answers would be: True–1, 2, 6, 10, 11, 12; and False–3, 4, 5, 7, 8, 9. If you differ on any answers, do two things. First, go back to the lesson where the subject is treated and, if the issue is still unresolved, bring it up for discussion in your group meeting.

My prayer for you is that the next few weeks will be a spurt in your spiritual growth. That's what preparing this study has been for me. Perhaps you can identify with my prayer response:

> **Holy Spirit, what a wonder You are! Thank You for making me with such high potential—to think and act like Jesus and to be one with You. When I mess up, You don't give up. Thank You for taking my broken model and transforming me into a new kind of person. Thank You for revealing to me what You want me to be and how I can become what You plan. Thank You for growing me up toward greater likeness to Jesus and thank You for all the growth that lies ahead. Thank You for companioning with me daily and for giving me those wonderful weapons to win out in life: prayer, the Word, the church. I want to be a faithful reflection of You. I want to be used by You to the maximum. I want to walk with You all the days of my life. I do trust You and love You. Here's my life—all of it, past, present, and future to do with as You please. I'm Yours, gladly and forever! Amen.**

---

[1] Andrew Reed, "Holy Spirit, Light Divine," 1817.

UNIT 2
DESIGNER MODEL

In unit 1 we overviewed Life in the Spirit. *In this unit we will examine the foundation for living a spirit-filled life. God designed you to have a love relationship with Him, but to have such a relationship you must be God-compatible. God made you as a special designer model—created in some mysterious way in God's likeness so you can experience intimate companionship with Him. When you have completed unit 2, I hope you will be elated with the potential God built into you!*

The off-duty flight attendant sitting beside me on the plane was an articulate conversationalist. As we talked, I learned that she was active in her church and occasionally listened to Billy Graham on TV. Yes, she believed what he taught, though she herself was not a member of an evangelical church. What about her husband?

"Well, he doesn't have any use for church," she said. "But he is very spiritual."

Spiritual? What did she mean?

She meant what many people today mean by the word spiritual. She meant that her husband believed in an unseen world and was interested in it. The contemporary fascination with the unseen represents a mega-shift in Western thinking. For several centuries we have concentrated on what can be seen and measured: scientific facts and the competence of the human mind to figure it all out. But now it seems feeling is more important than thinking; unseen forces are center stage. Spiritual is in, and the most ungodly people are said to be spiritual. But is this what the Bible means by spiritual?

Biblical spirituality grows out of the nature and activities of God. God is a spirit-being, not material; we were originally created in His image. In this unit we'll consider what it means to be created as a designer model—fashioned after God Himself.

Unit Memory Verse:
So God created human beings, making them to be like himself.
He created them male and female.
–Genesis 1:27, GNB

> What did God design me to be? What do people mean when they say we are spiritual? Is everybody spiritual? How can I be spiritual, and how can I know if I am?

DAY 1

WHAT DOES IT MEAN
TO BE SPIRITUAL?

The Spirit of God has made me;
the breath of the Almighty gives me life.
—Job 33:4

Three approaches to understanding the word *spiritual* coexist in our society. Generally people use the word spiritual in one of the following ways:

1. **Some people deny that we have a spiritual nature or that a spiritual world beyond the reach of science exists:** We might call this the naturalistic worldview. With the dawn of the scientific era, many people embraced the scientific method as the only way to valid knowledge and came to view the unseen world as non-existent or at least irrelevant. According to this view, the meaning of spirit must be limited to the processes of the natural world.

2. **Some people recognize our spiritual nature and dabble in the spiritual world:** They choose not to limit themselves to biblical guidelines for dealing with spiritual reality. We might call this the spiritualistic worldview. Today angels, magic, reincarnation, prayer, horoscopes, the occult, and life-after-death experiences fill newspapers, magazines, and talk shows. Maybe the interest came from the Eastern belief systems with New Age thinking. Some say it came from widespread disillusionment with a sterile, rational approach to life—the scientific outlook. Science, it turned out, wasn't solving our basic human problems. Wherever this new concept of spirituality came from, it influences many people today. This view recognizes the reality of the spiritual dimension but does not always distinguish between the good and the evil aspects of that spiritual world.

3. **Others recognize our spiritual nature and the spirit world but choose to deal with the Spirit world only through a relationship with the God of the Bible:** I call this the biblical worldview. Those who believe the Bible recognize that the material, visible world is not all that exists in life; it is not even the most important part. To treat what we can see, hear, touch, or taste as if the world we see were everything—or even the most important thing—will sooner or later lead to disaster. Paul reminded the people of Corinth of this truth in the verse appearing in the margin. Christians recognize the spiritual world, and they deal with it through obedience to the Triune God.

We fix our attention, not on things that are seen, but on things that are unseen. What can be seen lasts only for a time, but what cannot be seen lasts forever.
—2 Corinthians 4:18, GNB

Approach #1 denies or ignores the reality of the spiritual world. Attitude #2 recognizes the reality, but runs great risk of deception by evil. Only the biblical view of the world can provide a foundation for building a true and effective spiritual life.

I am grateful that people are beginning to recognize an unseen, "spiritual" realm, but we need to know just what really is out there. We need the ability to distinguish what part of that unseen world is good and what is not. If we want to understand spiritual reality and to link up only with the good part, we need to get better acquainted with the source of all spiritual good, the Holy Spirit of God.

In Christ all the fullness of the Deity lives in bodily form.
—Colossians 2:9

THE CHALLENGE OF BALANCE

The Bible teaches many truths that we cannot fully understand. Some of them seem contradictory. For example, the Bible teaches that Jesus Christ is fully and completely human. It also teaches that He is the fullness of God, dwelling in bodily form (see Col. 2:9 in the margin). In life, as in studying the Bible, to take one truth to an extreme is easier than to keep these complementary truths in balance. I call this need for balance the "center of biblical tension." To stay at the center of biblical tension means to hold complementary truths in balance.

We must maintain a biblical tension concerning the Holy Spirit. Since Jesus Christ is the center of our faith, we can easily ignore and treat the Spirit as if He didn't exist. Or we may go to the opposite extreme and so focus on the Spirit that we forget that the Spirit was given to glorify the Son. We may even try to use the Spirit by expecting Him to do things He never said He would, such as keeping us on a permanent emotional high. The following diagram illustrates the center of biblical tension concept:

Focus on Christ   **Fellowship with the Spirit**

Imagine the following: the President of the United States comes to speak at your local high-school auditorium. The band strikes up "Hail to the Chief" as the president strides to the microphone. The spotlight follows his every step. Suddenly the crowd, as one, rises and—what's this? They turn their backs to the stage and, pointing to the balcony, erupt in applause for the fine performance of the spotlight operator! Absurd? Of course, but it illustrates a truth about the Spirit. The Spirit glorifies—shines the spotlight on—the Son.

The Spirit points people to Jesus, and Jesus glorifies the Father (John 15:26; 16:13-14). Each member of the Trinity respects the others. They maintain a balance between individual personality and corporate identity. In the same way we need to have balance in our approach to the Spirit.

Proper theology and proper living are always a matter of balance. We must not focus so completely on the person and work of the Spirit that we lose sight of the central figure of time and eternity, the Lord Jesus Christ. We must also beware of and avoid the opposite extreme. We must not ignore the person and work of the Holy Spirit. Many churches and Christians treat the Spirit of God as if He did not exist. To ignore the Spirit is a tragic error.

We need the Holy Spirit to empower us for daily living. Jesus depended consciously on the Spirit for everything He said or did (John 5:30). We require the presence and power of the Spirit no less than did the Savior. We do not have to go to either of these extremes. We can strive to live in the balanced center of biblical truth about the Holy Spirit.

"When the Counselor comes, whom I will send to you from the Father, the Spirit of truth who goes out from the Father, he will testify about me."
—John 15:26

"When he, the Spirit of truth, comes, he will guide you into all truth. He will not speak on his own; he will speak only what he hears, and he will tell you what is yet to come. He will bring glory to me by taking from what is mine and making it known to you."
—John 16:13-14

🌀 **To go to an extreme is easier than to stay at the center of biblical tension. On the scale below place a check mark to indicate your relationship with the Spirit.**

Ignoring the Spirit									Excessive concentration on the Spirit

Unfortunately many people act as if all that really matters can be bought or sold, enjoyed by the body, or used to make them look good to other people. You might call such people unspiritual, since the realm of the spirit is not very important to them. On the other hand, to those who are spiritually minded the realm of the unseen is all-important, and God is the most important person in life. Relating to Him is the most important relationship. In fact, a spiritual life is one dominated by the Spirit of God.

Stop and think about this a moment. In which direction do you tend to actually live out your life—ignoring the unseen or constantly connected?

On a scale of 1 - 10, mark the place which best describes how much you think about unseen realities. I think of spiritual things…

1	2	3	4	5	6	7	8	9	10

almost
never

in church
or at prayer

periodically
throughout
the day

often
throughout
the day

When you think of "unseen realities," what specifically do you think about? What do you do? Check all that apply.

❑ I think about how each good event is a gift of God, and often I thank Him right then.
❑ When I face a problem or temptation I immediately call on God to help me.
❑ When I sin, I ask God to forgive me. I don't wait until bedtime.
❑ I spend some time alone each day reading the Bible and talking to God.
❑ I am faithful in church attendance, and most times I feel that I really met with God.
❑ God seems nearby all the time, and I talk things over with Him throughout the day.

Were you able to check each of the statements in the exercise above? If not, why not make those you couldn't check a set of goals for yourself?

KEEPING A JOURNAL

Since college days, I have greatly benefitted by keeping a journal. Often my entry will be a prayer telling the Lord how I feel about my situation, praising Him for something about Him I especially appreciate, or calling on Him to help.

As I finish preparing each day's lesson, I always pause to tell the Lord my personal response to what He has been teaching me. Often I will share my prayer response with you.

If you feel the same sort of response and wish to use those prayers as your own, please feel free to do so. Or perhaps my prayer will trigger something you wish to talk to the Lord about. Writing out that response in your own journal will help you.

Sometimes I will suggest something you may wish to talk to the Lord about. Whatever form your prayer response takes, be sure to close each lesson by talking directly to God about what you have been studying. My response to today's lesson on spiritual realities appears at the top of the next page.

> Heavenly Father, thank You that You are real and that Your unseen world, which goes beyond my senses and beyond scientific measurement, is more important than everything I see. Thank You for giving me Your blessed Spirit. Through this study may I grow to know Him better and to experience His presence and power. Teach me all I need to know about the Holy Spirit, but especially help me learn to walk with Him all my days. I ask this with confidence because I come in the authority of Jesus' name.

Write out Genesis 1:27, the memory verse for this week. Refer back to the unit introduction if necessary:

_____

_____

Now is the time to record in your journal something you understood or felt while studying this lesson, particularly anything about your own spiritual life or about your relationship to the Holy Spirit.

DAY 2

WHO IS THE SPIRIT?

At Halloween our street is crowded with little "ghosts." But no matter how much we play ghost or joke about ghosts, the idea of unseen spirit-beings still seems spooky. We may get uneasy, for example, when someone speaks of the "Holy Ghost."

I have encountered each of the following ideas about the Holy Spirit:

- Some people today conceive of the Holy Spirit as a force, a god-force, enveloping all things and determining the course of human events.
- Some understand the Spirit not as an impersonal force but as a person, an agent sent from God to do His will, sort of like a chief angel.
- For still others, the Spirit is simply another name of the one true God, a name that emphasizes His invisible nature.

Each of these concepts seem true to certain individuals, but none of these are biblical views.

If a new Christian asked you to describe the Holy Spirit, how would you respond? Below write your description of the Holy Spirit. Don't be intimidated by this exercise—it isn't a test! The purpose is to express your present understanding as a reference point. In this lesson you will establish a biblical description.

_____

_____

_____

EXAMINING SCRIPTURE

We must examine Scripture to answer our questions about life in the Spirit. A primary question relates to the nature of the Holy Spirit. Is the Spirit a person or an impersonal god-force? Consider what the following Scriptures indicate about the nature of the Holy Spirit.

> *"I will ask the Father, and He will give you another Helper, that He may be with you forever; that is the Spirit of truth, whom the world cannot receive, because it does not behold Him or know Him, but you know Him because He abides with you and will be in you. The Helper, the Holy Spirit, whom the Father will send in my name, He will teach you all things, and bring to your remembrance all that I said to you" (John 14:16-17,26, NASB).*

> *In the same way the Spirit also helps our weakness; for we do not know how to pray as we should, but the Spirit Himself intercedes for us with groanings too deep for words (Rom. 8:26, NASB).*

🌀 **Is the Holy Spirit a person or an impersonal god-force?**

❑ a person
❑ an impersonal god-force

Explain your answer. _____

_____

The personal pronoun demonstrates that the Holy Spirit is a person rather than an impersonal force. He knows you, lives in you, teaches you, and intercedes for you.

🌀 **Read Acts 5:3-4 and 1 Corinthians 3:16 (in margin). How would you respond to someone who said the Holy Spirit is not God but is merely an agent of God?**

_____

_____

_____

_____

You could point out to such a person that in many places the Bible speaks of the Spirit as God. In Acts 5:3-4, Peter said Ananias had lied to the Holy Spirit. Then when Peter restated the charge, he said Ananias had lied to God. Paul said we are God's temple and we are the Holy Spirit's temple. These statements make sense because the Holy Spirit is God. You could also refer this person to many passages that show the Holy Spirit is God because the Spirit has the power, attributes, and qualities of God. For example, in Psalm 139:7-10 the Spirit is all powerful and present everywhere.

How do we know that the Holy Spirit is a person distinct from the Father and Son? For one example, read John 15:26, appearing in the margin. The verse indicates that the Spirit goes out from the Father and testifies about Jesus.

Peter said, "Ananias, how is it that Satan has so filled your heart that you have lied to the Holy Spirit and have kept for yourself some of the money you received for the land? Didn't it belong to you before it was sold? And after it was sold, wasn't the money at your disposal? What made you think of doing such a thing? You have not lied to men but to God."
—Acts 5:3-4

Don't you know that you yourselves are God's temple and that God's Spirit lives in you?
—1 Corinthians 3:16

"When the Counselor comes, whom I will send to you from the Father, the Spirit of truth who goes out from the Father, he will testify about me."
—John 15:26

⊚ **Below describe other evidences that the Holy Spirit is a person distinct from the Father and Son. Remember the verses you read on the previous page.**

_____

_____

_____

You could have given many answers. Romans 8:26 tells us that the Spirit talks to the Father. John 14:17 says that the Father sent the Spirit. You may have drawn from your own Bible knowledge for instances such as Jesus' baptism. All three persons of the Trinity were present on that occasion, but they were separate and distinct (Matt. 3:16-17).

From these passages you see that the Holy Spirit is a person, and He is God; yet, He is distinct from the Father and Son. Furthermore, a division of responsibility exists between Father, Son, and Spirit. The Holy Spirit's role is that of executive—the one designated to carry out the purposes of God.

THE ACTIVITIES OF THE SPIRIT

You have identified some key elements of the identity of the Spirit. The following activity will help you identify some of the Spirit's activities.

⊚ **Read the following verses and name some of the activities of the Holy Spirit. The verses are printed in the margin.**

Genesis 1:2; Job 33:4 _____

_____

2 Peter 1:21 _____

_____

Luke 1:35; 3:22; 4:1 _____

_____

John 3:5 _____

_____

The Spirit is the One who created: "The Spirit of God was hovering over the waters" (Gen. 1:2). He is the One who revealed God and gave us the Bible: "Men spoke from God as they were carried along by the Holy Spirit" (2 Pet. 1:21). When the Son was to become man He was conceived by the Holy Spirit, and He taught and healed in the power of the Spirit.

In the same way the Holy Spirit works today. When God wants to act in our lives, He acts by His Spirit. The infinite God wants to relate to us personally to transform us into the likeness of Christ Himself. He transforms us through the work of His Spirit.

Now the earth was formless and empty, darkness was over the surface of the deep, and the Spirit of God was hovering over the waters.
—Genesis 1:2

"The Spirit of God has made me."
—Job 33:4

Prophecy never had its origin in the will of man, but men spoke from God as they were carried along by the Holy Spirit.
—2 Peter 1:21

The angel answered, "The Holy Spirit will come upon you, and the power of the Most High will overshadow you. So the holy one to be born will be called the Son of God."
—Luke 1:35

The Holy Spirit descended on him [Jesus] in bodily form like a dove. And a voice came from heaven: "You are my Son, whom I love; with you I am well pleased."
—Luke 3:22

Jesus, full of the Holy Spirit, returned from the Jordan and was led by the Spirit in the desert.
—Luke 4:1

Jesus answered, "I tell you the truth, no one can enter the kingdom of God unless he is born of water and the Spirit."
—John 3:5

⌖ **Read the following passages in your Bible and describe four more activities of the Spirit.**

John 16:7-11 _____

John 16:13-15 _____

Galatians 5:22-23 _____

1 Corinthians 12:4, 7, 11 _____

The passages describe four more ways the Holy Spirit works. He convicts of sin, righteousness, and judgment. He teaches and instructs, leading us into all truth. He produces the fruit of the Spirit in our lives, and He gives spiritual gifts—abilities for service.

⌖ **Has today's study changed your understanding of the Holy Spirit? Look back at your original definition and add anything omitted from your initial description.**

⌖ **Descriptions are good, but let's get personal. How do you relate to the Holy Spirit? Check all boxes which apply.**

❏ I love Him, and He loves me.
❏ I rarely think about Him or sense His presence.
❏ He talks to me through the Bible, and I talk to Him in prayer every day.
❏ I sense His presence often through the day.
❏ I'm not really sure how to relate to Him.
❏ I can see ways He is changing me into what I would like to be.

⌖ **This would be a good time to pray. First, reflect on your responses and talk to the Lord about them. Then reflect on the passages you studied in this lesson about the Holy Spirit. Spend a few minutes thinking about Him and thanking God for each of the things about Him you appreciate most.**

⌖ **In your journal write in your own words the memory verses.**

DAY 3

MADE TO BE LIKE HIM

"Just look at that boy! Why, he's the spittin' image of ol' Joe!"

I'm not sure how the "spittin'" got in there, but we get the picture: the boy is a replica of his father—looks like him, walks like him, talks like him. And so with us. In some mysterious way we were made on the model of God Himself. In a strategic planning session deep in eternity, the Father, Son, and Holy Spirit agreed, "Let us make man in our image." Read Genesis 1:26-27 (margin) to get a snapshot of this momentous decision.

God said, "Let us make man in our image, in our likeness, and let them rule over the fish of the sea and the birds of the air, over the livestock, over all the earth, and over all the creatures that move along the ground."

So God created man in his own image, in the image of God he created him; male and female he created them.

—Genesis 1:26-27

To know a person, keep an eye on his activity. In *Life in the Spirit,* we are concentrating on 10 activities of the Spirit. The first that impacts us daily is creation. God created us, in some mysterious way, to be like Him. That likeness we call the image of God. But what does His image look like? Theologians debate the meaning of image. Since the Bible doesn't give a concise definition, we have to draw from various passages of Scripture to find the meaning.

> **Below I have listed some of the meanings people have given for the image of God. Place a check by all those you think are included in human likeness to God.**
>
> ❑ the human spirit
> ❑ ability to communicate
> ❑ rational thought
> ❑ sexuality: maleness and femaleness
> ❑ a moral sense, ability to distinguish right from wrong
> ❑ the human body
> ❑ character, attitudes, and actions like God
> ❑ emotions, ability to love and be loved, to feel joy and sorrow
> ❑ ability to choose

For each of the items in the list, you can find a theologian to affirm that it is part of the image. Most of those listed are indeed human characteristics that God made to reflect His character. The list may contain some exceptions, however. For example, a few scholars suggest that our bodies reflect God's nature in some mysterious way, but most would leave our bodies off the list. God is spirit and not physical, apart from the incarnation of Jesus. Recently, some Bible scholars have added sexuality—maleness and femaleness—to the characteristics of God. They believe that God combines in His being all the characteristics of both sexes, but most would not include sexuality in the list.

OUR DESIRE TO TAKE GOD'S PLACE

Alexander the Great, Caesar, King Nebuchadnezzar, and Herod the Great all had two things in common—each claimed to be God and hated cats. They grasped for supreme authority, and the cats were the only ones who wouldn't obey!

Would supreme authority and power represent God's image? Today we are rapidly achieving corporately what some of the ancients futilely tried to achieve as individuals. With the assistance of computers we dream of accumulating infinite knowledge. With jets and telecommunications we think we can be everywhere—omnipresent. But these were not the aspects of God He intended for us to share. Not omnipotence. Not omniscience. Not omnipresence. Notice that I included none of these characteristics in the last learning activity.

Of course, we do have high potential for knowing and doing, since we are modeled after God Himself. That's why so much human achievement in the arts and sciences is truly magnificent, but God's infinities are forever beyond us. Yet, in one way God designed us to be just like Him.

> **Below list the way(s) in which you believe God intended you to be exactly like Him.**

Definitions:
omnipotence—all powerful
omniscience—all knowing
omnipresence—in all places at all times

_____

_____

Scientists tell us that porpoises communicate with signals; but they've written no dictionaries yet. Pandas make tools—they break off a stick to dig out the food they want; but they've built no automobiles yet. Ants build incredibly complex cities and even keep aphid-cows to milk; but no churches or temples have ever been found in those cities. Monkeys misbehave; but none have been known to blush.

When God created a special being in His own likeness, He designed one unlike the animals He had already created—one with a spirit who could communicate, create, know right from wrong, and, above all, love and be loved by God Himself. That is His "image," the stamp of the Designer. We are indeed a "designer model"—modeled after the Designer Himself. That was the work of the Holy Spirit in His first activity, creating us in God's image.

Some people have more intelligence, more authority, or more strength than others. Name a few people who have more authority, intelligence, strength, or skill than anyone else you know about. For example, you might name the strongest athlete, the most accomplished entertainer, or the most intelligent scientist.

_____

_____

_____

_____

Notice—even the greatest among us fall far short of the authority, intelligence, and strength of God. So, does being somewhat more intelligent, stronger, or having greater earthly authority really make a person that much more like God?

God made us to be like Him, not in power or authority but in our moral nature. He designed us to be loving, holy, trustworthy, just, good, peaceful, and joyful. We share, to a greater or lesser degree, some of His non-moral attributes, such as the capacity for abstract reasoning. But He designed us to be exactly like Him in His moral nature: "Be holy because I, the Lord your God, am holy" (Lev. 19:2).

Who are the people you know who are most like God in His moral nature, people you would call very godly?

_____

_____

_____

_____

In which of the above lists would you most prefer that people put you?

❑ known for my authority, intelligence, strength, or skill
❑ marked by godliness

You and I are designed on the model of the Creator. The joy of life comes from glorifying Him. We glorify Him as we more accurately reflect His character.

⊚ Pause for a few moments and tell God how humbled, honored, grateful, and thrilled you are to have been patterned after Him.

⊚ Your journal is a good place to record that prayer. Are there other special insights or experiences to note in your journal?

DAY 4

DESIGNED ON PURPOSE

Muriel was pretty, vivacious, talented, fun, a great lover of God—and a lover of me! Finally, she agreed to be mine and everything in life was aimed toward the wedding day, August 24. I was so intoxicated with love for Muriel that I constantly did irrational things like subsisting on one meal a day so I could save money for the great day; and reading her love letters the minute they arrived, in spite of the fact that they consistently preempted my history class.

Shortly before the big day, I gathered some of my family in South Carolina, borrowed my father's car, and headed for Nebraska. In a long, sweeping curve through the wheat fields of Kansas, a tractor had backed up traffic for what seemed like miles. The creeping traffic blocked our way.

Finally, my chance came. I could see around the curve, ahead of dozens of creeping cars, and no one was coming toward us. I whipped out into the left lane of that two-lane highway and put the accelerator to the floor—not very smart. But I was crazy in love. I had one objective: to get to the one I loved. Half-way through that curve, a speeding car appeared from nowhere, aimed right at us. I headed for the shoulder.

"Oh, no! Why did they put that telephone pole there?" The thought barely had time to flash through my mind. I closed my eyes and aimed at the narrow gap between the approaching car and the telephone pole. We left one of my father's fenders on that pole, but we limped on to Beaver City where Muriel and I began a lifetime odyssey together.

And now? Now Muriel lies in bed, unable to stand, walk, or feed herself. Knowing nothing, really, a victim of Alzheimer's disease. But her contented smile sometimes breaks through the dimness and brightens my day.

People speak of my care of Muriel as if it were something heroic—far from it. I love her more now than I ever did on that mad dash to Nebraska. When I'm away on a speaking engagement, I miss her more. I long to be with her, to feel the squeeze of her hand. But there is a big difference. Now the love flows mostly one way. The connecting point is gone.

We used to share our dreams, our work, our play, our children, our laughter, and our tears. We drew ever closer to one another. We became more and more like one another, actually. But we're not much alike now. The mutuality is almost gone.

Is that the way with God and you? He created you to be like Him so you could share His life and His love. He had a mutually satisfying love affair in mind.

The relationship started out so gloriously, didn't it? But for many Christians, something has happened. Oh, He still loves them and lavishes that love on them daily. But how do they respond? Communication is sporadic; love has lost its passion. Perhaps they can't even identify with Him, because they are so unlike Him now. Sad, isn't it? But that was never the Designer's plan.

THE DESIGNER'S PLAN

From all eternity God the Father, God the Son, and God the Holy Spirit were bound together in love, for God by nature is love (1 John 4:7,16). From the overflow of His loving nature, He wanted people to whom He could show His love and who would love Him back.

For communication and love to flow freely, the people God made would have to be like Him. The relationship couldn't be like you and your dog. Fido may be a great friend, but communication is limited and a dog is not exactly a "suitable helper" to you, as God said of the mate He was creating for Adam (Gen. 2:20). Fido is a different species, but Adam and Eve, that's another story. They were made for each other.

Just as God created Adam and Eve compatible with each other, He created us to be God-compatible. If that compatibility weren't there, in-depth communication would not be possible, intimate companionship would be missing. That is why God the Holy Spirit created humankind on God's own pattern. As a result, Adam and Eve walked with God in the garden of Eden, sharing His presence and love. They were created to love God and be loved by Him. They were created in His likeness so they could experience that love.

> **God's design determines genuine life purpose. What do you consider to be your supreme purpose in life? In the following list, check only one supreme purpose. I am here to—**

- ❏ serve in the church faithfully
- ❏ provide for my family
- ❏ become like Christ in my character
- ❏ love God
- ❏ rear children who are successful
- ❏ win souls
- ❏ be successful in my life's calling
- ❏ other _____

> **Read Matthew 22:37-38 that appears in the margin. Circle what you consider to be the essential part of the passage.**

Though the above list contains many worthwhile goals, the ultimate goal of our lives is to love God. Even becoming Christlike in character falls short of that supreme goal.

WHAT ABOUT CHRISTLIKENESS?

Becoming more like Jesus enables us to fellowship with God, but it is not the ultimate goal. The more like Christ we become, the more we will be able to love God and receive love from Him. Becoming like Christ is so important that the major emphasis of this study is how we become like Him, but keep in mind that becoming like Christ is not the final goal. The goal is to develop our love relationship with God. He created us on His pattern and provided the salvation process as a way for His image in us to be restored. He did all these things with the ultimate goal of loving us and us loving Him.

Before we close the study of God's purpose in making us like Him, let us reflect on ways we are becoming like Him and ways in which we are not.

Dear friends, let us love one another, for love comes from God. Everyone who loves has been born of God and knows God.

God is love. Whoever lives in love lives in God, and God in him.
—1 John 4:7,16

But for Adam no suitable helper was found.
—Genesis 2:20

Jesus replied: "'Love the Lord your God with all your heart, and with all your soul, and with all your mind.' This is the first and greatest commandment."
—Matthew 22:37-38

List five ways in which those who know you best would say you are growing in Christlikeness—ways in which He is making you more like Himself.

_____

_____

_____

List five ways in which you are least like Jesus, or ways in which people who know you best would say you least remind them of Jesus. If you fear someone may see this, you may want to list them on a separate sheet of paper, such as in your journal. But it will be very helpful to have them before you for reflection and prayer.

_____

_____

_____

Sometime during the next week ask someone close to you to answer those two questions about you. Ask someone who will tell you the truth. Write that person's answers in another color so you can see clearly and reflect on the differences between your own perceptions and those of the other person.

Comparing ourselves to Jesus could lead to discouragement. We fall so far short. In the next lesson we will consider our potential for actually becoming more like Him. That is the great desire of the true lover of God—to develop a character that is just like Him so that we can experience His purpose in making and redeeming us. We want to know an ever deepening love relationship that will bring Him joy and bring us joy, too!

Prayer time. As you conclude your study today spend some time talking with God about the following areas:
- First, thank the Lord for what He has done to change you into Christ's likeness.
- Spend time confessing the ways you haven't changed, but want Him to change you.
- Finally, thank the Lord that He loves you with an everlasting love, and tell Him how much you love Him.

Like the surge of joy I feel when Muriel responds with a smile, your Eternal Lover is waiting for your response.

Try to write the memory verse for this unit without referring back.

_____

_____

_____

DAY 5

CAPACITY OF YOUR DESIGNER MODEL

We were sightseeing in a giant computer mall. I discovered magical things like a program to landscape your yard. The program allowed you to plant shrubs and flowers and produce a picture of what it would look like six months later, a year later, or five years later. My son David, a software executive, was trying to explain things to me in simple terms I could understand. Finally, he said: "Dad, your computer just doesn't have the capacity for that program."

His statement reminded me of our reaction to the Bible. We browse through the Bible and see God's program for a growing, mature Christian. To be an effective disciple sounds marvelous, but does our model have the capacity to run that program? Can I really live the kind of life the Bible describes?

Remember, we were designed on the model of God's own character. He created us with plenty of capacity. We ought to be able to live out any plan God gives for thinking or behaving like His Son Jesus. But somehow, when we try to run the program we fail. We feel like the person who sits down at the computer, presses a button, and gets a message that says, "Enter the password." We have no idea what word to enter or what to do next. What has gone wrong? Why can't we get the results God promised? God's program for our lives looks something like this—

- loving responses toward the ungrateful, even the hostile
- joy in the midst of unhappy circumstances
- peace and hope when everything seems to be going wrong
- longsuffering with that persistently obnoxious person
- kindness even to the unkind
- obedience when others are disobedient
- faithful even when it is costly.

> Review the statements above. After each statement write one word to describe how difficult or easy you find that part of God's program.

Adam and Eve could run the program. They knew right and did it. They also had the capacity to choose wrong, and they did. They disabled their "computer" so it could no longer run God's program successfully. Theologians have a special word for the damage done by the entry of sin into humanity. They call it depravity. Depraved means that every human being has been damaged by sin.

THE NORMAL CHRISTIAN LIFE

We often use the term normal to mean "typical" or "average." Thus we call the way most people live *normal.* God never intended for Christians to be average. So I use the word normal to describe the life God offers—the norm or biblical standard for Christian living. For example, He designs us to overcome temptation, consistently obey His laws, and grow in self-control, contentment, humility, and courage. He intends for our thought processes to be so obedient to the Spirit and so instructed by Scripture that we authentically reflect the attitudes and the behavior of Jesus. Such a life and experience is the normal Christian life.

In the normal Christian life, God has first place in our lives. We value the welfare of others above our selfish desires. The functioning Christian has power not only for godly living but also for effective service in the church. Above all, he or she has the joy of constant companionship with the Lord.

⊚ **The next two paragraphs contain my evaluation of the spiritual condition of many church members. Read the paragraphs carefully. Then place a mark on the bar graph that follows the paragraphs. Indicate to what degree you agree that my evaluation is accurate or disagree that my opinion is overly pessimistic.**

The average church member typically thinks and behaves very much like morally upright non-Christians. They are decent enough but with nothing supernatural about them. Their behavior is explainable in terms of heredity, early environment, and present circumstances. They often yield to temptation, lusting when their body craves it, coveting what they do not have, and taking credit for their accomplishments. The touchstone for their choices is self-interest. Though they have a love for God and others, strained or broken relationships with others prove that the Spirit does not control their lives.

The average church member experiences little change for the better. In fact, many don't seem to expect much improvement and have little concern about the prospect for change. Scripture is not exciting, prayer is perfunctory, and service in the church demonstrates little touch of the supernatural. Above all, life seems to have an empty core, for it does not center around a constant, personal companionship with the Lord.

ACCURATE   PESSIMISTIC

⊚ **Is your experience more like the average church member or like the normal Christian? Perhaps it would help in answering that question to read slowly and prayerfully through the last four paragraphs again. Underline characteristics that best describe you, whether found in the normal Christian life described in the first two paragraphs or the more typical disabled version described in the last two.**

Each of us has areas of strength and weakness, some we are aware of, some perhaps not. But God knows, and when we acknowledge our need to Him, He will move in and begin restoring our broken-down models to function as He designed them to operate (1 John 1:5–2:2).

THE PRACTICAL QUESTION
"How, HOW, HOW, HOW can I ever live that kind of life?" A troubled graduate student scribbled the question on a scrap of paper and passed it to me after class. She had heard me talk about a Spirit-empowered life. She desperately wanted an answer. The answer to that student's question will comprise the remainder of our study, but let me summarize the answer briefly, in the words of Scripture:

For those God foreknew he also predestined to be conformed to the likeness of his Son (Rom. 8:29).

We, who with unveiled faces all reflect the Lord's glory, are being transformed into his likeness with ever-increasing glory, which comes from the Lord, who is the Spirit (2 Cor. 3:18).

The new self ... is being renewed in knowledge in the image of its Creator (Col. 3:10).

Notice that in all these passages the restoration to our original design is not in a study lesson, not in a formula, but in a Person. The transforming presence and power of God the Holy Spirit will enable us to be what God designed us to be.

In the weeks ahead I hope you will discover that the model you were built on, God's own pattern, when restored by the Master Repairman, can indeed run the program as designed. You can daily experience a beautiful life of spiritual effectiveness. You can begin to resemble Christ more and more.

THE TRANSFORMATION CONNECTION

How do we connect to let His power flow? How do we move from an average to a normal Christian life?

We connect with Him through faith. "'The righteous will live by his faith'" (Hab. 2:4) was the only message of an Old Testament prophet that was repeated, not once, but three times in the New Testament (Rom. 1:17; Gal. 3:11; Heb. 10:38). Faith is the uplink with divine power, whether for salvation or for being restored into the original design. God provides the power for living through the activity of the Holy Spirit. We respond to God's provision through faith. Faith releases the power of the Holy Spirit to work in our lives.

Faith means:
- believing what God has said
- choosing to trust God by putting your life in His hands even when everything seems to be going wrong
- placing your confidence in His love and knowledge of you and His ability to order your life for your greatest blessing
- yielding to do God's will.

God is the standard for our lives—we were meant to reflect His image. God also restores and empowers us to become like Him; the Holy Spirit can build character and make us more like Christ. We connect with God through faith. As you continue this study I pray that you will examine and experience those truths in all their exciting dimensions.

Here is my suggested prayer:

> **Thank You, blessed Spirit, that You have not abandoned me. You have shown me a secure hope that You personally stand ready to show me the way, enable me to travel it, and companion with me to the end of it. Amen!**

God is spirit. He created us on the same model—spiritual beings—so we could join His circle of love. We broke that relationship and damaged ourselves. But God pursues us with passionate love, intent on repairing us, remodeling us into His moral likeness so we can again be God-compatible.

Choose one item from your journal to share with your group or the partner you have chosen. This will strengthen your resolve, help others, and bring joy to the Holy Spirit.

UNIT 3

THE GREAT UNVEILING

In unit 2 we learned that the Holy Spirit created us in the image of God.
In this unit we will explore the role of the Holy Spirit in revealing truth to us
so we may know God and knowing Him, love Him.

As a young adult I began to doubt the truth of the Bible. I grew up in a Christian home, accepted Christ as a young child, and attended a Christian college, but I began to doubt the basic truths of the Christian faith.

My doubts grew until I became a full-fledged skeptic. I decided I must doubt anything I could not verify. I determined to be truly scientific—never to believe anything without proof. Since I couldn't prove the Bible scientifically, God was the next casualty of my "scientific" method.

As my skepticism grew, my world gradually darkened. I discovered that it was not just the Bible and God that I doubted. I began to feel that nothing was certain because I could never get all the evidence on anything. As a result, I believed less and less about more and more. I tried to convince myself that I was practicing "intellectual honesty," but trusting no one and no thing was a lonely existence.

Fortunately, I began to examine my own assumptions. If you are so "scientific," I asked myself, why have you ruled out in advance any investigation of the possibility of God? For the first time in a long while, I prayed. My prayer was simple, if a little arrogant: "God, if You exist, will You give me some objective evidence?"

In this unit we will examine revelation, the second activity of the Spirit. The Holy Spirit broke into history to reveal to us the existence and nature of God. He has worked in the world throughout salvation history—the process of God revealing Himself. The Spirit inspired the writing of the Bible and empowered the ministry of Jesus. Apart from the Holy Spirit we cannot know about God or know God.

Unit Memory Verse
All Scripture is inspired by God and is useful for teaching the truth, rebuking error,
correcting faults, and giving instruction for right living, so that the person who serves God
may be fully qualified and equipped to do every kind of good deed.
—2 Timothy 3:16-17, GNB

> **How do we know that the Bible is reliable? How did the Holy Spirit inspire the writing of the Bible? How does the Spirit lead us to understand and obey God's will?**

DAY 1

CONFIRMING THE WORD

My struggle with disbelief led to a lonely period of my life with no dependable truth. Finally, I prayed an arrogant but honest prayer. I asked God to prove to me that He exists.

I was surprised to find that God had answered my prayer before I was even born. My search took me back to the Bible. I had come to believe that the Bible was riddled with errors, yet the Holy Spirit began to use the Bible itself to build a foundation for my faith. For example, I realized that the Old Testament predicted many details about the Messiah–

- when and where He would be born
- what He would do
- how He would die
- that He would live forever.

These were predictions made hundreds of years before Christ's birth.

I was discovering revelation, supernatural revelation–the Bible, a miracle in my hand. I began, ever so tentatively, to embrace God with my mind. I was experiencing personally what God did through history–God revealed Himself. I call it the great unveiling. If God had not chosen to reveal Himself, He would remain forever a mystery to us. I have no doubt that the Holy Spirit was leading me into truth. That's His job. Jesus said, "When he, the Spirit of truth, comes, he will guide you into all truth" (John 16:13).

    Many believers go through periods of questioning or doubting. If you have, recall one or more of your concerns. In the margin describe how you dealt with them.

God provided a written record of everything we need to know about Him, so we can enter into relationship with Him. The Spirit of God led the writers of Scripture to communicate what we need to know to experience fellowship with God. But you may ask legitimate questions about the Bible:

- How do we know the words of the Bible are from God?
- How did the Holy Spirit inspire Scripture?
- Can we understand Scripture so that we know God's will?

Understanding the Bible and relating to God through His Holy Spirit go together. We cannot know God apart from Scripture, and we cannot understand the Bible apart from the Spirit.

    Read 1 Corinthians 2:14 printed in the margin. In your own words explain why any person without the Holy Spirit is unable to understand spiritual things:

_____

_____

Several terms describe the relationship between the Bible and the Spirit. Some of these terms are: revelation, authority, inspiration, interpretation, and illumination. God has chosen to disclose truth about the universe, about humanity, and about Himself–truth that we would not otherwise know. We call this self-disclosure

People who aren't Christians can't understand these truths from God's Spirit. It all sounds foolish to them because only those who have the Spirit can understand what the Spirit means.
—1 Corinthians 2:14, NLT

revelation. The Bible is our *authority* because it is the only completely dependable means through which God has revealed Himself to us. The Holy Spirit gave revelation through a process we call *inspiration.* We have the privilege and the responsibility to determine what each passage means through *interpretation.* For the task of interpretation we have the assistance of the Holy Spirit guiding us into all truth—the process of *illumination.*

Below are descriptions of the five terms related to the Bible that we will explore during this week's study. See if you can match the description with the proper term. Choices are listed in the margin.

Interpretation
Revelation
Illumination
Authority
Inspiration

_____ a. how the Holy Spirit gave Scripture
_____ b. the Spirit's activity in helping me understand the Bible
_____ c. the work of figuring out what the author meant in a particular passage
_____ d. God communicating what I otherwise couldn't know
_____ e. why I should trust and obey the Bible

About the Bible Herschel Hobbs wrote: "Revelation is God's unveiling of truth. Inspiration is receiving and transmitting truth. Illumination is understanding truth (cf. John 16:13). In the biblical sense revelation and inspiration were completed with the close of the New Testament. But illumination is a continuing activity of the Holy Spirit."[1] In the exercise above, the answers were: a. inspiration; b. illumination; c. interpretation; d. revelation; e. authority. You might have reversed inspiration and revelation or interpretation and illumination because the words describe related concepts.

When I began to recognize that the Bible is true, I began to trust and obey it. Let's examine how the Holy Spirit conveys truth to us through the Bible.

THE NATURE OF AUTHORITY

If I were to say, "A major earthquake will occur in California tomorrow," you have every right to ask, "And who are you?" Once you found out that I have no credentials to predict earthquakes, you probably wouldn't catch the first plane out of the state. But if I were a leading seismologist who never failed to make accurate predictions, you might take immediate action. Why? The trustworthiness of a statement depends on the speaker. So, the authority of the Bible depends on who said it. Because God said it, you can believe it. We call this book—and only this book—the Word of God. That's why it has supreme authority for our lives.

When, as a young man, I returned to faith in God, I still had problems with some parts of the Bible. Like waves of fog, the doubts would blow through my mind from time to time. After about a decade of this I said to myself, "McQuilkin, you've got to get this settled. You've got to get in or get out." I went to a lonely beach and camped out for three days. I read the Gospels again and again.

During those days the Holy Spirit used the Bible to impact my life. Something swept over me—a sense of awe in the presence of the historic person, Jesus Christ. Even if I accepted the arguments of the critics and did away with much of what the record says Jesus did and said, still there remained a figure that towers in absolute grandeur among men, an unprecedented revelation of God. On the third day as I stood gazing out over the vast Pacific, I had a sense that Jesus was with me, as if He put a hand on my shoulder and said, "Little brother, are you smarter than I?"

"Oh, no!" I cried, "of course I'm not smarter than You." The lights came on! The realization of who Jesus is and who I'm not cleared the shadowy doubts that had for so long lurked in my mind. That day I settled the issue of the authority of the Word of God in my life. Because the living Word of God—Jesus Christ—is my authority, His written word is my authority. From that moment, I determined to accept whatever Jesus said about the Father, heaven and hell, right and wrong—and the Bible. Throughout His ministry Jesus expressed His confidence in the Bible's authority. Who was I to question some passage I didn't understand? I am not implying that all the intellectual struggles of the Christian life are solved quickly or easily, but a solution begins with a decision to accept the authority of Jesus Christ and His view of the Bible.

🌀 **In the margin read the statements made by Jesus about the Scripture. Then below underline the sentence that best reflects Jesus' view.**

> a. Jesus believed most but not all of Scripture was true and enduring.
> b. Jesus believed Scripture is true, enduring, and necessary to spiritual life.
> c. Jesus set aside the Old Testament to make room for the New Testament.

Jesus answered, "It is written: 'Man does not live on bread alone, but on every word that comes from the mouth of God.'"
—Matthew 4:4

On the beach that day, I took the step of faith and chose Jesus as my authority. He viewed the Bible as God's Word. I'm not smarter than He! If you cannot honestly affirm that the Bible is the authoritative Word of God for you, would you be willing to ask God, as I did three decades ago, to show you in some way how He views Scripture? You may have to struggle as I did over a period of time, but you will be demonstrating a willingness to change if He wants you to. In the exercise above, I underlined choice b.

"Do not think that I have come to abolish the Law or the Prophets; I have not come to abolish them but to fulfill them. I tell you the truth, until heaven and earth disappear, not the smallest letter, not the least stroke of a pen, will by any means disappear from the Law until everything is accomplished."
—Matthew 5:17-18

🌀 **What is your attitude toward the authority of Scripture? Put a check by the description that best fits:**

❏ I can't believe some things in the Bible are true.
❏ The Bible is good literature, but it doesn't have divine authority.
❏ I believe the Bible is true, but I still want to choose my own values.
❏ The Bible is true in all its parts, and thus is the final authority for what I believe and how I behave.
❏ Other? _____

Now would be a good time to thank the Lord for His authority in your life. Thank Him for the Bible. Ask Him to empower you as we progress through this week to understand more clearly the role His Word should play in your life. Would it help to write out your response to God in your journal entry for today?

🌀 **In our unit memory verse Paul gives at least five ways the Holy Spirit interacts with us in Bible study. Can you find them in 2 Timothy 3:16-17? List them below, using your own words.**

1. _____

2. _____

3. _____

4. _____

5. _____

All Scripture is inspired by God and is useful for teaching the truth, rebuking error, correcting faults, and giving instruction for right living, so that the person who serves God may be fully qualified and equipped to do every kind of good deed.
—2 Timothy 3:16-17, GNB

I worded my responses this way: The Holy Spirit (1) helps me understand the truths of God's Word; (2) corrects false beliefs or teachings; (3) convicts me of sinful attitudes and actions; (4) disciplines me in choosing a lifestyle pleasing to God; (5) helps me develop the skills and abilities I need to accomplish God's purposes for me. Maybe you chose different words, but check to see if the meaning is similar.

DAY 2

INSPIRING THE WORD

The Bible claims to be inspired by God, and that makes me curious. Exactly what did the Holy Spirit do to the Bible authors? How did He make sure they wrote what He wanted to say? Since He doesn't tell us, we try to figure it out. Some conclude the Spirit must have dictated the Bible to the authors like executives dictate to their secretaries. He obviously did dictate parts of the Bible; for example, when He gave the Ten Commandments to Moses. However, I do not believe much of Scripture was dictated in that way.

Many have undertaken to draw up an account of the things that have been fulfilled among us, just as they were handed down to us by those who from the first were eyewitnesses and servants of the word. Therefore, since I myself have carefully investigated everything from the beginning, it seemed good also to me to write an orderly account for you, most excellent Theophilus, so that you may know the certainty of the things you have been taught.
–Luke 1:1-4

🌀 **In the margin read the prologue to Luke's Gospel. What does Luke tell you about how God inspired him to write?**

❑ God dictated the book to Luke.
❑ Luke just wrote what he "felt led" to write.
❑ Luke did careful research.

Some of the Bible comes from historical research, as in the case of the Gospel of Luke and the Book of Acts, as Doctor Luke himself tells us.

On the human side, the experiences and writing style of each author are evident throughout Scripture. But in some mysterious way those authors were inspired by the Holy Spirit, so that what they wrote was consistently called, "the Word of God." Our unit memory verse reminds us that "all Scripture" is inspired.

Above all, you must understand that no prophecy of Scripture came about by the prophet's own interpretation. For prophecy never had its origin in the will of man, but men spoke from God as they were carried along by the Holy Spirit.
–2 Peter 1:20-21

🌀 **Read 2 Peter 1:20-21 written in the margin and circle yes or no in response to the following questions:**

yes no 1. Bible writers thought up the ideas expressed in Scripture.
yes no 2. Peter believed Old Testament writers were expressing the thoughts of God.
yes no 3. The Holy Spirit transmitted God's thoughts to human writers.

Though we may not know how the Spirit carried out this activity, we know from Scripture itself that He so guided the writing process that the human authors, using their own experiences and vocabulary, wrote what the divine Author wanted communicated. This cannot be said of any other book, no matter how helpful it is. Other books may be called "inspired" in the sense that they inspire the reader, but none can be said to be God-breathed as is Scripture. The Bible alone carries that guarantee. That's why we can trust it. The answers to the exercise were 1. no, 2. yes, and 3. yes.

🌀 **From the ideas about inspiration listed at the top of the next page choose the one that is closest to your view.**

❏ 1. The Holy Spirit dictated the words to human authors, much as a person would dictate a letter to a secretary.

❏ 2. The Bible is inspired like Shakespeare's work or any other great piece of literature.

❏ 3. The Holy Spirit influenced the minds of the authors so that they wrote in their own words exactly what He wanted to communicate.

❏ 4. Scripture inspiration is a mystery I don't understand.

Since the Bible does not define inspiration, we might be tempted to take the option of calling it a mystery and letting it go at that! I hope you were able to select the third option above. If not, would you be willing to reflect on the implications of any other choice?

My son Kent, well-versed in the creation story of Genesis, first encountered an alternative view of human origins in the third grade. His righteous indignation ran so hot that he conducted his own inquisition at the lunch hour. Going down the line of little people waiting to be fed, he asked each one, "Do you believe the monkey business?"

When he reached his best friend Darwin, his friend replied, "Of course I do." (He seemed to live up to the name his parents gave him!)

Kent then leveled his accusation: "Then you don't believe the Bible."

Darwin replied, "Oh yes I do, I just don't believe the part about creation."

With the wisdom of his advanced years, untutored by any elder, Kent responded, "Well, how do you choose which part to believe?"

🌀 **If you are uncertain about the reliability of the Bible, how would you answer Kent's question, "How do you choose which part to believe?"**

_____

_____

I remember hearing W. A. Criswell, pastor of First Baptist Church of Dallas for more than half a century, thunder, "They tell me the Book is inspired in parts and I'm inspired to pick the parts!" Eight-year old Kent and the 80-year-old pastor each identified the key issue. If I do what Jesus Christ never did and affirm error in Scripture, then I put myself over Scripture. By deciding what to accept and what not to accept as trustworthy, I must sit in judgment on the Book; I consider my inspiration superior to the inspiration of Scripture. In that way I would reduce the inspiration of Scripture to the size of my intellect, and that's not a very impressive "revelation!" Paul assures us in our unit memory verse that "All Scripture is inspired by God."

🌀 **King Josiah of Judah believed the Scriptures were the inspired message from God to His people. Read the verses in the margin. Below describe in your own words how Josiah reacted when he received the long-lost copy of the Book of the Law.**

_____

How did the people react?

_____

He read in their hearing all the words of the Book of the Covenant, which had been found in the temple of the Lord. The king stood by the pillar and renewed the covenant in the presence of the Lord—to follow the Lord and keep his commands, regulations and decrees with all his heart and all his soul, thus confirming the words of the covenant written in this book. Then all the people pledged themselves to the covenant.
—2 Kings 23:2-3

What difference does affirming that Scripture is the inspired Word of God make in a believer's life?

_____

The Bible helps us in the following ways:
- It describes God's character so we may know Him.
- It tells us how to become a child of God.
- It gives us moral direction for our lives.
- It assures us of our final destination.

The Holy Spirit gave us a fully reliable revelation of God's will for us. What a magnificent gift! He unveiled the character and purposes of God. We can know God! Knowing Him we will surely love Him. Love leads us to obedience as we seek to conform our wills to that of the Father. In the next lesson we will look more closely at Scripture as God's revealed will for what we think and how we behave.

This is my prayer response as I think about the inspiration of the Word. Pray along with me or voice your own prayer concerning the Bible.

> Father thank You for the good gift of Your Spirit who has revealed all the truth I need to know You, to love You, to please You. Thank You that the Bible is reliable. Help me to understand it more clearly and obey its teachings more fully.

Write the unit memory verse by filling in the missing words below:

All Scripture is_____by God and is useful for _____the truth, rebuking_____, correcting _____,and giving _____ for right _____,so that the man who serves God may be fully _____and _____ to do every kind of _____ _____

—2 Timothy 3:16-17, GNB

"How Firm a Foundation" is one of the great hymns of the faith. The song describes what God has done for us through Scripture. Take time to sing the song—you can get in the shower if necessary. Go for a walk. Tell God what you think and feel about His Word.

How firm a foundation,
* ye saints of the Lord,*
Is laid for your faith
* in His excellent word,*
What more can He say,
* than to you He hath said,*
To you who for refuge
* to Jesus have fled?*

But these are written that you may believe that Jesus is the Christ, the Son of God, and that by believing you may have life in his name.
—John 20:31

DAY 3

REVEALING GOD'S WILL

Revelation means that God has spoken. Inspiration means that the Holy Spirit so worked with the authors of Scripture that they wrote what He wanted written. We have a book we can rely on. But what is its purpose?

The Bible leads us to saving faith through Christ Jesus (John 20:31), the beginning point for our lifelong journey toward Christlikeness. It also reveals what we will be like when we are spiritually mature (Eph. 4:13). Our unit memory verse says Scripture "is useful." Its purpose is to teach us, rebuke and correct us, train us in righteousness, and equip us for every kind of good deed.

PRINCIPLES AND SPECIFICS

The Holy Spirit uses Scripture to guide us, but we often want specific—and simple—answers to our questions. The Bible does give "do's" and "don'ts," but it is much more a book of principles than a list of rules. I'm glad the Bible gives both. I need specific instructions, but I especially need principles.

Unlike rules, principles are comprehensive—covering all possibilities, but how the principle applies to life may elude me. So specific examples are also in the Scripture. "Love your neighbor as yourself," is a principle that covers all relationships, but the Bible also describes specifics of how love will behave. For example, when someone sins against me, if I truly love him or her, I will go to the person alone and confront him or her (Matt. 18:15-17). That's specific, but by giving the underlying principle of love, the Bible covers all potential attitudes, actions, and relationships.

When the Bible gives a general principle, we have the responsibility to apply the principle to specific situations. To make that application, we have help from the Holy Spirit.

First Corinthians 13 describes loving behaviors without tying them to specific situations. For the following descriptions of love, give a specific illustration of a loving behavior that would demonstrate this quality:

1. Love is patient (v. 4). _____

_____

2. Love is kind (v. 4). _____

_____

3. Love does not keep a record of wrongs (v. 5). _____

_____

How long would the Bible be if it gave specific examples or precise commands covering every possible attitude and activity for all people of all time? Even if God put all that detail on some mega-computer, how could we possibly access our specific directive at the moment of decision? No, the Spirit has given us something far better—principles to guide in the decisions of life.

In the exercise above, I listed these examples of love: I can be patient while waiting on a child to get ready in the mornings. I can be kind in my choice of language when I am expressing hurt feelings to my spouse. I can choose to forgive and not hold a grudge against a fellow employee.

We also encounter non-moral questions like: Should I take this job? What school should I attend? Should we stay here or move to another place? Even in those dilemmas of life, the Bible provides principles for guidance. God deals with us as individuals. His plan for your life will not be just like any other person's. Abraham's experience was unlike Moses', and Moses' experience did not resemble Jonah's. But Abraham, Moses, and Jonah lived by the principles of God's Word. Their example is given to help us understand God's will for us.

Until we all reach unity in the faith and in the knowledge of the Son of God and become mature, attaining to the whole measure of the fullness of Christ.
—Ephesians 4:13

Love is patient, love is kind. It does not envy, it does not boast, it is not proud. It is not rude, it is not self-seeking, it is not easily angered, it keeps no record of wrongs. Love does not delight in evil but rejoices with the truth. It always protects, always trusts, always hopes, always perseveres.
—1 Corinthians 13:4-6

GOD'S WILL REVEALED IN BIBLICAL EXAMPLES

The Scripture teaches both by precept and example. It states truth, and it demonstrates the truth at work in the lives of people.

Read each of the principles below. Write an example from the life of some Bible character such as Abraham, Moses, or Jonah that illustrates each principle. Many examples are possible; you may use your own examples or you may look up the Scripture passages I suggest.

a. God loves everyone, even sinners (Jonah 1:2; Rom. 5:8).

_____

b. God disciplines His children when they are disobedient (Deut. 32:48-52; Heb. 12:6).

_____

c. God wants us to trust Him even when we don't know how things will turn out (Gen. 12:1; Heb. 11:39).

_____

We could compare the Bible to a road map. It shows us the route from our beginning point as sinners without hope (Eph. 2:12). From our beginning we move to our point of conversion where we accepted Christ as the "way" (John 14:6). It leads us through the triumphs and pitfalls of everyday living to our ultimate destination (John 14:1-3).

Trace some of your life's journey on the path below, labeling each square with a significant spiritual event or insight you have experienced.

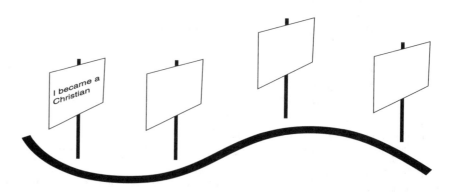

GOD'S WILL REVEALED IN SPECIFIC INSTRUCTIONS

Like any road map, the Bible has specific directions. What good would a map do if it only gave general directions for your journey through life? I recall a trip Muriel and I took to London. Muriel always wanted to go there. An artist, my wife never tired of visiting art museums; and London was, in her opinion, the art capital of the world. But with six children at home, we only traveled when necessary. However, a window of opportunity opened when I had a speaking engagement in England.

We knew where we wanted to go. We talked with people who had been there, we accumulated videos, travel books, and maps. We learned, for example, that the

There will be a highway there,
called "The Road of Holiness."
No sinner will ever travel that
road;
no fools will mislead those who
follow it. …
Those whom the Lord has
rescued
will travel home by that road. …
They will be happy forever,
forever free from sorrow and
grief.
—Isaiah 35:8-10, GNB

Tate Museum contained the largest collection of paintings by our favorite artist. But examples, descriptions, and principles would never have gotten us to the Tate Museum. We needed specific directions.

The principles and commands of Scripture are never in conflict. You cannot justify violating a direct command by appealing to some broader principle. The specific commands are God's official application of some principle and must be obeyed. My application of the principle doesn't have God's authority, so I must not set my interpretation in opposition to a clear directive from God.

Furthermore, the fact that no command covers a specific situation doesn't set us free to do as we please. We are still bound by the principles of Scripture. Thus we need both the principles and the commands to know God's will.

GOD'S WILL REVEALED IN JESUS

God didn't just make up rules. God's laws actually flow from His own character. They express His will that we be like Him. We might not understand if He just sent instructions and gave us examples of Bible characters. He Himself came to show us what the Father is like (John 14:7-11; Heb. 1:1-3). The exciting thing is this: Jesus in person is our standard for life. He is the supreme revelation of God's will.

God's will is that we be like Jesus. Four Scripture verses appear in the margin. After each reference below write the attribute of Jesus the verse describes. I have written the first response as an example. Put a check beside the attributes you want to develop more fully during this study.

❏ Luke 22:27   <u>Servanthood</u>
❏ John 15:9 _____
❏ Philippians 2:8 _____
❏ Hebrews 5:8 _____

God's revelation is not merely truth about the unseen world, given to satisfy our curiosity. Revelation shows us what God wants us to be and do. The Holy Spirit enables us to become like Jesus; He is God's standard for the Christian. Seeing how far we fall short of reaching that standard can be discouraging, but if we don't first see our need, we'll never attempt to meet it! The characteristics of Jesus that I listed were servanthood, love, humility, and obedience.

Even with our map for living we will make wrong turns. But God always provides a way back! A serious disciple of Christ has at least two reasons to obey:

1. We want to know what will bring joy to the one we love. We want to please Him by doing what He wants. "You are my friends," Jesus said, "if you do what I command you" (John 15:14). Love makes obedience to God's rules a joy because the result is fellowship with Jesus.
2. Obedience is practical. I need direction for my life. Only on the tracks laid out by divine wisdom will I find the fulfillment of life's purpose. As the Psalmist said, "Oh, how I love your law!" (Ps. 119:97).

In Psalm 119:105 David said, "Your word is a lamp to my feet and a light for my path." Give an example from your experience of how Bible study has guided your path.

_____

_____

"Who is greater, the one who is at the table or the one who serves? Is it not the one who is at the table? But I am among you as one who serves."
–Luke 22:27

"As the Father has loved me, so have I loved you. Now remain in my love."
–John 15:9

Being found in appearance as a man, he humbled himself and became obedient to death—even death on a cross!
–Philippians 2:8

Although he was a son, he learned obedience from what he suffered.
–Hebrews 5:8

In summary, God reveals His standard for Christian living in four ways, each reinforcing the other:

1. Principles of Scripture
2. Example of Bible characters, whether good or bad
3. Direct commandments
4. The example of Jesus.

In the next lesson we will discuss how to interpret the road map. Interpretation—determining the meaning the author intended—is the next step in knowing the will of God. And that is crucial for living life in the Spirit.

Has any truth become clear or especially important to you, perhaps demanding some response on your part? If so, you may wish to enter it in your journal for today.

○ **Write the unit memory verse in the space below, using these key words listed in the order they appear: inspired, useful, teaching, rebuking, correcting, giving, fully qualified, equipped, good work. Then check your accuracy by looking back at page 42.**

_____

_____

_____

DAY 4

INTERPRETING HIS MESSAGE

What do we mean when we say we need to interpret the Bible? How does depending on the Spirit affect interpretation? What about those passages that we find confusing or controversial? Interpretation must be the most abused word in discussing the Bible. Many people believe that everyone's "interpretation" is valid, no matter how outrageously it twists the meaning of the Scripture. Curiously, the popular view of "interpretation," as if no objective truth exists, is most often used of the Bible. Can you imagine two engineers debating whether or not 2 x 2 = 4?

Interpretation always begins by determining what the author intended to communicate. Interpretation does not mean justifying my view of an issue by twisting the passage into a new shape. When we assume that the Bible communicates specific meanings, some people call our approach "literalistic." I want to ask them, "Do you mean literalistic like literalistic news, history, or law?"

As we approach any written communication, we assume that the author intended to say something. The writer may have used literal or figurative language, but the task is to understand the intended meaning, not impose our own "interpretation" on the written material.

○ **Can you name an issue which tempts you to make the Bible say what you want it to say? Write one or more examples below.**

_____

Do your best to present yourself to God as one approved, a workman who does not need to be ashamed and who correctly handles the word of truth.
—2 Timothy 2:15

We all struggle with some issues in the Bible. Some passages in the Bible I still don't understand.

When we read the Scriptures, our assumptions condition how we understand what we read. Our culture, life experiences, understandings of words and ideas come with us. Sometimes what we bring with us can lead us astray. We must always be willing to challenge our own thinking to allow the Spirit to lead us into His truth. Interpretation means working diligently to make sure exactly what the author intended to say. Bible scholars call the study of Scripture *hermeneutics*–the science of determining the meaning of a text and applying it authentically to life. Good interpretation follows principles to separate the message of the Bible from my own thoughts, opinions, and ideas.

THREE BASIC APPROACHES

Bible interpreters use one of three basic approaches to the Scripture. These three approaches reflect the fact that the Bible is both a human and a divine Book–"holy men spoke," to be sure, but they were "carried along by the Holy Spirit" (2 Pet. 1:21). As is so often the case, we tend to go to one extreme or the other. Some people understand Scripture strictly as a man-produced document, while others treat it as exclusively supernatural, almost magical. We will surely miss what God wants us to understand by using either one of those approaches.

1. Those Who Treat the Bible as Purely Human

Some people reject any miraculous event recorded in Scripture as impossible. For example, they might say that the "feeding of the five thousand" was actually a story of sharing. A selfish crowd that had been hoarding their lunches responded to the generosity of a boy who was willing to share and brought out their own picnic baskets. For people using this approach, miracles–like the reluctant missionary Jonah and his savior/taxi, the fish–are no more than mythological accounts given to teach spiritual lessons.

What are some pitfalls of a purely human approach to the Bible?

_____

_____

_____

With this approach, the interpreter's own natural reason sits in judgment on the Scripture, screening out the true from the false, the authoritative from the dispensable.

2. Those Who Treat the Bible as Exclusively Supernatural

Some interpreters, throughout the ages, have treated the Scripture as if it were exclusively supernatural. Instead of working to understand the original meaning of a passage, they look for hidden meanings to be discovered by the reader. They think the Bible is a mysterious, almost magical Book. They use the Bible as a means of gaining insights, feeling impulses, or getting directions which may be wholly unrelated to what the Bible author intended to communicate.

Some so-called Bible studies do this. Members share what struck them as they were reading the Bible, and none of their responses need agree with one another or with the meaning of the text. They consider all ideas equally valid. Some Christians seek guidance for life this way. An impression which comes to them while reading

Scripture lends God's own authority to the guidance whether or not the text implies that course of action. This approach, though common, is magical; the reader looks for hidden, secret, or personalized meanings in the text.

I've done this myself. I was aimed toward overseas missionary service, but found myself in the mountains of North Carolina, principal of a Christian prep school. I considered it a temporary assignment, however, because Muriel and I kept thinking about those people who were out of reach of the gospel witness. Maybe God would let us be His ambassadors to those who had never heard.

The problem was that no one thought we should go. Everyone said we should stay where we were. Wasn't God blessing the work? So Muriel and I went to the Bible to find guidance. We searched for verses that would tell us what to do. And we found them! We read in Deuteronomy 1:6, "You have stayed long enough at this mountain." We did not realize that we were using the Bible like a ouija board, a magical divining rod. In those passages we read we were trying to get the biblical writers to speak to our current situation. Our "guidance" had nothing to do with the meaning intended by the authors. We were using a "supernatural" or magical approach to Scripture.

> **I'm not the only one who has used the "magical" approach to Scripture at one time or another. Can you describe below an occasion when you used the Bible in the way I have described?**

_____

_____

The Bible views itself as supernatural—God the Spirit is the Author behind the authors. But the authors were inspired to communicate a specific meaning as the revealed truth of God. In a newspaper, political cartoons and comics may have a double meaning or a hidden agenda, but the bulk of the newspaper is written in language intended to communicate a single meaning. So the Bible may have some "picture language" in which the meaning is not obvious, but the Bible is intended to convey meaning, not hide it. It is revelation. So our objective should be to understand the meaning the Author Himself intended to communicate.

> **What are some dangers to the search for a "magic text" to answer a pressing life need?**

_____

Though several dangers exist, such as missing the Holy Spirit's genuine leadership and making wrong decisions, the greatest danger may be in our relationship to God's Word. When we use the "magical" approach, we automatically stop looking for the authentic meaning of the Scripture; and that is a tragic loss.

3. Those Who Treat the Bible as Divine/Human

We need to view Scripture as more than a human book from which we pick and choose, or a magical book that grants our wishes. We need a balanced view that involves looking to Scripture as a divine revelation of things we could not otherwise know; but, as with any human communication, we must search out the meaning intended by the authors. If we diligently study the Bible, we will not find it a complicated puzzle. The Holy Spirit wants us to understand the meaning He intended. And by His grace we can do it!

◎ **Label the approach to interpretation you believe is being used in each of the following examples. (l) human; (2) magical; (3) divine/human.**

___ "You have dwelt long enough at this mountain" means that I should move from my present location in the mountains.

___ Jesus didn't really die; He was drugged. On the third day He woke up and was able to free Himself.

___ "Go into all the world and preach the gospel" means that my church must share in the responsibility of world evangelization.

___ "If your brother offends you, go to him alone" means that I should not talk to anyone else about a person who has wronged me, at least not till I have confronted him and tried to solve the problem.

If our goal in Bible study is to find out what the Holy Spirit wants to say to us, we must treat the Book as both human and divine, not going to one extreme or the other. My answers to the exercise above would be 2, 1, 3, 3.

We may have used a "magical" approach to get to Japan, but during the next 12 years we developed a more biblical approach to finding God's will. It's a good thing we did, because we faced the most difficult decision of our lives. While serving as missionaries, we were invited to come to Columbia, South Carolina, to lead Columbia Bible College and Graduate School; but our hearts were in Japan. We intended to "bury our bones" there. What should we do?

As was our custom when faced with a major decision, we scheduled time alone with the Lord to seek His will for our lives. This time I wasn't looking for some personalized special hidden meaning in the Bible. Instead God guided us through the principles of Scripture. For example, I found that in the Book of Acts, God guided His servants on most occasions through His church. That would suggest that one of the ways I should seek to find God's will would be to ask the church and my mission colleagues. I had resisted going to my mission council because I knew they would never agree to my leaving, nor would the leaders of the Japanese churches. And the little church I was in the process of starting surely would not understand. But finally I gave in and agreed to follow the pattern I found in Scripture. To my amazement, the "church" was virtually unanimous in urging me to accept the call to Columbia as God's call.

Perhaps God wanted to use us in another way to reach His goal of sharing the good news with all the world. And that is exactly what happened. During the 22 years I was president of what has now become Columbia International University, we sent thousands of missionaries around the world, many to places of strategic leadership in the mission enterprise of the church. I could not foresee all of that years before when I wrestled with God in a hotel room in Tokyo. I had learned to use Scripture for what it was intended, treating it as a divine Book with God's own authority, but treating it also as a book in human language that can be understood.

A BOOK AND A GUIDE

As we study, we may become confused or discouraged, so I have good news for you. We have more than a Book, we have a Guide! The Holy Spirit comes alongside to guide us in understanding the Book. That enlightening work of the Spirit will be our study next time.

◎ **Any notations for your journal? Anything to talk over with your partner? Be sure to thank the Lord that He has given you a wonderful Guidebook which you can understand, and ask the Holy Spirit to guide you as you study.**

⊚ **Write out your memory verse for this unit. Underline the key phrases you feel reflect needs in your life as you study the Scriptures:**

_____

_____

_____

DAY 5

ILLUMINATING MY MIND

Friends said I should get on the information super highway so I could send and receive electronic mail. They said things like, "You could send letters to Zimbabwe free of charge! Instantly!" But I was intimidated. I'd used a computer for years, but had never read one of the manuals on my shelf. They might as well have been written in a foreign language. If I hit a snag, instead of picking up a manual, I'd call an expert.

Some people approach Bible study the same way. The Bible sits on the shelf, so intimidating. How could I ever understand it? I'll just give the expert a call; I'll just wait to hear what the preacher says. But the Bible was given to us to use. It's so much more important than a computer manual. But like the manual, it takes effort to comprehend its message. How can I understand it?

Isn't it great that we can have our own personal guide? The Holy Spirit will guide us into all the truth we need (John 14:26).

Peter, a computer whiz, was my guide on the information highway helping me understand those mysterious manuals. The difference is I can see Peter, but I can't see the Spirit. So how does the Holy Spirit "illumine" my mind, throw light on the pages of Scripture? It's as mysterious as His activity in inspiring the Bible writers. How He does it, we may not know; that He does it we can experience daily.

⊚ **The course map pictures the activities of the Spirit. As a review fill in the two activities you have studied so far.**

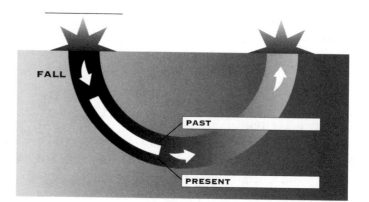

⊚ **The second activity of the Spirit is *revealing*. Now customize the course-map portion. Beside *past* write the revealing activity of the Spirit that is completed in the past. Beside *present* write the revealing activity the Spirit carries on in our lives today.**

The Spirit inspired the written Word. Inspiration is a past action. The Spirit illuminates the Word as believers read and study. Illumination is the present action.

DISCIPLINE REQUIRED

I haven't always had a hunger for God's Word. I once heard a Chinese evangelist say, "No Bible, no breakfast." I thought it made sense and started reading my Bible every day. But it was like eating sawdust. So I let it slip—the Bible, not breakfast. Sometimes I'd have my morning devotions, often I wouldn't. This went on for years. Finally, I became so spiritually malnourished that I became desperate.

At that point, I made a vow to the Lord that no matter what happened I would start the day with His "bread, milk, and meat," as the Bible calls itself. I thought He'd be pleased and work a miracle—the Bible would taste better than breakfast! But it didn't happen. It was still like eating sawdust.

I kept my vow, doggedly reading Scripture before the day got under way. Several months later I noticed a radical change had come over me, stealthily, all unannounced. I had a ravenous appetite, I loved my time in God's Word. If I had to miss the Bible or my breakfast, it would be no contest. I was thoroughly hooked.

What made the difference? I actively engaged in Bible study. I gave the Spirit time to teach me. The Spirit will not direct me if I sit passively by waiting for His inspiration. Bible reading demands that I give my best intellect, attitude, and time.

🌀 **When is the best time for you to be alone with God?** _____

What is the best place? _____

What "attitude adjustment" would make your time alone with God more

productive? _____

How do we insure that the Spirit is guiding our Bible study? Here's my approach. Before the day begins—while I am still in bed—I tell God good morning, thank Him that He is with me; and ask the Spirit to guide my reading. I have become so confident He will keep His promise, I anticipate with excitement what the Spirit will do with my mind and heart. Then as I open the Bible I often have an "ah-ha" experience. "Wow! Why didn't I think of that before?" "Look how this attitude needs to change! Now I see how to do it. What a wonderful God you are!" The light comes on, lifting my spirit, empowering my will, pointing out the right path.

🌀 **When you read Scripture, how would you evaluate your encounter with God? Check the item below which best describes your feeling.**

❑ The Bible really doesn't make a lot of sense to me, though I keep trying.
❑ I know God inspired the Bible writers, but I try to figure out the meaning with my God-given common sense.
❑ Sometimes I have an "ah-ha" experience when reading the Bible, and I give the Holy Spirit credit for helping me understand the meaning and what I'm supposed to do about it.
❑ Without some teacher or preacher to explain it to me, I'm not very confident I can understand most of the Bible.
❑ To be honest, I haven't really worked very hard at understanding and applying the Bible to my life.
❑ Other _____

> *To one there is given through the Spirit the message of wisdom, to another the message of knowledge by means of the same Spirit.*
> —1 Corinthians 12:8

⊚ Do you have a firm life-habit of reading the Bible regularly? If not, would you like to make a commitment to read the Bible more often? If so, check the response that indicates your commitment:

❑ I will seek to read the Bible daily.
❑ I will read the Bible on a regular basis.

⊚ If you aren't satisfied with your present relationship to the Bible, why not pause right now and ask God to do a new thing in you? You might want to talk over your experience in studying the Bible in your next group meeting, perhaps learning from the experiences of others.

The Bible speaks of a Spirit gift of knowledge and wisdom (1 Cor. 12:8). It may be God's purpose to gift you in that way. If not, ask Him to enable you to recognize that gift in others who may already have it. Whatever the gifted among us may experience, the Holy Spirit enlightens the mind of every believer.

ANOTHER SUBTLE DANGER

Growing disciples easily can encounter another problem. Christians who have a life of intimate conversation with God may begin to think that what they understand about the Bible is infallible–that their understanding is as certain as the Bible itself.

We must never confuse the activity of the Spirit in inspiring Bible writers with His activity in illuminating our minds today. Both are part of His "revelation" activity–the Spirit gave us an objective record of God's truth and He also helps us, subjectively, to understand it. However, a major difference exists. He inspired the Bible authors to write infallibly, but my understanding of the Bible's meaning is not infallible. I may err; and when I do, I rarely know it.

God does speak to us through His Word. He does lead us to understand the Word, but we need to beware of confusing our authority with that of Scripture. Some people attempt to claim authority by saying "God told me...," but we need to be a bit more modest. Though Scripture is fully trustworthy, we may err in our understanding of it.

Having given that caution, however, we must affirm His revelation in Scripture. It is so clear that Bible-believing Christians can agree on its major teachings.

⊚ Give an example of a major teaching on which most Bible-believing Christians would agree:

_____

Now give an example of a doctrine or teaching Christians disagree about:

_____

⊚ Why do you think there is not universal agreement on every point in the study of the Bible? Should there be? Explain your answer.

_____

_____

_____

We have the comforting assurance that the Holy Spirit comes alongside to help us understand the Bible. Each time you open it, ask the Author to do His work and illuminate its pages. You may have noted that Christians agree on issues such as the divinity of Christ and certainty of His second coming. We often cannot agree on such matters as the details of future prophecy or the way we describe the meaning of baptism.

Perhaps you've been helped by the Spirit more than you know. Review your journal entries—you may have as many as 15 so far. Underscore at least 5 things you have come to understand. Perhaps it's something about the nature of God or your own nature, something about your relationship to the Spirit or about His Book. What evidence do you find that the Holy Spirit is at work? How diligently have you been working to understand His self-revelation? Do you make the time necessary to get better acquainted? Are you committed to do what will bring Him joy?

The Bible is a love letter showing us the face of our Beloved and pointing out what we'll be like when we reach our destiny of becoming like Him. Here's my journal entry for today:

> **Spirit of the Living God, thank You that in ancient times You unveiled God's character through the prophets and apostles, and that today You lift the veil of my heart to understand Your Book. I want to walk with You all the days of my life, listen carefully to Your whispers, follow the light You shine on my way, and bring You joy. Amen.**

Perhaps you would like to express in your own words your response to the activity of the Spirit in giving you the Bible and in helping you understand it. You may have some frustrations and failed expectations. Whatever you feel about the Bible and your relationship to it would be a good journal entry for today.

Write 2 Timothy 3:14-16 from memory.

_____

_____

_____

In the second unit, we considered how the Holy Spirit created humankind on God's pattern. In this unit we examined the activity of the Spirit in revealing God to us through inspiring the Bible authors and in helping us understand Scripture today. In the next unit we will consider three major activities of the Spirit: (1) His activity in bringing about the birth, life, death, and resurrection of Jesus Christ, (2) His activity in convincing me of my need for a Savior, and (3) His activity of re-creating a disabled me into an altogether new person.

---

[1]Hershel H. Hobbs, *What Baptists Believe* (Nashville: Broadman Press, 1964), 65.

A NEW
CREATION

*In units 2 and 3 we studied the first two activities of the Holy Spirit in creating us
originally in His image and revealing Himself to us in the Bible. In unit 4
we will turn our attention to the third activity of the Holy Spirit:
God's masterful plan of redemption.*

"Dad, I have terrible news. Bob has been badly hurt in a diving accident. Please pray." Susan's voice at the other end of the line was controlled, though terror lurked around the fringes of her words.

I sat at my desk, stunned. I cried out to God to spare my son. Bob had just made a fresh commitment of his life to Jesus Christ. I thought of the conversation only three days earlier when he told me, "Dad, it's time for me to stop circling the harbor and launch out to sea." He was reaching the summit of his career as a photo-journalist, his marriage to Susan was idyllic, and I had just received another of those exquisitely crafted love letters he periodically wrote me. What a terrible time to die.

"Please, God," I cried. I felt so helpless; dared I even hope?

Ten minutes later the phone rang again. "Dad, Bob's with Jesus..." Hot tears flowed as if to wash away the pain, and friends gathered to embrace me; but the wound was too deep to be healed. Sons are meant to bury their fathers, not fathers to bury their sons.

In the following days I began to think about a father's love. I would have done anything to protect my son. If given a choice, how gladly I would have taken his place. I would never choose to let him go, not for anyone. Yet, God did just that. He chose to give His son for me. That's how much God loved me. I was not a family member, not even a friend. An enemy. And, unlike me, God did not have two sons left. He gave His only Son for me. Outrageous love motivated God to redeem a hostile, selfish, and angry world.

I had always thought of Jesus' love as supreme. Now I felt the impact of the Father's sacrifice. To give up one's own life is one thing, but the life of your beloved son? I wondered if the pain I felt was like the pain of the brokenhearted God.

Unit 4 begins with the sacrificial love of the Father that made our redemption possible; His sacrificial love resulted in the death of His Son.

Unit Memory Verse
If anyone is in Christ, he is a new creation; the old has gone, the new has come!
−2 Corinthians 5:17

> **What did the Spirit have to do with the birth, ministry,
> and death of Jesus? What does the fact that Jesus depended
> on the Spirit mean to me?**

DAY 1

OUTRAGEOUS LOVE

Our study, *Life in the Spirit*, does not focus on the activity of the Father and Son. But because God is indivisible, before we consider the specific activity of the Holy Spirit in our redemption, we need to be reminded of the sacrificial love of the triune God.

Through the work of the Holy Spirit, God sent Jesus to die—to become our Savior. What could motivate God to such sacrifice? When Bob died, I realized as never before how much it cost God to love us. In this lesson we will explore the love that motivated redemption.

"The Father's Cross" appears in the margin. Choose from the following list the statement you think best describes the main idea behind the poem, or you may write your own response.

❑ Sending Jesus to pay for our sins broke the heart of the Father.
❑ Only Jesus suffered on the cross.
❑ Giving His Son was more difficult for the Father than giving His own life.
❑ Out of love for us, God endured more pain than we can imagine.
❑ Other _____

The poem tells of the Father's love. I cannot imagine how God could love me enough to give His son to die for me. The learning activity asked for your opinion. You may have checked any but the second answer. Obviously, Jesus was not the only one who suffered on the cross.

Perhaps you, too, have suffered a great loss. Would you have chosen to suffer that loss for the benefit of someone else?

Think of the most painful loss you have experienced. From the list of words below, circle the word or words that best describe how that loss felt.

Reflect for a moment on the greatest sacrifice anyone ever made for you. Parents may give a son or daughter for love of country, a firefighter may give life in a rescue attempt, but when do we sacrifice for an enemy? The Scripture says "God has shown us how much he loves us—it was while we were still sinners that Christ died for us!" (Rom. 5:8, GNB).

Isn't it time to tell the Father again how very grateful you are that He loved you that much? If you feel gratitude, why not pause right now in your study and thank God for His incredible sacrifice.

The Father's Cross
Father,
What was your Gethsemane?
And when …
And where …
Did you decide,
Against all heart and reason,
To abandon your beloved one?
And that for me—
Oh, worthless substitute!

Like the piercings of a sword
We hear the cry,
"My God, my God, why
"Hast thou forsaken me?"
"What love!" we say
And yet …
Was not the Savior's piteous lament
A mere echo
Of that broken-hearted cry
Reverberating down the endless
Corridors of heaven,
"My Son, my Son,
"My beloved Son,
"Why have I forsaken you?"

No greater human love,
Christ taught, than when one
Gives his life.
But Father's love explodes
Beyond the reach of
Highest, deepest, and most untamed
Flight of human thought—
God gave not life, but Son.
His only Son.
For me …

LOST IMPACT

Once the word *blood* had power to move us. That single word summoned a vivid image of sacrifice and death. It stabbed our hearts with the pain of torture and senseless death. But no more. Television and movies have so washed the screen with blood that the writers must work to invent fresh images of increasingly violent death to grab our emotions. And we, by our bouncy hymns about the blood of Jesus, have trivialized the most sacred of sacrifices. We repeat the word *blood* like a mantra or chant it like a cheerleader's slogan. It no longer evokes strong passions within us.

The image of the cross also used to have powerful effect. Today we have difficulty understanding the image a cross had in the New Testament church. We have so glamorized the cross, who would be startled by the image? Who would think of wearing on his lapel the replica of a hangman's noose or an electric chair? People would think it weird and shudder. How do we regain the sense of loss, of outrage, of profound gratitude when we speak of the cross?

Before the crucifixion Jesus pled for a way out; His sweat poured to the ground like drops of blood. His heart was not bouncing with some jingle about blood. He was not fascinated with a diamond-studded replica of a cross. What was the agony for Him? Pause and read again the story in Luke 22:39-44 (also see Matt. 26:36-45). Meditate on what you have read and try to put yourself in Jesus' place in the garden of Gethsemane.

> **Reflect for a few minutes on what His agony must have been. From the following list of possible reasons for Jesus' agony in Gethsemane, number your choices, beginning with the most likely reason for His inner struggle. Leave blank any emotions you think He did not feel.**
>
> ____ fear of death
> ____ dread of so torturous a death
> ____ the pain of separation from His Father
> ____ the horror of being identified with our sin
> ____ terror of experiencing hell
> ____ other _____

He may have feared death, especially so torturous a death, but I doubt that was His greatest struggle. History is full of heroes who faced death unafraid. Jesus knew His death wasn't permanent; He knew that He would rise again on the third day. He had predicted it. Perhaps He shrank from the mysterious identity with our sin— He was about to experience the foul moral pollution of a whole world of sinners (2 Cor. 5:21). Or perhaps something deeper caused the Savior's agony.

Have you ever been betrayed by a friend? Even more painful—have you been abandoned by someone you thought would stand by you no matter what? But at the critical moment that person was silent or absent. Perhaps you have felt such pain, not from a mere friend, but from a parent or family member.

THE DEEPEST AGONY

I believe the deepest agony of Gethsemane was not the betrayal by Judas, painful as that must have been; nor the abandonment by Peter, deep sadness that it caused. The agony of Gethsemane was the horror of a break in the Trinity itself. From all eternity, the Son was the delight of the Father's heart, the crowning joy of heaven. And now, the Son would embrace our sin and the wrath of God would fall on Him instead of us. The heart of God, in a moment of time, would suffer an eternity of grief. "My God, my God, why have you forsaken me?"

Jesus went out as usual to the Mount of Olives, and his disciples followed him. On reaching the place, he said to them, "Pray that you will not fall into temptation." He withdrew about a stone's throw beyond them, knelt down and prayed, "Father, if you are willing, take this cup from me; yet not my will, but yours be done." An angel from heaven appeared to him and strengthened him. And being in anguish, he prayed more earnestly, and his sweat was like drops of blood falling to the ground.
—Luke 22:39-44

God made him who had no sin to be sin for us, so that in him we might become the righteousness of God.
—2 Corinthians 5:21

How do you feel about the cross, the blood? Have they lost their power? Do you need to take time to pour out to God your astonishment, your love, your gratitude? If you don't feel the passion, ask Him to restore it, or perhaps to engulf you with such love for the first time.

Whatever your emotions—whether you feel grief for His loss and gratitude for your gain, or passionless familiarity with the old story of our salvation—isn't it time to tell Him? Whatever your heart's true condition, share it with Him in writing.

◎ **Add to the prayer you've already written in your journal, or perhaps you would like to revise it altogether.**

◎ **This unit's Scripture memory verse appears in the margin. Write the verse on a card and begin memorizing it. If you have already memorized this or any of the suggested memory verses, choose an alternate verse from your time spent with God's Word. Substitute the alternate memory verse and begin to memorize it.**

If anyone is in Christ, he is a new creation; the old has gone, the new has come!
—2 Corinthians 5:17

DAY 2

THE INCARNATION: GOD WITH US

The unspeakable sacrifice of the Father and the Son amazes us, but what does the Holy Spirit have to do with the sacrifice? The Bible doesn't spell it out clearly, though it does give a hint: "Christ, who through the eternal Spirit offered himself unblemished to God" (Heb. 9:14). In some way the Spirit enabled Jesus to do what He did on the cross.

Scripture only hints about the Spirit's role in the crucifixion, but it goes into great detail about the role of the Spirit in the birth of Christ. We need to examine the importance of the incarnation to God's whole plan of salvation. As a matter of fact, if the Spirit had not given human life to the eternal Son in the womb of a virgin, all the other activity of the Holy Spirit in our behalf would be meaningless.

Scholars debate the exact year of Christ's birth, but Jesus didn't begin at Christmas! He's always been. As a member of the Trinity, He is included in Genesis 1:26, "Then God said, 'Let *us* make man in *our* image, in our likeness.'" John's Gospel begins with the declaration that "In the beginning was the Word, and the Word was with God, and the Word was God. He was with God in the beginning" (John 1:1-2). John credits Jesus with creation itself. He says, "Through him all things were made; without him nothing was made that has been made" (John 1:3).

◎ **Paul agrees with John's declaration. Read Colossians 1:15-17. Based on these verses, who**

created all things? _____

holds all of creation together? _____

He is the image of the invisible God, the firstborn over all creation. For by him all things were created: things in heaven and on earth, visible and invisible, whether thrones or powers or rulers or authorities; all things were created by him and for him. He is before all things, and in him all things hold together.
—Colossians 1:15-17

The Second Person of the Trinity, Jesus Christ, has always existed, just as the Father and the Spirit have always been. Time is a part of our human experience, but God is beyond our imprisonment in time. "'I am the Alpha and the Omega,' says the Lord God, 'who is, and who was, and who is to come, the Almighty'" (Rev. 1:8).

GOD'S TIMETABLE

When did God decide to send Jesus to earth? Was the decision a last-minute attempt to straighten out the mess we had made of God's plan? Did God think up the idea in a moment of inspired musing? Again, the Scripture tells us that the incarnation was an accomplished fact long before mankind sinned.

> **Read Ephesians 1:4-5. When did God decide to choose us as His adopted children through Jesus Christ?**

Paul praised the Ephesian Christians for being among the first to put their hope in Christ (v. 12). He affirmed that God's plan of redemption was put into place before the creation of the world.

> **In two other letters Paul affirms that the plan of salvation was in place before mankind sinned. In the margin, read 2 Timothy 1:9 and Titus 1:2. Underline the phrase common to both verses that tell when God's plan was formulated.**

God foreknew we would sin and, therefore, need a Savior. Man's sin did not create a need for the incarnation. Man's sin confirmed God's foreknowledge that a supernatural second birth would be necessary to re-create us in His image, capable of being like Him in His moral nature. God's plan was formulated before the beginning of time. Revelation 13:8 describes Jesus as the Lamb "that was slain from the creation of the world."

PROPHECIES OF THE INCARNATION

The Old Testament is the story of the preparation of Israel, God's chosen people, for the coming of the Messiah. The covenant with Abraham and later with Moses, the setting up of the kingdom and the throne of David, the ministries of the major and minor prophets, the fall of Judah and Israel, and the Exile—all demonstrate that "a man is not justified by observing the law, but by faith in Jesus Christ" (Gal. 2:16).

The Old Testament prophets announced the coming Messiah. The prophet Isaiah introduced the Suffering Savior who would bear our sins. (See Isa. 53 and 61.) Jeremiah, Daniel, and Malachi also foretold aspects of the Savior's life. Micah even told us Jesus would be born in Bethlehem (Mic. 5:2)!

> **From your Bible, read the following verses from the Gospel of Matthew. Write the phrase common to all the verses. Matthew 1:22; 2:17; 3:3; 4:14.**

Matthew was writing to a primarily Jewish audience. He wanted his readers to know that the birth of Jesus happened just as the prophets predicted. In the blank I wrote the phrase *through the prophet.*

The last, and according to Jesus, most significant of the forerunners announcing the coming of the Messiah was John the Baptist who was "filled with the Holy Spirit even from birth" (Luke 1:15). According to his father, Zechariah, John would "go on before the Lord to prepare the way for him, to give his people the knowledge of salvation through the forgiveness of their sins" (Luke 1:76-77).

For he chose us in him before the creation of the world to be holy and blameless in his sight. In love he predestined us to be adopted as his sons through Jesus Christ, in accordance with his pleasure and will.
—Ephesians 1:4-5

This grace was given us in Christ Jesus before the beginning of time.
—2 Timothy 1:9

A faith and knowledge resting on the hope of eternal life, which God, who does not lie, promised before the beginning of time.
—Titus 1:2

Who were "forerunners" of the gospel who announced to you that Jesus Christ is the Savior of the world? Perhaps they were parents, teachers, or neighbors. List their names below. Pause and thank the Father for their ministry in your life.

_____

_____

THE ROLE OF THE HOLY SPIRIT IN THE INCARNATION

Both Matthew and Luke credit the Holy Spirit with the mystery of the incarnation. In Matthew's account, Joseph is told in a dream that he should take Mary as his wife because "what is conceived in her is from the Holy Spirit" (Matt. 1:20).

Luke tells us that the angel Gabriel announced to Mary that she would conceive. Mary asked a legitimate question: "How will this be … since I am a virgin?" (Luke 1:34).

The angel replied, "The Holy Spirit will come upon you, and the power of the Most High will overshadow you. So the holy one to be born will be called the Son of God" (Luke 1:35).

The virgin birth is a supernatural phenomenon we will never fully comprehend this side of heaven. Both Matthew and Luke clearly attributed this miraculous event to the activity of the Holy Spirit. God's plan fashioned before the beginning of time was now put into motion. The holy child born in a manger in Bethlehem was named Jesus, "because he will save his people from their sins" (Matt. 1:21).

Why did Jesus come to earth in first-century Palestine? Why not centuries before or after? In his letter to the Galatians, Paul said "the time had fully come" (Gal. 4:4). Many factors converged to make first-century Palestine the right time and the right place for the birth of Jesus:
- The Roman roads and postal system made the spread of the gospel possible.
- It was a time of relative peace.
- Greek was the universal language.

The most important factor, however, was that the legalistic Pharisees, the religious elite of their day, had demonstrated the futility of trying to keep the law in man-made systems. Paul explained the Jewish dilemma this way: "Before this faith came, we were held prisoners by the law, locked up until faith should be revealed. So the law was put in charge to lead us to Christ that we might be justified by faith. Now that faith has come, we are no longer under the supervision of the law" (Gal. 3:23-25).

Read Galatians 4:4-7 in the margin. What does this verse say the Spirit accomplishes in the life of a believer? Put the following words in the proper order to complete the sentence: *heir, slave, son.*

You are no longer a _____ but a _____

and an _____.

No longer prisoners of the law or slaves of sin, believers are rightful heirs of all the Son's inheritance. For your prayer time as you close today's lesson, thank God the Father for each of the following: 1) His plan from the beginning of time to save you from your sins; 2) the work of the Holy Spirit in the incarnation of Jesus; 3) that you can be a child of God and an heir of all the riches of the Heavenly Father with Jesus Christ.

But when the time had fully come, God sent his Son, born of a woman, born under law, to redeem those under law, that we might receive the full rights of sons. Because you are sons, God sent the Spirit of his Son into our hearts, the Spirit who calls out, "Abba, Father." So you are no longer a slave, but a son; and since you are a son, God has made you also an heir.
—Galatians 4:4-7

If anyone is in Christ, he is a new creation; the old has gone, the new has come!
—2 Corinthians 5:17

◎ Record in your prayer journal what being called a child of God means to you. List some of the benefits you receive because you are a child of the King.

◎ Read the unit memory verse. Close your eyes and say it to yourself. If possible, have a family member check your accuracy.

DAY 3

JESUS RELIED ON THE SPIRIT

All that Jesus did to accomplish our redemption, from birth to ascension—the entire incarnation—was by the power of the Holy Spirit. In this lesson you will identify some of the ways Jesus depended on the Spirit.

◎ The following Scriptures each describe one of the ways the Spirit worked in the life of Jesus. From the list in the margin match the activity of the Spirit with the passage describing that activity.

A. accomplished Jesus' sacrificial death

B. enabled Jesus to preach and minister

C. guided Jesus

D. healed the sick

E. brought about Jesus' birth

F. raised Jesus from the dead

G. visibly identified with Jesus

___ 1. Luke 1:35—"The angel answered, 'The Holy Spirit will come upon you, and the power of the Most High will overshadow you. So the holy one to be born will be called the Son of God.' "

___ 2. Luke 3:22—"The Holy Spirit descended on him in bodily form like a dove."

___ 3. Luke 4:1—"Jesus, full of the Holy Spirit, returned from the Jordan and was led by the Spirit in the desert."

___ 4. Luke 4:18-19—"'The Spirit of the Lord is on me, because he has anointed me to preach good news to the poor. He has sent me to proclaim freedom for the prisoners and recovery of sight for the blind, to release the oppressed, to proclaim the year of the Lord's favor.'"

___ 5. Luke 5:17—"One day as he was teaching, Pharisees and teachers of the law, who had come from every village of Galilee and from Judea and Jerusalem, were sitting there. And the power of the Lord was present for him to heal the sick."

___ 6. Hebrews 9:14—"How much more, then, will the blood of Christ, who through the eternal Spirit offered himself unblemished to God, cleanse our consciences from acts that lead to death, so that we may serve the living God!"

___ 7. Romans 8:11—"If the Spirit of him who raised Jesus from the dead is living in you, he who raised Christ from the dead will also give life to your mortal bodies through his Spirit, who lives in you."

The Holy Spirit was at work in every event in Jesus' incarnation. When Jesus healed, overcame temptation, taught, prayed, and endured His crucifixion—everything was attributed to the Spirit's power. If the powerful Son of God, Himself deity, needed the Holy Spirit's presence and power, how much more do you and I! And yet, too often, we try to live the Christian life as if the Spirit did not matter. Many parallels exist between what the Spirit did in Jesus' life and what He can do in ours. You may have responded: 1-e, 2-g, 3-c, 4-b, 5-d, 6-a, and 7-f.

🌀 **Consider your life. In the exercise below, identify ways the Spirit works in you that parallel what He did in the life of Jesus. I have completed the first comparison as an example. Read the Scriptures below each statement if you need assistance.**

How the Spirit Helped Jesus   *How the Spirit Helps Me*

1. Jesus' birth by the Spirit's power   my new birth
   (John 3:5)
2. Jesus' prayer life   _____
   (Rom. 8:26)
3. Jesus' service empowered by the Spirit _____
   (1 Cor. 12:4-7)
4. Jesus' crucifixion enabled by the Spirit _____
   (Rom. 8:13)
5. Jesus' resurrection by the Spirit's power _____
   (Rom. 8:11)

🌀 **You will find the answers to the last learning activity in the following paragraph. Circle actions of the Spirit in the life of the believer.**

Like Jesus we must completely depend on the Holy Spirit from new birth to our own death and final resurrection. Born again by the power of the Spirit, we gain any knowledge or wisdom we have through Him. We live godly lives and minister with power only to the extent that He enables.

In powerful picture language, Paul draws parallels between Christ's death and our own "death" to the old life. Our death marked our entrance into life. Paul says Christ's death paradoxically also points to how we are to continue that new life. The apostle also draws parallels between Christ's resurrection and our own—spiritually in the past and physically in the future.

These analogies will prove to be rich lodes of truth for us to mine throughout this study—how to live out our own lives in the Spirit. For the moment, remember that if Jesus needed the Holy Spirit—we need the Spirit even more.

If Jesus accomplished His Father's will by exercising His divine powers, then we can never hope to follow in His steps. Yet that is exactly what we are told to do: "Follow my example, as I follow the example of Christ," said Paul (1 Cor. 11:1). Paul then explained how: "If we live by the Spirit, let us also walk by the Spirit" (Gal. 5:25, RSV). Jesus Himself said He was sending the Spirit to be "with you" and "in you" (John 14:16-17). So we have exactly the same resource Jesus had to live His life: the Holy Spirit within.

Before He ascended, Jesus told His disciples it was to their advantage that He was going because only then would they receive the Holy Spirit (see John 16:7-14). Just before He ascended to heaven He said, "You will receive power when the Holy Spirit comes on you" (Acts 1:8).

Jesus attributed His powerful ministry on earth to the work of the Holy Spirit. "The Spirit of the Lord is on me," Jesus said in Luke 4:18. Believers today have access to that same power source. Jesus intended that we live a victorious Christian life. He never meant for us to flounder, bound in the same prison of sin, defeated and discouraged, as though we had no Holy Spirit to set us free and empower us.

At the top of the following page is my prayer response to these truths. If it reflects your own response, I invite you to join me in the prayer. If not, take time to tell God your thoughts, feelings, and concerns.

"I tell you the truth: It is for your good that I am going away. Unless I go away, the Counselor will not come to you; but if I go, I will send him to you. When he comes, he will convict the world of guilt in regard to sin and righteousness and judgment: in regard to sin, because men do not believe in me; in regard to righteousness, because I am going to the Father, where you can see me no longer; and in regard to judgment, because the prince of this world now stands condemned.

"I have much more to say to you, more than you can now bear. But when he, the Spirit of truth, comes, he will guide you into all truth. He will not speak on his own; he will speak only what he hears, and he will tell you what is yet to come. He will bring glory to me by taking from what is mine and making it known to you."
—John 16:7-14

Holy Spirit of God, thank You for the gift of a Savior. From Bethlehem and Nazareth to the streets of Jerusalem and the paths of Galilee, then on to Golgotha and the empty tomb, You hovered over the Son, empowered Him, enabled Him. What a wonder You are! Though it is beyond my ability to understand, You now stand ready to do the same things for me. I don't have the words to let You know how thankful I am, but how I long that my life itself will prove my gratitude. My life will honor You only by Your work in me, so I now ask for that powerful work with confidence that You keep Your promises. Amen.

Do you need to rely on the Spirit more in your life? Write about your need in your journal. Is there something you need to share with your accountability partner? God loves to overhear you talking about Him to someone else.

DAY 4

CONVICTION: WE NEED REDEMPTION

The Holy Spirit touches me deeply and personally when He convicts me of my sin. All that Jesus did would be wasted, at least for me, unless the Spirit convinces me that I need a Savior. The rebirth experience Jesus spoke of to Nicodemus in John 3 begins with the Holy Spirit convicting us of our sin. The Spirit must show me my sin so that I may repent, ask forgiveness, and receive salvation.

In this lesson we will focus on John 16:8-11. Below answer the following question: "Why do we need the convicting power of the Holy Spirit?"

_____

_____

_____

_____

"When he comes, he will convict the world of guilt in regard to sin and righteousness and judgment: in regard to sin, because men do not believe in me; in regard to righteousness, because I am going to the Father, where you can see me no longer; and in regard to judgment, because the prince of this world now stands condemned."
—John 16:8-11

Without conviction we would never become new creations in Christ Jesus. In John 16:8 Jesus explained that a key role of the Holy Spirit would be to "convict the world of guilt in regard to sin and righteousness and judgment." We can depend on the Spirit to show us our sin if we are open to His conviction.

Even believers can shut out the Spirit and deny that they are sinning. Fortunately, the Spirit does not give up and go away, for the Father loves and disciplines His children (Rev. 3:19). Anytime we feel the conviction of the Spirit, we should rejoice. The Father loves us so much He doesn't want us to continue hurting ourselves or others. Conviction of sin is a blessing in the life of a believer.

In John 16:7, look for why Jesus said His return to the Father was "for our advantage." Check the best answer, or write your own response.

❑ They would never have the Holy Spirit in them as long as Jesus remained with them.
❑ The Holy Spirit in them is better than Jesus only with them.
❑ The Holy Spirit will not come to you until you turn from all your sins.
❑ other _____

I would never have come to Christ if the Holy Spirit had not convinced me that I need forgiveness. You could correctly check either of the first two responses. The third response is false. We cannot summon the Holy Spirit by leaving our sins. The Holy Spirit comes to us first and shows us our sins.

THE WORLD'S RESPONSE TO CONVICTION

The work of the Holy Spirit includes some painful aspects. When the Spirit convicts me that I am a sinner or that a particular thought or behavior is wrong, I feel guilty. Many in our culture tell us that guilt is the greatest roadblock to human happiness and fulfillment. They believe that guilty feelings are the "root of all evil." Their goal becomes to get rid of guilt feelings. But just as physical healing sometimes involves physical pain, the route to spiritual restoration involves confronting our own guilt and sin.

My friend Pramod had a disease—a form of leprosy. Because of his disease, he could feel no pain in his hands and feet. Pramod caused himself serious injuries, eventually hastening his own death, because of his lack of feeling. A person with leprosy may feel no pain, but the absence of pain is harmful rather than good.

Write your own moral to the story of Pramod—comparing our need to recognize our sin to Pramod's need to feel physical pain.

_____

_____

I wrote that apart from the convicting work of the Spirit, we are something like Pramod—only ours is a form of spiritual leprosy, deadening our sensitivity to sin.

The ability to feel guilt is a wonderful gift. We've been given a sense of soul-pain, a conscience to warn when we are spiritually ill. The greatest danger is to feel no pain of guilt. Guilt is like the warning light on the dashboard of a car, letting us know that something is in need of attention. Just as we appreciate a warning light, we should appreciate guilty feelings as an indicator that something in our spiritual life needs attention.

Read Psalm 139:23-24. Would you consider making these verses a regular part of your prayer life? Cultivate an appropriate sensitivity to the Spirit as He convicts you of sin.

THE OPPOSITE EXTREME

We can also have a sense of guilt when we actually are innocent. Spiritually sensitive people often confuse temptation for sin. For example, young men have often come to me with a burden of guilt for the attraction they feel for a particular girl.

"Have you tried to seduce her with words or actions?"

"Oh no, I wouldn't do that."

"It is to your advantage that I go away; for if I do not go away, the Helper shall not come to you; but if I go, I will send Him to you."
—John 16:7, NASB

Search me, O God, and know my heart;
test me and know my anxious thoughts.
See if there is any offensive way in me,
and lead me in the way everlasting.
—Psalm 139:23-24

"Well, have you entertained sexual fantasies about her?"

I explain that finding a girl very attractive is not a sin, but can easily become a temptation to sin. As long as you keep saying no to the temptation, it remains that—a temptation, not a sin.

Of course the enemy gets in there and mixes us up—he's called the Accuser for good reason. If he can't trip us into sinning, his next ploy is to make us believe we have sinned; because misplaced guilt is destructive. For example, many of us feel bad when we stand up to another person or say no. Christians often must face rejection for standing up for the truth. The price of obedience often includes rejection or anger from those who disregard biblical standards. We may feel regret when we have been rejected, but regret is not guilt.

⊚ **Can you think of a time when you suffered some kind of penalty because you chose to stand up for what you knew was right? ❑ Yes ❑ No If so, did you feel either guilt or regret?**

If what I did was not wrong, the feeling isn't legitimate guilt. A feeling of sadness about what we have done can come when we do the difficult but right thing, like confronting a person over some sin. Feeling bad about it, especially if we did the right thing poorly, is legitimate; but a feeling of guilt is not legitimate. Feelings of guilt at such times are the work of an over-sensitive conscience or the accusations of our enemy.

MAKING THE DISTINCTION

How can you tell when guilt is appropriate and when it's not? The answer is the Word and the Spirit! First examine the Bible and see how it defines the attitude or action in question. Our conscience can be our guide only if we have an informed conscience. Our moral judgment must be molded by what God has to say. For example, many people have come to me in great distress, feeling they have committed the unpardonable sin. In every case they've been set free from this terrorizing sense of guilt by turning to Scripture and allowing the Bible itself to determine what the sin is. Certainly no person who cares about the sin of grieving the Spirit has committed this unpardonable sin.

We also need the leadership of the Holy Spirit to guide our moral judgment. We humans have infinite capacity for rationalizing, excusing that selfish impulse or unworthy motive. We need the Holy Spirit to sensitize our conscience.

If we could go to a counselor who would be right in the advice he or she gave each time, we would probably choose to go often! We have access to such a counselor and He is free of charge. The word *Helper* in John 16:7 (NASB) is also translated *Comforter* (KJV) or *Counselor* (NIV).

⊚ **Can you think of one or more times when you have gone to the extreme of undeserved guilt or lack of deserved guilt? Briefly describe a time when you felt guilt for something that probably was not your fault. Then briefly describe a time when you needed to feel deserved guilt.**

I felt undeserved guilt when _____

_____

I felt (or needed to feel) deserved guilt when _____

_____

The exercise called for a difficult level of self-examination. Most of us have experienced undeserved guilt. Some people struggle every day under a sense of personal worthlessness and shame. But ultimately every one of us has done wrong. We need to recognize our deserved guilt. When all the arguments of innocence and guilt are fully explored and the Judge renders the verdict, it is "guilty as accused." We are guilty, every one of us, of violating God and others. We are guilty of harming ourselves. I do not readily admit my guilt, even to myself, until the Holy Spirit sensitizes my conscience to see things truthfully. He was sent "to convict the world of guilt in regard to sin and righteousness, and judgment" (John 16:8).

THE SPIRIT CONVICTED ME

The greatest crisis in my life came at an early age. I was desperately afraid of hell. I went to my mother, naturally, where a fearful child is accustomed to go; but she sent me to my father. Upon hearing my fear, he asked me an old-fashioned question: "Have you sinned?"

Such a question for an innocent child! I nodded. Even worse, he followed up with, "And what was your sin?" That was my pain; I needed no heart-searching probe to find a possible answer.

Sobbing, I blurted out, "I lied." It was finally out. Surely he would let me off the hook as a confessed sinner. But no.

"Any other sins?" I couldn't remember any more, so focused was I on that lie. So Daddy helped me remember some more.

Finally we were ready to pray. We knelt by his bed, the same bed on which I had been born the first time, and I gave my life to the Savior. Since I was only a child, I could not begin to appreciate all that the Holy Spirit did in my life that day. I was sorry enough for my sin, but primarily I feared punishment. I had heard of hell, and I knew hell was for sinners. Jesus was for sinners, too. I ran to Him, opened my heart to Him and felt His warm embrace. With that embrace came peace.

I am ashamed to admit it, but 18 long years passed before I shed the first tear over my sin. As a church member, I had been asked to prepare a message on the death of Christ. As I prepared, for the first time in my life I felt sorrow that Jesus was on that cross because of my sin. Not Hitler's. Not Stalin's. Not the world's. Mine. My heart was broken by grief, not grief for what my sins might do to me, but grief for what they did to Him.

Like a deep reservoir trapped for years beneath a stony heart, the gusher burst free and I mourned the hell I caused my Beloved. That was the work of the Holy Spirit. Not everyone will have the same outward response, but the evidence of the Spirit's work is grief for the wrong I have done my Savior.

Hopefully, you have had a similar experience. How did the Holy Spirit convince you of your sin when you first turned to the Savior to rescue you? Was it through the painful consequences of some sin? Was it your sense of weakness before a persistent temptation? Or was it not a sin, but a sense of need: loneliness or a feeling of futility? Who brought your need home to you? A parent? A preacher? A Sunday School teacher? A book? The Bible?

Below list all the ways you can remember that God used to make you aware that you needed a Savior.

_____

_____

_____

"Son of man, I have made you a watchman for the house of Israel; so hear the word I speak and give them warning from me. When I say to a wicked man, 'You will surely die,' and you do not warn him or speak out to dissuade him from his evil ways in order to save his life, that wicked man will die for his sin, and I will hold you accountable for his blood."
–Ezekiel 3:17-18

Indeed, when Gentiles, who do not have the law, do by nature things required by the law, they are a law for themselves, even though they do not have the law, since they show that the requirements of the law are written on their hearts, their consciences also bearing witness, and their thoughts now accusing, now even defending them.
–Romans 2:14-15

What shall we say, then? Is the law sin? Certainly not! Indeed I would not have known what sin was except through the law. For I would not have known what coveting really was if the law had not said, "Do not covet."
–Romans 7:7

Those who sin are to be rebuked publicly, so that the others may take warning.
–I Timothy 5:20

In the margin read Ezekiel 3:17-18; Romans 2:14-15; Romans 7:7 and 1 Timothy 5:20. As you read, write below any means the Spirit uses that were not part of your experience.

_____

_____

Though the Spirit convinces people of their sin and its consequences, the Bible does not explicitly teach all the methods He uses. It does tell us what the Spirit uses to bring conviction: the preached Word, one's own conscience, the law, and the example of those who sin, along with the consequences of their sin. In these ways and in direct whispers to the heart, the Holy Spirit convicts us.

At the time of my rebirth I felt liberated and forgiven. Never again would God see me as a polluted, self-dominated sinner. He sees me as clean and innocent as Jesus. I never again must quake before Him. My relationship to God is that of a loved child to his Father. To this day I still continue to learn and appreciate more what His love for me cost Him.

OUR RESPONSE TO THE SPIRIT'S CONVICTION

Have you heard the convicting whisper of the Spirit as you read? Do you have a repetitive sin that the Spirit continues to bring to your attention? If so, resolve to confess your sin, repent, and receive forgiveness before you continue this study.

Perhaps you are safe in Jesus and sure of it. For you, the Spirit's work of convicting the world of judgment to come is no longer your dread, but do you grieve over what your sin did to Jesus? Do you dread bringing Him pain again? Have you ever felt deeply what your sin means to Jesus? Perhaps today is the day the Spirit will break open your heart and let your love burst forth in grief and gratitude.

Today, rather than my suggesting a prayer, reach out to Jesus and tell Him of your sorrow for whatever sin the Spirit may convict you of. If no moral violation comes to mind, consider the sin of running your own life for your own benefit. Tell Him your gratitude for what He did to wash away the guilt. You can do this whether you have never done it before or whether you have done it often. He will delight to hear what is on your heart.

Below write this week's Scripture memory verse from memory if you can. Review your other Scripture memory verses.

_____

_____

DAY 5

THE MAGNIFICENT RE-CREATION

In this unit we've studied the Spirit's activity in providing through Jesus our salvation from sin, death, and hell. Redemption, we call it. Actually, all the Spirit's activity since the fall has been redemptive. God has taken the initiative to provide a way back into loving oneness with Him.

In this unit we've focused on God the Son coming to pay the redemptive price. We've seen how the Holy Spirit prepares us through His convicting power to want salvation. All of this would come to nothing if something didn't happen to change us into a different kind of person, a God-compatible person. That's the theme of this lesson. Theologians call it regeneration. God the Spirit who "generated" us in creation, now "re-generates" us, transforming us into altogether different people. That's the turning point in our spiral down, away from God. But regeneration is only one part of what happens at the turning point.

BIBLICAL DESCRIPTIONS OF SALVATION

Salvation is a word that encompasses all God ever did for us and all He ever will do. Regeneration describes one part of the total salvation process. Other words, such as justification, describe other aspects of our salvation.

The following is a list of terms that describe facets of salvation. Try to describe in simple language each one as you now understand it.

Conviction _____

Faith _____

Repentance _____

Forgiveness _____

Justification _____

Regeneration _____

The following paragraphs describe what takes place when a person becomes a believer. As you read, watch for key words and phrases. Underline any of the terms from the list above and circle any synonym I used in place of the technical word.

The Spirit first convinces us that we are sinners in need of a savior. His work may take a long period of time, depending on the resistance He meets. Finally, He breaks through our denial, and we recognize our need of a Savior! We believe certain basic facts about Jesus and about our own condition. We feel sorrow for our sin. We turn from our sin in repentance and trust our lives to the Savior. That is a description of complete or biblical faith. As you see, biblical faith means much more than simply believing.

When we respond to God in faith, He forgives our sins; He blots out the record of our sin and declares us righteous. This we call *justification*—just-as-if-I'd never sinned! At the same time, in some mysterious way we may never fully understand, God transforms us at the core of our nature into something wondrously new and different. We call this change *regeneration*.

Not all would agree with the order of the salvation process as noted above. Some would put regeneration at an earlier stage, but all would agree that the activity of the Spirit in re-making us is a glorious essential in our salvation.

If you are already a Christian, reflect for a few minutes on what happened in your life when you were "born again" (regenerated, re-created). What changed? Actually, God changed something about every part of your personality—the way you think, how you feel, and what you choose.

Below give an example of the major changes as you remember them, or as others saw them in you. Note: If you were too young to remember, you may want to make your list from a later time in life when you encountered God afresh and renewed your commitment to live for Him.

Your mind (how you thought)—what viewpoints changed? How did your thinking change about your values, priorities, and purpose?

_____

_____

Your heart (how you felt about things)—what attitudes changed? What changed in your likes and dislikes, who you liked to be around, who your heroes were? How did your feelings about yourself and God change?

_____

_____

Your will (your ability to make choices for God and against sin)—did any bad habits stop, good habits start? Did you experience any changes in lifestyle and activities?

_____

_____

A MAGNIFICENT NEW CREATION

You have just described a magnificent new creation. You! Regeneration is only the beginning of the transformation God brings in our lives. It sets in motion a great restoration project. We will explore that restoration process in the rest of our study of *Life in the Spirit*. Restoration begins when we trust in Christ and begin a continuing process that lasts a lifetime.

Today, fathers routinely assist in the delivery of their children. When our daughter was born such ideas were considered outrageous. Fortunately, our doctor was young and willing to consider new approaches. I argued that we were going to the mission field, and I might need to assist in a birth the next time. He told me to stand just inside the door where I wouldn't be in the way. When the time came, however, I could see nothing but a sheet-draped figure on a table across the room!

Then it happened. The doctor rose from behind the sheet canopy, holding aloft a tiny creature by her heels. "Is she supposed to be blue?" I wondered. "And why is she so silent? I thought babies started off with a bawl." Nurses scurried to retrieve a suction syringe and—what's this?—the doctor whacked my baby across the behind! Suddenly little Mardi let out a wail, startling me with her lung power, and bringing relief to a tense delivery room.

INCREDIBLE POTENTIAL

Who was this new creature? She was the same little person who had been residing for a time in her mother's womb. But now that she had been born, she experienced new dimensions of life! She could communicate, breathe on her own, develop loving relationships, and grow, unimpeded by the restrictions of her former life.

The following paragraph describes three new potentials a believer receives that he or she did not possess before spiritual birth. Circle the three abilities I identify. In the margin write any additional examples of how you would compare physical birth with the new birth.

Jesus taught that we must be born again (John 3:3). When we experience the new birth, we are the same person physically as before. But what a radical transformation we have experienced! Now we can communicate with God, we can develop a relationship of intimate companionship with Him, and we can grow more like Him. We have become a new creation through the process called regeneration. We were originally generated through conception and birth. Now we are re-generated, born again.

You might identify other ways a believer receives new potential. Did you circle the opportunity to communicate, to develop a relationship, and to grow more like Him?

THE COMPLETION OF OUR TRANSFORMATION

Odd as it sounds, the Bible also compares the new birth to dying (Rom. 6:1-11). You may have heard these words during a baptism ceremony: "dead to sin, raised to walk in newness of life."

I sat on the side of my bed, head bowed, tears flowing. I was grieving the loss of my eldest son, Bob. My youngest, Kent, stood by me, trying to comfort a heartbroken father. All the what-ifs paraded through my mind—what if he had caught fire for God sooner? What if I had been a better father?

"Dad," said Kent, "if you ever failed Bob, I'll guarantee he has forgiven you now. And all you ever wanted him to be, he is. And more. Just like Jesus. He's free and fulfilled. Why, I'll bet he's winging it off to some distant galaxy on a photo assignment, planning exciting new adventures for you to share when you get there, like he always did here."

The same Bob, who lay dying on a hospital gurney one moment, now experiences new dimensions of life, new potentialities!

And so it is with us. The same person who lived out life in a dim shadowland, now has come alive in Jesus. We died, as it were, and have been resurrected to a new life. We don't know exactly how it was done or even exactly what happened, but we experience a radical transformation into a whole new dimension of being. "The old is gone, the new has come." Sort of like a death. Or a birth. That's the work of the Spirit.

Both the Bible and history are filled with people whose lives were transformed by the power of the Holy Spirit. John Newton was a slave trader, without regard for man or God. After the Spirit convicted him of his sin and brought him to repentance and faith, Newton became a pastor and the author of one of the most beloved Christian hymns of all time. He wrote:

> *Amazing grace! How sweet the sound,*
> *That saved a wretch like me!*
> *I once was lost, but now I'm found,*
> *Was blind, but now I see.*

That old, old story never ceases to amaze. You know it well. But how would you tell the story to someone who came to you and said: "I really want to be a Christian. I want to be sure everything's OK between God and me"?

Don't you know that all of us who were baptized into Christ Jesus were baptized into his death? We were therefore buried with him through baptism into death in order that, just as Christ was raised from the dead through the glory of the Father, we too may live a new life.
—Romans 6:3-4

Write out in non-technical words how you would answer, explaining God's plan of salvation and telling how to commit his/her life to Jesus.

_____

_____

_____

_____

_____

Your words may be different, but did you include each of the following ideas?
- I'm a sinner. I deserve God's judgment. I can't save myself. I can't get rid of the guilt of my sin.
- Jesus took my penalty. He died in my place.
- Jesus rose from the dead. He demonstrated the Spirit's power to conquer sin, death, and hell.
- I personally receive Him by faith.

When I turn to Jesus Christ in faith, I—
1. confess to Him my sin and desire to turn from it.
2. trust Him to keep His promise to forgive all my sin and make me His child.
3. acknowledge Him as Lord of my life.

In an instant He forgives my sin, makes me His child, and changes me into a new person, from the inside out. He comes to live in me as a daily companion.

Did the gospel story you wrote above include each of those actions on God's part and on yours? Circle any item you omitted. Now the most important question of your life: have you taken those steps?

A Story of New Birth

Yesterday I received a phone call from Kimie. In Japanese she blurted out, "Kesshin shimashita!" (I decided) is all she said, and for a moment I wondered what she had decided—where to live? what courses to take? Then my heart leaped for joy. For weeks Kimie has been visiting me, bringing with her a gift of Japanese crackers and long lists of questions about the Trinity, God's sovereignty and her choices, the deity of Christ, and the state of her father who recently died. Gradually, this young woman who had never heard of a personal God until six months ago began to understand. In fact, last week she said she believed all I told her was true, and sometimes she was excited about it all. But she wasn't ready to turn her life over to this new acquaintance named Jesus, at least not unconditionally.

Oh, Kimie knew that she was a sinner, not a notorious sinner, but a self-oriented person, not deserving God's favor. She was grateful that God loved her enough to give His Son to die for her, but what would she do about it? I said, "Kimie, you can study and study, pray and pray, and attend church faithfully, but that will never make you a Christian." She was startled. She had been sure that by doing those things and trying hard to be a better person she would gradually become what she so much wanted.

"No, Kimie," I told her last week, "you can't grow into it. Sooner or later you must make a choice. You must decide."

"But what about my feelings?" she asked.

"That depends on your personality and how you have lived out your past rebellion against God. The feelings, the joy, will follow, but first comes the choice."

"Sono uchi ni," (one of these days) she said and left for school in another city. That was last week. Yesterday she called to tell me, "Sensei, I did it! I decided for Jesus!" And her joy had already begun to surge.

🌀 Have you done what Kimie did? If not, I encourage you to do it now. Go back to what you and I wrote of God's plan of salvation and make that into a prayer of faith. Commit your life to Him unconditionally and forever. Then thank Him that He's a promise-keeping God; He has indeed forgiven you and made you His child.

🌀 If, on the other hand, you are sure that you have already made the salvation transaction with God, whether you can remember all the details or not, tell Him again how grateful you are for His great salvation, including remaking you into an altogether new person. That new you has all sorts of potential the old you never had. That potential will be our exciting study in the units ahead.

We have considered the redeeming activity of the Spirit. The Spirit's redemptive actions stretch from bringing about the life and ministry of Jesus to applying Christ's work to our lives.

🌀 On the course-map portion below fill in the three activities of the Spirit we have examined thus far. Next we will consider how the first three actions of the Spirit come together in the fourth. The Spirit comes to live in the life of the believer.

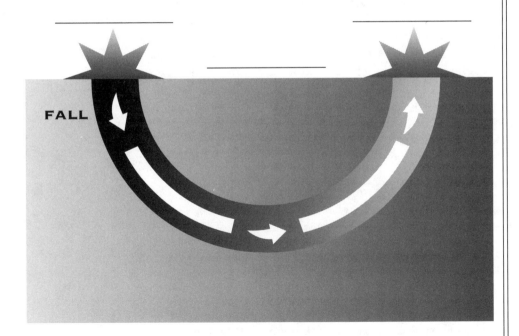

INDWELLING:
FAITH AND OBEDIENCE

*We have considered how the Spirit created us, revealed God to us through the Bible,
and set about to redeem us through Jesus. In this unit we will consider what comes next:
how can we maintain the close relationship that comes with regeneration?*

Jim, the school bully, stalked me after school every day, week after terrifying week. Like some evil presence, he haunted my life by day and my dreams by night. Finally, I ran out of ways to evade him. I lingered in the school building long after everyone else had gone home. Everyone but Jim, that is. From the second floor window I could see him by the front entrance. Suddenly, I saw something that had never happened before. Walking down the sidewalk was the most marvelous vision I had ever seen—my father!

Down the stairs and out the door I ran. MY comforter had come. What relief! Holding my father's hand, I marched bravely past my nemesis and waved cheerily, "Hi, Jim!" What strength! What joy!

We may not be 10 years old, but we, too, are haunted by the evil presence of an enemy set on destroying us. We have experienced a lifestyle of worry—about a job we have or don't have, about the children, about old age or health. We have been ambushed by greed or booby-trapped by an explosive tongue. The Bible and church are supposed to help, but the enemy just keeps stalking us.

To cope with the enemy, we try one strategy and another, but nothing works for long. Then down the street comes help. The Comforter has come! (John 14:16, KJV). That name means "the one called along side," but He doesn't just shepherd us through the crisis of the moment. Unlike my father, the Holy Spirit is with us forever. Better than that—the strong Comforter doesn't just walk beside us; He resides inside us! "The one who is in you is greater than the one who is in the world" (1 John 4:4).

"'I will ask the Father, and he will give you another Counselor to be with you forever—the Spirit of truth. The world cannot accept him, because it neither sees him nor knows him. But you know him, for he lives with you and will be in you'" (John 14:16-17).

The Spirit acts in me, however, only to the extent I respond. The connection is faith. He acts, but I must respond for the power to flow. So there are two parts to the "close connection"—His part and mine. These two activities—His work inside me and my faith response—are our themes in this unit. The Holy Spirit takes up residence inside me, and I keep a close connection through faith.

Unit Memory Verses
*Do you not know that your body is the temple of the Holy Spirit,
who is in you, whom you have received from God?
You are not your own.—1 Corinthians 6:19*

*The righteous will live by his faith.—Habakkuk 2:4
(also see Romans 1:17; Galatians 3:11; Hebrews 10:38)*

> **Now that I have been regenerated by the power of the Holy
> Spirit, how do I maintain my close connection with Him?
> What does it mean for me to have the Spirit dwelling in me?**

DAY 1

THE "IN" RELATIONSHIP

God's Spirit within us supplies the resources we need for successful Christian living. What a mystery! He whom the heaven of heavens cannot contain, the infinite One, in some mysterious way lives inside me.

The Holy Spirit is not the only one who lives in us. Read the verses in the margin and complete the following.

John 14:16-17–The _____ lives in believers.

John 14:23–The _____ and _____ live in Christians.

Ephesians 3:17– _____ resides in the believer.

> *"I will ask the Father, and he will give you another Counselor to be with you forever–the Spirit of truth. The world cannot accept him, because it neither sees him nor knows him. But you know him, for he lives with you and will be in you."*
> —John 14:16-17

The Bible indicates the Father and the Son also live in the believer. The relationship we call the Trinity expresses our finite minds' attempt to understand God. We see from Scripture that God relates to us as three persons, but He is only one God. So in this amazing love relationship the fullness of the Godhead–Father, Son, and Holy Spirit–all love and live in the believer.

> *Jesus replied, "If anyone loves me, he will obey my teaching. My Father will love him, and we will come to him and make our home with him."*
> —John 14:23

What is the physical aspect of this relationship? Does God–the Trinity, what theologians call the Godhead–live somewhere inside my body? Perhaps a key to unlock the mystery is the way the Bible uses the word *in*. The focus is not on the physical. For example, Jesus speaks almost interchangeably of being *in* us and our being *in* Him (John 14:20; 15:4-5). They seem to mean the same thing. Obviously we are not *in* Jesus in a physical sense.

> *So that Christ may dwell in your hearts through faith.*
> —Ephesians 3:17

In your Bible read John 15:1-17 and circle every "in" you can find.

Most but not all of these "in's" speak of our being in Christ and Christ being in us. However, in verses 7, 9-11 we find a different perspective. From the list below circle the items Jesus said we are to have in us.

His love   His joy

    His commandments   His words

Jesus seems to be talking more about a relationship than a physical location. He intends for His words (v. 7) and His joy (v. 11) to remain in us. He also said He wants us to remain in His love. In bypassing the physical aspect, which is a mystery we may never fully solve, Jesus moves on to something far more important. He speaks of a relationship.

The Theological Dictionary of the New Testament calls the "in Christ" relationship the "in" of fellowship.[1] We might call it *intimacy*–a relationship with another Person so close the only way to describe it is to speak of His being in us and us in Him. Believers share with Jesus an identity of life, an interpenetration so intimate you could call it being "in love" (v. 9).

Have you ever been so in love that you couldn't think of anything but your beloved? The human experience of love is a mere shadow of this spiritual in-love-ness. God loves you with a love that dwarfs any human example.

"Anyone who has seen me has seen the Father. ... I am in the Father, and the Father is in me."
—John 14:9-10

Do not cast me from your presence or take your Holy Spirit from me. Restore to me the joy of your salvation and grant me a willing spirit, to sustain me.
——Psalm 51:11-12

I pray that out of his glorious riches he may strengthen you with power through his Spirit in your inner being. Now to him who is able to do immeasurably more than all we ask or imagine, according to his power that is at work within us.
—Ephesians 3:16,20

"'I will put my Spirit in you and move you to follow my decrees and be careful to keep my laws.'"
–Ezekiel 36:27

The fruit of the Spirit is love, joy, peace, patience, kindness, goodness, faithfulness, gentleness and self-control. Against such things there is no law.
–Galatians 5:22-23

The only adequate way to describe the love relationship God intends with us is to say it's the way the Father and the Son relate (John 14:9-10)! The Father and the Son love each other. They love me. They are in each other and they are in me. The Father, the Son, and the Spirit—one God—is in me, and I am in Him!

Incredible as it may seem, God has planned my life around Himself—uninterrupted companionship with the greatest Lover who ever lived! He doesn't require an appointment a month in advance. I do not have to take a number and wait my turn, and He doesn't just tolerate me. Outrageous mystery—God actually desires my company! He wants to be best friends. That's a hint of what it means to be "in Christ" and for Christ to be "in me"—a new relationship that defies analysis or description. While we wonder about the mysterious physical aspect of our bodies as a residence for the triune God, we can rejoice in the mystery. We can focus our attention on building the relationship between us.

WHAT THE SPIRIT DOES INSIDE

The Holy Spirit of God has always been at work. In the Old Testament He worked primarily in an external way. Since Jesus' death and resurrection, however, the Spirit has a new relationship. His relationship is no longer limited to certain people. Now He lives inside every one of His people.

The Holy Spirit not only created us in God's likeness, He re-created us as altogether new people. He takes up residence in our lives. But what does He actually do in us?

Match each of the following passages with one or more activities of the Spirit inside you. See if you can match at least one Scripture beside each activity I have listed. This and the next activity will take longer than most assignments; but it is strategic for understanding how the Spirit works in your life, so don't skip it!

____ 1. Gives us peace and joy	a. John 14:26
____ 2. Directs us	b. John 16:13
____ 3. Assures us that we are His	c. Acts 13:2
____ 4. Guides us into the truth	d. Acts 16:6-7
____ 5. Calls us to serve Him	e. Romans 8:14-16
____ 6. Teaches us the thoughts of God	f. Romans 14:16-17
	g. 1 Corinthians 2:10-11
	h. 1 John 4:13

In the margin read the following Scriptures and write in your own words how they describe the activity of the Spirit in your life.

Psalm 51:11-12 _____

_____

Ephesians 3:16,20 _____

_____

Ezekiel 36:27; Galatians 5:22-23 _____

_____

Zechariah 4:6; Matthew 10:20; Acts 1:8 _____

_____

1 Corinthians 12:7,11 _____

_____

Ephesians 6:18; Jude 20 _____

_____

🌀 **I've given you several activities of the Spirit in the following five paragraphs. Underline each activity you identify.**

Isn't it incredible? And remember, these passages are just a few of the ones we might check. First of all, the Spirit gives me assurance that I belong to God; He whispers to my spirit, "Remember, the heavenly Father is your daddy [the English for *abba*] and we—the Father, Son, and I—will be here forever, no matter what bully is stalking you" (Rom. 8:14-16; 1 John 4:13).

The Holy Spirit is the master teacher, enlightening our minds to understand all the truth we need to know about God and His will for us (John 14:26; 16:13; 1 Cor. 2:10-11; 1 John 2:20). He not only helps us understand Scripture, He guides us in the personal decisions of life. Sometimes He impresses us with the way to go; sometimes He blocks the way we planned to go (Acts 16:6-7; Rom. 8:14).

His name is Comforter because that is what He does. When we are in trouble He gives peace and joy that can't be explained in terms of our early environment or present circumstances (John 14:16; Rom. 14:17). When we stumble, even falling like David into gross sin, the powerful Spirit of God lifts us up and recommissions us. He never abandons us (Ps. 51:11-12).

The Spirit strengthens us with the same power He used when He loosed Jesus from the grip of death (Eph. 1:19-20; 3:16,20). The Spirit energizes us for godly living (Ezek. 36:27; Gal. 5:22-23), for powerful ministry (Zech. 4:6; 1 Cor. 12:7,11), and for bold witnessing with wisdom (Matt. 10:20; Acts 1:8).

God's Spirit even assists us in our prayers (Eph. 6:18; Jude 20). Often we don't even know how to pray or what to pray (Rom. 8:26). But He knows, and He inspires our prayers. Even inspired prayers may fall short, however. That's when the Spirit, who knows the mind of the Father, goes straight to the throne and tells the Father exactly what we needed to pray.

🌀 **Of the activities you identified, which are most personal and valuable to you? Circle the two or three activities you appreciate most.**

With such an inside partner, nothing can stop you! Life in the Spirit is no fantasy, nor is it reserved for the spiritually elite. Effective Christian living is here, now. God the Spirit lives in you in such a close relationship that everything He promises is within your reach.

You could have identified the activities any of several ways. I listed the activities this way: the Holy Spirit gives me assurance, lets me know God is my Father, teaches me, guides me in personal decisions, comforts me, gives peace and joy, lifts me out of sin and recommissions me, provides strength for godly living, ministry, and witnessing, assists me with prayer, and intercedes for me when I don't know how to pray.

"Not by might nor by power, but by my Spirit," says the Lord Almighty.
—Zechariah 4:6

"For it will not be you speaking, but the Spirit of your Father speaking through you."
—Matthew 10:20

"You will receive power when the Holy Spirit comes on you; and you will be my witnesses in Jerusalem, and in all Judea and Samaria, and to the ends of the earth."
—Acts 1:8

Now to each one the manifestation of the Spirit is given for the common good. All these are the work of one and the same Spirit, and he gives them to each one, just as he determines.
—1 Corinthians 12:7,11

Pray in the Spirit on all occasions with all kinds of prayers and requests. With this in mind, be alert and always keep on praying for all the saints.
—Ephesians 6:18

Dear friends, build yourselves up in your most holy faith and pray in the Holy Spirit.
—Jude 20

Isn't it time to tell the Comforter how much you appreciate Him? If you've never addressed the Spirit by name in prayer, why not now? Tell Him several of the things about Him you especially like, how much you love Him, how grateful you are for what He has done, is doing, and will yet do. Then reflect for a few minutes on what you need Him to do in your life. What one specific change in your life requires the work of the Spirit? What one attitude or behavior do you need to develop to improve your relationship with Him? Ask Him to develop those areas of your character today. If you want to remember today's encounter with the Spirit, jot down those thoughts in your journal.

DAY 2

INDWELLING AND BAPTISM BY THE SPIRIT

The Spirit brings about the "in" relationship–Jesus in you and you in Him. You probably have some questions about this relationship, such as:

- How does a person get into the "in" relationship?
- How can I be certain that I have such a relationship?

One biblical expression used to answer the "how" questions is the phrase *baptism by the Spirit.*

A BIBLICAL PHRASE: BAPTISM BY THE SPIRIT

One of the ways the New Testament talks about the "in" relationship is with the phrase *baptism by the Spirit* (some people use the term *baptism in* or *of the Spirit*). Read 1 Corinthians 12:13 that appears in the margin. Much confusion exists over the phrase. One reason for the confusion is that people use the phrase, *baptism by/in/of the Spirit* to describe different aspects of the Christian experience.

The following paragraphs describe three ways people commonly use the phrase *baptism by the Spirit.* Circle the number beside one that most nearly describes what you understand when you hear the term.

1. Some believers experience a transforming encounter with the Holy Spirit when, after being unyielded or doubting, they come back under the control of the Spirit. They use the term as a way to explain the experience.
2. Some use the expression as synonymous with being "filled with the Spirit" and mean a one-time experience of the Spirit that happens after their salvation experience.
3. Some use the phrase *baptism by the Spirit* to describe the salvation experience.

I want to avoid controversial issues in order to focus on the central theme all believers can agree on–that God provides a supernatural quality of life by His Spirit to all who surrender to, obey, and trust Him to do what He promises.

Each of the three interpretations of *baptism by the Spirit* contains at least an element of practical truth. Different believers use the term in various ways in an attempt to describe their experience of the Christian life. The confusion comes from using the phrase *baptism by the Spirit* to describe these different situations.

We were all baptized by one Spirit into one body—whether Jews or Greeks, slave or free— and we were all given the one Spirit to drink.
—1 Corinthians 12:13

The first description is a way to explain what happens in some Christians' experience. Many Christians wander or drift away from a close, trusting and obedient relationship with the Lord. Some then experience a profound turnaround. Their experience feels like a post-salvation conversion—as if they have been saved all over again. When unbelievers turn to Christ, we call the experience *repentance and faith*. When a believer experiences repentance, we might describe such a turn around as *yieldedness and trust*. Some Christians use the phrase *baptism by the Spirit* to describe this renewing experience.

The second description is closely related to the first. It uses baptism in a way that some Christians use the term *filling*. Those who hold the second view understand the baptism or filling of the Spirit to be a one-time experience like salvation. After salvation a person seeks the additional experience of baptism by the Spirit. This baptism provides the power to live a more effective Christian life. Some Christians who hold this understanding believe Spirit baptism is accompanied by sign gifts, particularly speaking in tongues.

This second view is not the kind of "filling" Paul tells us to have when he says, "keep on being filled with the Spirit" (literal translation of Eph. 5:18), or the kind of fresh "anointing" of courage the disciples received by being filled with the Spirit a few days after their filling at Pentecost (Acts 4:31). Plainly Scripture uses the term *filling* to refer to different experiences with the Spirit as we shall see in unit 7.

Both the above approaches describe some people's personal experience. Using the term *baptism by the spirit*, however, creates a communication problem. The only way the Bible actually uses the phrase is to describe entry into the original salvation relationship (description number 3). Carefully read again 1 Corinthians 12:13.

The phrase in biblical usage refers to initial regeneration by the Spirit. That's because the term *baptism* was commonly used to mean "initiation" or "act of joining." When you are initiated into Christ, you are "baptized" by the Spirit into that relationship. As I understand Romans 6:3-5 the act of water baptism demonstrates in a visible way what the Spirit of God has already done in the life of a new Christian.

Since the Bible uses the phrase *baptism by the Spirit* to describe regeneration, am I saying that those who use the term differently are wrong? No, I am personally more comfortable using the term to refer only to the salvation experience; but those who use the term to describe a life-changing, after-salvation experience also have a point. They draw on another use of the term *baptism*.

Remember that we are dealing with picture words. The word *baptism* is sometimes used to mean "suffused with," as in a baptism by fire, or an overwhelming experience like the crucifixion—"I have a baptism to undergo," said Jesus (Luke 12:50). So, for people to use the term to describe an overwhelming experience is legitimate. But since the Bible never describes a second encounter with the Spirit with the term *baptism*, it may be confusing to use it that way. That's why I've avoided using the word, choosing rather to describe in biblical terms exactly what you can expect in your Christian experience.

BAPTISM AND FILLING

The term *filled* is a picture word, like baptism, and therefore capable of conflicting interpretations. Filled, rather than baptism, is the picture word the Scripture uses to describe how the Spirit works in the life of Christians. Because being filled with the Spirit is so important, all of unit 8 will be devoted to what you can expect from living a Christian life filled with the Spirit.

BAPTISM AND INDWELLING

Since I am using the phrase *baptism by the Spirit* to describe your entry into the Christian life, baptism is the beginning of a life with the Holy Spirit living in you.

We were all baptized by one Spirit into one body—whether Jew or Greeks, slave or free—and we were all given the one Spirit to drink.
—1 Corinthians 12:13

Don't you know that all of us who were baptized into Christ Jesus were baptized into his death? We were therefore buried with him through baptism into death in order that, just as Christ was raised from the dead through the glory of the Father, we too may live a new life. If we have been united with him like this in his death, we will certainly also be united with him in his resurrection.
—Romans 6:3-5

You, however, are controlled not by the sinful nature but by the Spirit, if the Spirit of God lives in you. And if anyone does not have the Spirit of Christ, he does not belong to Christ.
—Romans 8:9

We can use the term *indwelling* to describe the same reality. Indwelling means to live in. When we have been regenerated or baptized by the Spirit, the Spirit lives in us.

🌀 **Read Romans 8:9 in the margin. Circle the phrase that speaks of indwelling. Below write your own paraphrase of the verse.**

_____

_____

🌀 **According to Paul, who is indwelt by the Spirit?**

❑ all Christians   ❑ only certain Christians

All Christians are baptized by the Spirit in the sense that I use the term and in the sense of 1 Corinthians 12:13. Not all Christians, however, are led by, filled with, or controlled by the Spirit.

Since Paul was so clear that every Christian has the Spirit dwelling in his or her life, why do so many seem to experience defeat? In tomorrow's lesson we will examine the practical hazard of unbelief. Unbelief prevents the Spirit who lives in us from guiding and controlling us.

🌀 **See if you can recall this week's memory verses by writing them in the margin. Check your work on page 78.**

DAY 3

PRACTICAL EXPERIENCE: THE HAZARD OF UNBELIEF

The Spirit of God lives inside me. He has all the resources of heaven to empower me. But what if I don't seem to experience a supernatural quality of life? What's wrong? A key source of difficulty comes from the connection between the Spirit and me. The current doesn't flow automatically. I have to throw the switch, and the "switch" is faith. "The righteous will live by his faith," our memory verse reminds us. Not only are we justified by faith, but we also live out the Christian life by that same faith. The Holy Spirit within does His work when we throw the switch of faith.

When the Spirit of God confronts us with the challenge to believe, we must make a choice. We choose to practice either belief or unbelief. We need to examine our attitudes and actions carefully. When we choose to disbelieve we refuse to obey Him. Our disbelief and disobedience says some significant things about our attitude toward God.

🌀 **Before you continue, you may want to pray the prayer in the margin.**

WHAT UNBELIEF SAYS ABOUT GOD

The father was distraught. Jesus' disciples had failed to live up to the advertisements. They couldn't cure the son's terrifying condition. Then Jesus came on the scene and the father said, "If you can ... help us!" (Mark 9:22). "If you can?" What kind of question is that?

Spirit of God, please guide me now as I study what Your Book teaches about how I can actually experience Your life flowing through me. More than anything, that's what I want. Thank You.

"If you can do anything, take pity on us and help us."
—Mark 9:22

By his statement, what was the boy's father saying about Jesus?

_____

_____

The hired mourners had lots of experience with dead people. They knew death when they saw it. So they slapped one another on the back and scoffed as they pointed at the itinerant preacher, "Some healer he is! He doesn't even know the kid's dead. We know better!" You know better? What kind of talk is that?

By their laughter, what were they saying about Jesus?

_____

_____

They laughed at him, knowing that she was dead.
—Luke 8:53

The wind howled and the waves lashed the little boat mercilessly, terrifying the seasoned fishermen. But one passenger on board leaned back against a pillow in the stern and went to sleep. "Enough of this!" The fishermen shook their leader awake. "What's wrong with you? Don't you care if we drown?" "Don't you care?" What kind of question is that?

By their question, what were the disciples saying about Jesus?

_____

_____

Jesus was in the stern, sleeping on a cushion. The disciples woke him and said to him, "Teacher, don't you care if we drown?"
—Mark 4:38

These people were making statements of unbelief. The father wondered if Jesus could handle his tough situation; the professional mourners were more confident in their own judgment than His, and the disciples accused Him of being uncaring.

You remember my struggle with doubt in unit 3. One day when I was stumbling down a dark alley of doubt, these three Bible stories startled me with what I was actually saying about God. I saw my "innocent" flirtations with unbelief as actually calling into question the very character of God. I was insulting Him!

Can you describe a time when you have allowed, or are now allowing, unbelief rather than faith to govern your thoughts and actions?

_____

_____

When we fail to trust God we are actually questioning His power, His wisdom, or His love. We're saying, in effect, "You're not strong enough to handle my rotten boss, to make me victorious with my impatience, to meet my needs while I'm unemployed." We're saying, "I'm not sure you're smart enough to figure out how to get me out of this jam, to guide me in the best way. I think I know a better way than yours." Or we're saying, "You're powerful enough, all right, and you're smart enough. You just don't care that much about me." We call into question the character of God.

Without faith it is impossible to please God.
—Hebrews 11:6

WHAT UNBELIEF DOES TO GOD

The first problem with unbelief is that it displeases God. God is displeased when we don't trust Him; He has been dishonored, and by a family member at that!

 According to Hebrews 11:6, what is absolutely essential to please God?

_____

WHAT UNBELIEF DOES TO ME

When we don't trust Him, it makes God sad, just as it makes us sad when someone we love doesn't trust us. But the tragedy of unbelief does more than just hurt God. It hurts us as well. Unbelief short-circuits the flow of divine energy—the Holy Spirit won't act freely in the life of one who doesn't trust Him. For salvation, for growth, for success in the Christian life, for power in ministry, faith is the connection through which God's power flows.

Are you finding trusting God difficult in some areas of your life? Your finances? Your health? Your job? Your children? Some temptation you fall before? Some task you're afraid to undertake for God?

 List below your main areas of fear, defeat, or worry. Then, to the right of each note the characteristic of God you need to trust: His power, wisdom, or love. In other words, why are you unable to trust; what about God are you uncertain of? If you have been calling into question, by your responses to the Holy Spirit, more than one of those characteristics of God, list both or all three. I have given you an example.

MY AREAS OF FEAR, DEFEAT, OR WORRY	GOD'S CHARACTERISTIC THAT I NEED TO TRUST
my temper	His power to change me, and His wisdom in controlling situations

I know someone who went through this very exercise. My wife Muriel called herself a chain worrier. With six children she thought, *What's a mother for but to worry those children through to maturity?*

One night she lay in bed doing her usual thing, worrying about Jan, a teen, who hadn't gotten home yet. Her precious daughter was out in a terrible storm. What might have happened? An accident? Would the phone ring? A call from the state highway patrol? At that point, Muriel said the Lord spoke to her: "Do you really want to keep on like this the rest of your life?"

"Oh, no," she cried out in the darkness. "Please, Lord, please. I really don't want to live this way. Deliver me, I pray."

God heard her prayer. As she turned those children over to the Lord, He made a basic change in her personality. She began to trust God with her children instead of seeking to do His work for Him. In the days following that encounter with the trust-worthy God, she penned the following couplet:

Anything, anytime, anywhere,
I leave the choice with You;
I trust Your wisdom, love, and power
And all I need You'll do.

Muriel began to identify the characteristics of God she needed to trust. She developed her relationship with Him, and she consistently turned her worries over to Him. She learned to express her fears to God, and then spend her time focusing on His attributes rather than concentrating on her fears. Muriel experienced deep, lasting change in her pattern of worry.

☉ **Analyze Muriel's experience with worry. From the list below, check the best description of how God changed her pattern of thinking, feeling, and acting.**

    ❏ Muriel chose to change, and she made the change in her own power.
    ❏ God challenged Muriel, and she responded in obedient faith.
    ❏ God enabled Muriel to see what she was doing to herself. She then chose to trust Him and began practicing different behavior.
    ❏ God simply acted; Muriel had nothing to do with the change.

Genuine, lasting life-change must involve two parts—His and ours. The Holy Spirit confronts us with our need and supplies the power to obey. We must choose to obey. You might have chosen either the second or third response. The third response explains the process in greater detail.

☉ **Look again at your list on the last page. Choose one or two areas in which you really want to see the Spirit's victory. Tell the Lord how much you want to change and tell Him you're turning it over to Him right now. Trust His wisdom, power, and love for you. If your faith is not that strong, you might want to add a prayer: "I believe, help my unbelief."**

DAY 4

HOW MUCH FAITH IS ENOUGH?

"All justified people live by faith" is a good paraphrase of the recurring passage from the prophet Habakkuk (Hab. 2:4). Life is to be lived in the power of the Holy Spirit. But, how much faith do we need to live a Spirit-powered life? Do different people have varying levels of faith?

☉ **Read the following passages that appear in the margin and describe in your own words how much faith Jesus saw in each of these different—and unlikely—people.**

The disciples in Matthew 8:26 _____

The foreign woman in Matthew 15:28 _____

He replied, "You of little faith, why are you so afraid?" Then he got up and rebuked the winds and the waves, and it was completely calm.
—Matthew 8:26

Then Jesus answered, "Woman, you have great faith! Your request is granted." And her daughter was healed from that very hour.
—Matthew 15:28

When Jesus heard this, he was amazed at him, and turning to the crowd following him, he said, "I tell you, I have not found such great faith even in Israel."
—Luke 7:9

The Roman army officer in Luke 7:9 _____

Little. Great. Greatest. The disciples asked for more faith. Jesus responded: "If you have faith as small as a mustard seed, you can say to this mulberry tree, 'Be uprooted and planted in the sea,' and it will obey you" (Luke 17:6).

According to Luke 17:6, how much faith does a person need for God to work in great power?

❏ little ❏ great ❏ greatest

Jesus taught that if you had faith as big as a tiny seed you could say to this mountain, "Up! Into the Mediterranean," and it would jump (Matt. 21:21). Jesus says, "If you have ever-so-little confidence in me, you're connected to all my resources."

Let's think back to those three Bible stories at the beginning of yesterday's lesson. Notice that, though they doubted, Jesus acted anyway.

- The father's timid faith was enough: he cried out, weeping, "I do believe; Help me overcome my unbelief!" (Mark 9:24), and his son was set free.
- The professional mourners didn't believe; but Jairus, the religious leader whose daughter had died, did believe and the little girl rose to embrace her father.
- The disciples were in fear of their lives in the grip of the storm. Jesus rebuked them for their low-level faith (Matt. 8:26), but He stilled the storm-driven seas anyway.

In a sense, the issue is not how much faith you have but what your faith is in. I once heard someone say: "Timid faith in thick ice and you'll make it across; robust confidence in thin ice and you're sunk." God is trustworthy; He will bear up under your heaviest loads.

HOW CAN I TELL IF I HAVE ENOUGH FAITH?

How can I tell whether or not I have any faith at all? For example, how do I know if my faith will endure when confidence in God seems to waver as a broken relationship tears me apart?

What do you think determines whether or not we have faith? In the margin write what distinguishes faith from unbelief.

The difference between hesitant, apprehensive faith and sinful unbelief occurs at the point of choice. Do I choose to follow God's way no matter how fearful my timid steps, or do I choose to say no to Him and go my own way?

The critical evidence of faith or lack of it is obedience. If I believe Him enough to do what He says, that will connect.

Theologians differ as to whether obedience is part of faith or simply the necessary evidence of genuine faith. Either way, Scripture teaches that we can't connect with God while saying no.

In our next lesson, we'll discover that when we refuse to do what we know is right, we disconnect from intimate companionship with God; and the Holy Spirit's power won't flow. For now, let's just underscore the fundamental truth of Scripture that faith is the only human response that will connect with God. It's the connection that lets the Spirit flow to us and through us.

The secret to successful Christian living is trusting God to do what He says He will do. So how is your F.Q., your *Faith Quotient*? Average? Above average? Painfully low? Now is the time to ask the Spirit of God to give you a robust faith.

> Spirit of the Living God, like the father with a demon-possessed son, I cry to You, "I do believe. Help me overcome my unbelief." I want to be strong in faith so that Your power may flow freely and effectively to enable me to be all You designed me to be. I commit to You my body and my mind. Guide me with your great wisdom in the directions You plan for me to go. Thank You for loving me so.

In the margin write out your memory verses for this unit, referring back to page 78 as necessary.

DAY 5

THE "SPIRIT" OF FAITH: OBEDIENCE

A friend of mine knows that moving in with her boyfriend is against God's will, but she does it anyway. Why?

From what you studied in day 3, what may my friend be having difficulty believing about God?

_____

_____

She might believe that God isn't powerful enough—either to provide her a life partner or empower her to live a full life on her own. She may believe God isn't smart enough to know what's best for her, or she may think He doesn't care enough about her to work things out for her best interests. So she chooses to disobey God.

What might have happened if she had chosen instead to obey God, even though she felt utterly miserable and abandoned? She would have acted in faith–timid, faltering faith, to be sure. But her obedience would be evidence she had enough faith to connect with the powerful Spirit of God.

In the margin, read what James wrote about the relationship between faith and obedience. Below write your own paraphrase of the verses from James.

_____

_____

_____

_____

_____

What does it profit, my brethren, if someone says he has faith but does not have works? Can faith save him? You believe that there is one God. You do well. Even the demons believe—and tremble! But do you want to know, O foolish man, that faith without works is dead? For as the body without the spirit is dead, so faith without works is dead also.
—James 2:14,19-20,26, NKJV

"Trust" and "obey" are so intertwined that James says you can't have one without the other. A body without a spirit is truly a human body, but it is dead. James says our connection with God is the same. Faith that does not embody obedience is no more than a corpse.

TWO COMPLEMENTARY TRUTHS IN SCRIPTURE

The Bible uses hard or challenging words like *repent, obey,* and *confess.* Those words emphasize the importance of positive, active effort on the part of the believer.

> **Remember the principle of balance? If the hard words of Scripture are taken alone, what kind of Christian lifestyle and attitude will develop?**

_____

The hard words emphasize the responsibility of the Christian life. Taken by themselves, they can lead to a works-oriented view in which we think we must earn God's favor. They lead us to become rigid and self-righteous like the Pharisees in Jesus' day.

The Bible also uses soft words like *love, trust,* and *surrender.* Those words emphasize God's activity rather than our effort.

> **If the soft words of Scripture are taken alone, what kind of Christian lifestyle and attitude will develop?**

_____

Taken by themselves the soft words of Scripture can lead us to a passive, "I just have to believe; I don't have to do anything" mentality. Good theology and Christ-honoring living always involve balance. Let's consider these hard and soft terms to see how they contribute to a balanced view of faith and obedience.

> **We sometimes speak of the "hard" words as lordship and the "soft" words as grace. The following list contains words and phrases that describe aspects of our Christian experience. Draw an arrow pointing each concept either to the soft list (grace) or the hard list (lordship).**

"Hard" words/   "Soft" words/
Lordship   Grace

1. salvation
2. obedience
3. holiness
4. repentance
5. no conditions
6. once for all
7. law as guide
8. moment by moment rather
   than once for all

We see the importance of balance in that Scripture uses both concepts. We are to believe and emphasize both salvation and lordship. I drew arrows to grace from numbers 1, 5, and 6. I connect numbers 2, 3, 4, 7, and 8 to lordship. You might choose differently. The important fact is that we recognize the balance present in Scripture. In the following section I will attempt to maintain that balance.

⟳ **Practice a little self-examination. Do you tend more toward the hard (law) or the soft (grace) words of Scripture? On the scale below place a check for where you see yourself.**

LAW   GRACE

⟳ **Do you think other people see you in the same way you see yourself? If your spouse or a close friend were completing the exercise about you, where would the mark appear? Why not ask him or her?**

SAVED BY GRACE

We must begin with the grand affirmation of the Protestant Reformation: salvation is by grace alone through faith alone! In your Bible, read Ephesians 2:1-10.

⟳ **In what way does Paul's view of faith/works seem to differ from the view expressed in James 2:14, 19-20, 26?**

_____

_____

Ultimately, James said, "Faith works." Obeying God is the worked-out evidence that I have genuine faith. What does Paul say? I paraphrase Ephesians 2:8-10 this way: By grace you have been saved through faith–a gift, not earned by your own effort. That salvation is accomplished by the work of the Holy Spirit who re-created you on purpose to do good. That was no afterthought, but God's original plan.

Paul rejoices in God's grace–God's free gift of full salvation to those who have earned damnation. You can't earn a smidgen of it he says. But notice that Paul ends up in the same place James did: faith works. In fact, Paul seems to say here that the purpose of salvation is a changed life.

On the other hand, if my salvation depended on my goodness I would be forever insecure, continually asking myself, *Have I done well enough to make it?* In my case, I wouldn't be uncertain at all; I'd be quite certain I'd never make it! I know my performance, even for a moment, would never make me eligible for membership in the family of a holy God. So the glorious news that broke into history two millennia ago and into my life six decades ago is that "Jesus paid it all, all to Him I owe!" That's why we can be confident, which is another way to say, "trust," or "faith." Salvation is by grace alone through faith.

SANCTIFIED BY GRACE

The Bible speaks of our salvation in another way. Through our salvation we were "sanctified." The word *sanctified* literally means "set apart." When God saved you He set you apart from sin for Himself. Sometimes the word is translated *holy*, so we are called a "holy" or "set-apart" people. Other times the word is translated *saint*, so all believers are called saints. That has a nice ring to it, doesn't it? "Saint Robertson!" So saint Robertson by new birth has been sanctified–made holy, set apart from sin and its consequences to God and His use.

The term *sanctify* has another meaning the way it is most commonly used. I may be officially declared a saint on the merits of Christ, but am I saintly?

Saintly means to be like Jesus. So the second use of the term *sanctification* speaks of the activity of the Holy Spirit in me from the time of my initial salvation till I

What does it profit, my brethren, if someone says he has faith but does not have works? Can faith save him? You believe that there is one God. You do well. Even the demons believe—and tremble! But do you want to know, O foolish man, that faith without works is dead? For as the body without the spirit is dead, so faith without works is dead also.
—James 2:14,19-20,26, NKJV

91

reach heaven. As a Christian, I undergo the process of continually changing from what I was by natural inclination to what God desires for me to be. I become more like Jesus. This second use of the word *sanctification* is the term that best describes the whole process of living life in the Spirit.

The case studies below picture what happens when we get law and grace out of balance. Write either "law" or "grace" beside each case study.

- John lives by the creed, "I'll work 'til Jesus comes." He lives with continual self-scrutiny, always asking, "Have I done enough?"

- Jill is convinced she'll never be a consistent Christian. Her motto is, "God knows and loves me anyway."

- Andy excuses his lack of discipline with a shrug. "Nobody's perfect," he says.

Balance is the key. Many people who know they have no part in saving themselves other than to believe act as if working out that salvation were all up to them. Paul writes: "Are you so foolish? Having made your start by the Holy Spirit are you now going to perfect yourselves in your own strength?" (Gal. 3:3, my paraphrase). Just as salvation began with a response of faith to God's promise of life and the activity of the Holy Spirit, so you will now be continuously sanctified. You are transformed by the activity of that same Holy Spirit.

Others leave their sanctification completely up to God. They do nothing to obey or grow. In the case studies above, John is out of balance on the law while Jill and Andy are out of balance on grace.

REPENTANCE FOR SALVATION, OBEDIENCE FOR SANCTIFICATION

The transforming grace of God in our lives comes in response to the same kind of faith as did His saving grace in the first place. But, just as saving faith included repentance or turning away from sin as well as believing what He promised, so sanctifying faith includes obedience as proof that we really do trust Him. There's no way to succeed in the Christian life other than to trust and obey.

Name a skill you have developed that required learning and growing.

_____

If you've learned to use a computer program, snow ski, or play an instrument, your learning experience included getting instruction from someone else. It also involved trying and failing, learning from mistakes, and practicing to develop proficiency. In exactly the same way, we develop our ability to trust and obey God.

Read Romans 6:16 that appears in the margin. In what way does offering ourselves and becoming "slaves" fit the process of developing any life skill? Check all that apply.

❑ The more I practice, the easier a behavior becomes—up or down.
❑ My insignificant daily choices have little effect on my life direction.
❑ Tough decisions may lead to a life of greater meaning and purpose.
❑ Past choices have little influence over my ability to choose right or wrong today.

Don't you know that when you offer yourselves to someone to obey him as slaves, you are slaves to the one whom you obey— whether you are slaves to sin, which leads to death, or to obedience, which leads to righteousness?
—Romans 6:16

This profound passage may be a good one to discuss in your next group session. I checked the first and third response.

THE LAW AS GUIDE

Galatians 5:25 says, "If we live in the Spirit, let us also walk in the Spirit" (NKJV). But how does He guide me in my walk; how does He tell me the difference between right and wrong?

God gave His will, written out for us to see. The Spirit and the Bible work together to guide us. The first purpose the Spirit had in giving the law was to condemn us and bring us to our senses. By the law we understood how sinful and hopeless we were, so that we would flee to the Rescuer (Gal. 3:24). But once we have recognized our sin and fled to Jesus for grace, we no longer have to fear the law. "Therefore there is now no condemnation for those who are in Christ Jesus" (Rom. 8:1).

Now the law has another function. To the believer it serves as a guide, pointing out the attitudes and behaviors that are pleasing to God. Nothing the Holy Spirit suggests to my spirit can be contrary to what He revealed in the Bible. His function is to cast a spotlight on God's intention expressed in Scripture. To the sinner, the law is like a light over the bathroom mirror, showing the dirt to be removed, condemning. To the saint that same law is like a flashlight, piercing the darkness to show us clearly the way to go.

> **Read the words of David from Psalm 119 that appear in the margin. How are you doing on the transition from fearing the law to loving the law? On the scale below place an S to indicate how you felt about God's law when you first became a Christian and an N to indicate how you feel now.**

Oh, how I love your law! I meditate on it all day long.
—Psalm 119:97

FEAR   LOVE

To fear the Word of the awesome and holy God is an appropriate response. When we first come to know Him fear may be our only response to the law. Then, as we grow in grace and obedience, we learn that the law is for our benefit; and we come to love the words God has given us.

God's part of our "close connection" is so incredible and so beautiful. It isn't merely a set of instructions we try to follow, but the Holy Spirit coming to be an intimate, inside companion! Our part is so incredible, too—that all God would ask of us is to trust Him! That's the beginning and end of the Christian life—oneness with God through faith, a truly close connection. But how does it work out so I can grow in that faith and oneness? That will be our theme in unit 6.

---

[1] *Theological Dictionary of the New Testament, Vol. 2* (Grand Rapids, MI: Wm. B. Eerdmans Publishing Co., 1964), 543.

SPIRALING

UP

This week you will be half way through Life in the Spirit. We began with God's purpose in creating humanity compatible with Himself. We've seen how the Spirit worked in history and in our lives to bring us into an intimate love relationship with Himself. Now we begin to look at how the Spirit leads us to become progressively more and more like Jesus—how He leads us on the upward spiral of spirit-filled living.

Matsuyama slumped cross-legged on the wooden floor of his third-floor apartment. Apartment? One room for a family of four in a former army barracks now serving as ramshackle housing for dozens of poor families.

"What's wrong, Matsuyama San?" I inquired.

"I'm not a Christian any longer." He explained, "I was drunk, got in an argument with some guy, and chased him with a baseball bat. What's worse, when I got home and told my wife, she handed me the butcher knife and said, 'The Bible says, if your right hand does wrong, cut it off.' I'm no Christian."

Matsuyama had been saved from a life of drunkenness. A skilled electrician, he descended down the river of alcohol to poverty, taking his wife and three children with him.

"Did you ever get drunk and fight before you became a Christian?"

"All the time."

"Did you feel bad about it?"

"Only if I got beat."

"Don't you see, Matsuyama San? Since the Holy Spirit lives in you, when you sin you're miserable. Your misery is evidence that you really are a Christian!"

Six months passed. Matsuyama's business had been reestablished. One Sunday morning he arrived at church with shoulders sagging. "What's wrong?" I asked. "Chase someone with a baseball bat?"

He smiled wanly. "No, but I really chewed out one of the young fellows who works for me. A Christian doesn't blow his top like that."

A year passed and time came for the greatest celebration of the year: New Year's Day. But Matsuyama wasn't celebrating. I found him in his little office, slumped over his desk. He had built the leading electrical contracting firm in the city, but he wasn't a happy man.

When I asked him what was wrong he replied, "The check bounced." In Japan people commit suicide when they can't pay their bills by December 31. He owed many people and was counting on being paid for his work on the high-rise department store under construction. Finally, he had been paid by check on the 31st and rushed to the bank. But the check was worthless.

"Did you beat up the contractor?" I asked.

"No. But my stomach is standing up" (that is, "I'm very angry").

One Sunday a year later Matsuyama bounced into church with that crooked, boyish grin I'd come to love. He told a story hard to believe. He discovered two of his employees had been deceiving him for months. Everyone in the company knew it, but no one told him. These employees called in sick, took a company truck, and drove to a distant village to moonlight, drawing sick pay for the time off. Matsuyama got suspicious and phoned the next employee who called in sick. The child who answered the phone said, "Oh, Daddy's gone to Hojo town."

Matsuyama rode his motorcycle to the fork in the road where his "sick" employee must pass on his way home, hid his bike in the bushes and waited. As he sat there, contemplating the mayhem about to happen, he began to think about Jesus–how Jesus forgave him of a life-time of evil, and how much loss Jesus had suffered to provide that forgiveness. "As I sat there, thinking about Jesus," Matsuyama said, "I choked up. I pulled out my bike and went home."

That Sunday morning we celebrated the incredible victory of the Holy Spirit in the life of a sinner saved out of Buddhist idolatry, from hopelessness to hope, from failure to success, from bondage of an explosive temper to freedom and power. Matsuyama was developing Christlikeness. I encouraged him to deal with his employees, but I knew he would do so with compassion and a forgiving spirit.

> **The Bible verse that best summarizes our theme in this unit was our memory verse for unit 1. Do you remember 2 Corinthians 3:18? Write it in the space below.**

_____

_____

The spiral pictures all of life since every person is spiraling *upward* toward God or *downward* toward destruction. Once we repent and believe, we start the spiral up.

DOWN TO DESTRUCTION   **UP TOWARD GOD**

Second Corinthians 3:18 speaks of our transformation from one degree of Christ's glorious character to another. We've used the image of a spiral to picture that. In our course map however, we've used the activities of the Spirit that bring about that transformation. Those activities of transforming, filling, overcoming, gifting, and sending don't happen in linear fashion—one after the other. The Spirit works them all simultaneously. It is we who are transformed. So in this unit we can picture the growth pattern with another spiral. In this unit we will be considering how we participate with the Spirit in bringing about that growth.

Many verses in Scripture describe this upward spiral in different ways, but one of my favorites actually reads like a spiral. It's a little longer than most of our memory passages; but the verses are short, and it really does flow upward in a beautiful spiral toward likeness to Jesus.

Unit Memory Verse

For this very reason, make every effort to add to your faith goodness; and to goodness, knowledge; and to knowledge, self-control; and to self-control, perseverance; and to perseverance, godliness; and to godliness, brotherly kindness; and to brotherly kindness, love. For if you possess these qualities in increasing measure, they will keep you from being ineffective and unproductive in your knowledge of our Lord Jesus Christ. —2 Peter 1:5-8

> Can the Holy Spirit really change the deeply-ingrained patterns in my character? How can I "spiral up" to become Christlike in my behaviors, thoughts, and feelings?

DAY 1

TURNING POINT: A CRISIS IN LIFE

Nonbelievers can make choices that move them closer to or farther from a saving encounter with Jesus Christ, but a nonbeliever cannot produce the fruit of the Holy Spirit. In this study we are dealing with the believer's faith walk. The spiral we now consider begins with the salvation experience. From that point believers move either toward Christlikeness or away from Christlikeness by lifestyle choices.

Matsuyama was on a spiral, and so are you! In fact, every believer is. The only question is whether the spiral is going up or down. We are not all spiraling at the same rate—some are on the fast track and others on the slow track, either up or down. This spiral represents our movement toward or away from Christlikeness.

The spiral does not picture our standing with God in terms of salvation. Rather it pictures our practical transformation into the character of Jesus. Believers have the opportunity to "work out your salvation with fear and trembling" (Phil. 2:12). When we experience regeneration, the process of sanctification begins. We can now begin to grow in faith and grace day by day. Now we are on the spiral, moving toward or away from Christlikeness as we make choices for or against Christ's Lordship.

⊚ **To help picture the spiral, here are some descriptions of people with certain characteristics: faithful, cheater, braggart, peaceful, ill-tempered, loving, hateful, moral, humble, worldly. Write these words beside the appropriate heading below:**

SPIRALING AWAY FROM CHRISTLIKENESS

SPIRALING TOWARD CHRISTLIKENESS

How do I tell if I am on an upward spiral? I will begin to display character traits like these:

- loves unlovable people more each year
- has joy and peace in the midst of life's storms
- endures difficult times with strength and grace
- gentle with those who are hurting
- humble about personal accomplishments
- rejects sinful impulses with increasing strength.

What have I described? The fruit of the Spirit (Gal. 5:22-23)! That's how to tell whether I'm on the upward spiral. Do I feel, think, act, and react more and more like Jesus?

⊚ **To get an initial feel for your own spiral, go back and rate yourself on each of the characteristics in the last paragraph. In the margins beside each characteristic, put an F by any fast growth items, S by any slow growth items.**

Did you find yourself wanting another label to place on some of the characteristics? Like "stable" or "steady." Sometimes I'd like to think I'm on a plateau spiritually–not growing, but not spiraling down either. But that's not possible. We're always on the move, either up or down.

⊚ **Read Matthew 12:30. In the space below explain what the passage teaches about the possibility of being in "neutral" spiritually.**

_____

_____

"He who is not with me is against me, and he who does not gather with me scatters."
—Matthew 12:30

If I'm in neutral, I'm not parked. I'm rolling backward downhill. If my sails are not raised to the wind of the Spirit, I'm not dead in the water; the tide is pushing me toward enemy territory.

ANALYZING THE PROBLEM

What's the problem of believers who aren't "being transformed from one degree of Christ's glorious likeness to another?" Consider three possibilities. They are either:

1. ignorant of some basic truth essential to growth
2. living in rebellion against God
3. drifting from God.

⊚ **In the margin see if you can summarize in a single word each of the three problems just described.**

1. _____

2. _____

3. _____

God gives us the ability to choose. We can consciously choose to move away from His revealed will, or we can drift away unconsciously. Either course is movement away from the abundant life Christ came to give us. I wrote *ignorance, rebellion,* and *drifting,* but any synonyms for these words will do.

⊚ **Below draw a line graph of your growth as a Christian from the time you met Christ to the present.**

Are you confident that you're spiraling up to greater likeness to Christ? Can your family and fellow workers see it? If you have some uncertainty, or you're not satisfied with your present rate of progress, reflect on which of the three problems contributes most to the slow growth or decline.

⊚ **Circle the word or words you feel describe what may be hindering your progress.**

    ignorance   rebellion   drifting

REVERSING THE DOWNWARD SPIRAL

God plans for Christians to keep growing. While none of us leads a sinless Christian life, our lifestyle should reflect this upward journey. We may have twists and turns along the way as we deal with our sin nature. But for many of us, because of ignorance, rebellion, or drifting, our Christian life is not one of growing and maturing. We slip into a downward spiral, out of touch with the Spirit.

In your Bible read Jesus' explanation of the parable of the sower in Mark 4:14-20. How does the soil analogy help us understand why not all Christians blossom?

_____

_____

When we come to a realization that we are on a downward spiral away from God, we need to make a U-turn. Theologians call this a "crisis" experience. However, that term can be misleading. For some a crisis means an emotional upheaval or some miracle sign from heaven. Certainly, a "crisis experience" may be a dramatic event. The apostle Paul saw a light from heaven that knocked him to the ground and left him blind for three days (Acts 9:3-9). For others this experience may be less dramatic. Jesus recommissioned Peter through a quiet conversation beside the Sea of Galilee (John 21:15-19). The basic meaning of the word *crisis*, both in the dictionary and in biblical teaching, is simply "a turning point." And without that, no one spiraling downward will ever spiral upward.

My father was a successful young businessman and active church leader, but something was missing. He felt defeated by his sins, his work for God was powerless, he was agitated within. Though no one in his family or church would have guessed it, he was fighting a losing battle in his attempts to spiral upward toward God. Then came the turning point.

Challenged by a dramatic turnaround in the life of a friend, he went to his room and methodically yielded to God each part of his life: first the sins he was aware of; then the disputed things that some said were wrong and others said were OK; after that, his past, both failures and successes; and finally, his future. Everything. As a result of that experience, his life was transformed. He said there was no special emotion, no vision, but from that time on doing the will of his Lord became his first priority.

Like my father, a person can have a crisis, a turnaround, that is an unemotional transaction with God. The intensity of the turning experience may depend on one's personality, expectations, or how long and how deliberately he or she has resisted the will of God.

Have you had a turning point since your initial conversion? If so, describe it briefly:

_____

_____

_____

Once we have made the decision to turn around, the Holy Spirit is free to begin the process of transforming us into greater likeness to Jesus.

> Wherever a person may be on the spiral of life, the way to change direction from downward to upward is to turn around. We call that turn-around *repentance*. Repentance means a change of mind that results in a change of behavior. Without this turning, the only direction possible is down.

◎ **Where are you in life's spiral? In which direction are you headed? Check one response below:**

❑ upward ❑ downward ❑ not sure

If you aren't sure or you are quite sure you aren't spiraling upward, at least so anyone would notice it, isn't it time to make a turn around? Or do you need to make sure you have fully turned around?

Jesus wants to be Lord of our lives. He has to be Lord if we are moving upward in the spiral. We can choose between two masters: Christ or sin. We cannot choose to put ourselves in control. When we think we are in control, sin is our real master. Of these two choices, which do you want to control you: Christ or your sin nature?

Are you ready for the big turnaround? If you are, now is the time to settle the direction your life is headed. In repentance, acknowledge the factors that have led you away from God. Yield to Christ's control. Ask for the Spirit's guidance as you seek to carry out your commitment in the days ahead.

In our next lesson we will look closely at how the Holy Spirit moves us up the spiral toward Christlikeness.

◎ **On the graphic below, list the "add-ons" from our memory verse, beginning with "faith" and ending with "love."**

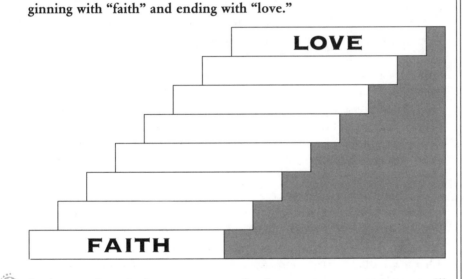

◎ **In the margin write in your own words what our memory verse says will result if we don't keep spiraling.**

DAY 2

KEEPING STEP WITH THE SPIRIT

"If you have come into life by the power of the Spirit," says Paul, "by that same Spirit keep on walking" (Gal. 5:25, my paraphrase).

Have you ever thought of the word *companion* as a verb? To companion means to spend time with or be friends with. The Holy Spirit invites us to companion with Him all day every day. Companionship with the Spirit is not just a mystical, internal experience. In the process of transforming us the Spirit gives us resources we can see, touch, and experience. Theologians call these resources *means of grace.*

So I say, live by the Spirit, and you will not gratify the desires of the sinful nature. For the sinful nature desires what is contrary to the Spirit, and the Spirit what is contrary to the sinful nature. They are in conflict with each other, so that you do not do what you want. But if you are led by the Spirit, you are not under law.
—Galatians 5:16-18.

The means of grace include our devotional life, prayer, the Bible, the church, and adversity. In this unit we will consider how we can faithfully use these means of grace to participate with the Spirit in His work of remodeling our lives.

THE DEVOTIONAL LIFE: COMPANIONING WITH GOD

The devotional life is one key to spiritual growth. The general term *devotional life* includes anything we do to increase our fellowship with God. Prayer and Bible reading are the cornerstones of a devotional life. God is our source of power. Intimate communication with Him is the only way to live a victorious Christian life.

Jesus said, "I am the vine; you are the branches. … apart from me you can do nothing" (John 15:5). The only way to avoid a dry, lifeless Christianity is to consistently abide in Christ by meditating on God's Word and communing with Him in prayer. Companionship with God is not confined to a daily devotional time. Christian mystics speak of constant, conscious communion with Christ. I've not attained such a constant contact with the Spirit, though I would like to.

Each of us can be aware of God's abiding presence and turn to Him spontaneously throughout the day. We can share our gratitude when things go well and call on Him to help when they don't. We can develop the habit of sharing our hearts with our best friend who is always there. I'll never get over the wonder that the Infinite One actually desires my companionship!

How would you describe your devotional life? Put a check by each item that plays a significant role in your life.

❑ I have a set time each day for devotional activities.
❑ I read and meditate on Scripture.
❑ I praise God and give Him thanks for my many blessings.
❑ I confess my sins to Him when I fail.
❑ I pray not only for my own and family needs, but also for other individuals and causes.

A Christian can go through a routine of reading the Bible, offering praise, and praying, without any tangible awareness of God's presence. The devotional life can be mechanical, something to check off a list of good things to do. Going through the motions can lead to spiritual pride and self-righteousness. The big question is, What is the quality of your encounter with God? What kind of fellowship do you experience with Him?

On a scale of 1 to 10 rank your perception of what your recent devotional times have been like.

1	2	3	4	5	6	7	8	9	10

Dull routine,
mostly just going
through the motions

Intimate companionship,
exhilaration with a
sense that I really
companioned with God

I, like you, seek to develop more intimacy with God. Since we find help in seeing how others experience God, I'll share some of my approach to the devotional life; but please remember that my way isn't the only way. It's one way a fellow pilgrim has pursued companionship with God.

MY APPROACH

I began a personal quiet time following my surrender to Christ at age 12, but reading the Bible was more like eating sawdust; and praying–well, was God listening at all? I tried to keep that morning appointment with Him, but more often than not I skipped it in favor of more sleep or breakfast. Finally, at age 21, I told the Lord I would read the Word daily whether it had meaning for me or not, just as an act of obedience. Things didn't change except that I kept that promise faithfully, week after weary week, eating sawdust. Then one morning I realized I had changed. I couldn't get along without that time with God. In fact, the Bible had come alive to me. It's been that way ever since.

My appointment–every morning at 6:00 a.m. Why morning? Well, David said God would hear his voice every morning (Ps. 5:3). Jesus set a powerful example by praying early in the morning, and a friend of mine once said he couldn't see tuning your violin after the concert was over! Some say they just aren't morning people; but it is important to have a set time or other things will crowd out your time with God. The enemy will see to that! I prefer early morning because there aren't many interruptions at 6:00 a.m.

How much time should I set aside for my "date" with God? The editor of a religious magazine wrote that he cannot get along without spending 15 minutes a day alone with God. Many Korean pastors say for them 4 hours is necessary. For myself, I can hardly unwind and settle my restless mind in 15 minutes. I set aside an hour, and it is always too short! One thing is sure, a hasty salute toward heaven is not sufficient for building a meaningful relationship with God. The goal is companionship, not dutiful routine.

First, I sing aloud a couple of hymns. That tunes my heart. He doesn't care about my lack of solo quality! The Bible contains many commands to sing. See the examples in the margin.

Praise the Lord.
Praise the Lord, O my soul.
 I will praise the Lord all my life;
 I will sing praise to my God
 as long as I live.
—Psalm 146:1-2

That's how I get started, but remember, that isn't the only way. How do you do it? This would be a great time to note your approach and then set some goals if you would like to change.

	Present Practice	*New Plan*
Time and place of appointment	_____	_____
Length of time spent in your "quiet time"	_____	_____
How you begin	_____	_____

Let the word of Christ dwell in you richly as you teach and admonish one another with all wisdom, and as you sing psalms, hymns and spiritual songs with gratitude in your hearts to God.
—Colossians 3:16

SCRIPTURE READING

After tuning my soul with song, I turn to the Bible: I use a different translation each time I read through the Bible to keep it fresh and gain new insights. I read consecutively through each book. I pause before reading and ask the Spirit to speak to me through His Word.

As I read I underline passages that speak to me–
• a new insight into God's ways
• comfort for my present heartache
• conviction of sin
• a principle of life I didn't understand or had neglected.

Then I go back through and think about (meditate on) the parts I underlined, often praying these back to the Lord in His own words or asking Him to work them out in my life. If the underlined portion is something I want to be sure not to forget, I type it on a 3-by-5 inch card and rotate those on my "refrigerator collection" so I can memorize them.

⟳ **That's my approach to devotional Bible reading. What's yours? Again, note your present practice, and set some goals if you desire to change:**

	Present Practice	*New Plan*
How often do you read the entire Bible?	_____	_____
From what version(s) do you read?	_____	_____
How do you "capture" what God is saying?	_____	_____
How do you reflect on what you read?	_____	_____
How do you memorize key passages?	_____	_____

PRAYER

Thanking God for His blessings, exulting in His beauty, and worshiping Him with adoring praise often come naturally through songs or passages of Scripture. If not, I spend some time in worship, not asking for anything, just focusing on God.

Then I turn to "intercessory" prayer. I commit each plan for the day to the Lord, asking Him to use me to the maximum for His purposes in each encounter and each activity–planned or unplanned. I talk to God about everything in my life–He invites us to, but I don't want to be egocentric in prayer. It won't do to stop with intercession for my own needs and those of my family. I pray for the needs of others.

One way I pray for others is to have a current list–people who are a special concern, divided by categories: unsaved, Christians in spiritual trouble, people with health needs or bereavement, and a general catch-all of those making hard decisions, or having special ministry opportunities. Some people I pray for daily–family, close friends, and others for whom I have assumed a prayer responsibility. Others I pray for less frequently. Finally, I pray for the nations and for missionaries seeking to reach them. I want to be a world Christian on my knees! God loved the world; I want to love it also.

⟳ **How would you evaluate your prayer life?**

	Present Practice	*New Plan*
Is there a vital time of praise/worship/thanksgiving?	_____	_____
Do I routinely confess sin?	_____	_____

Intercession
for personal needs   _____   _____

Intercession
for others   _____   _____

Other prayer activities   _____   _____

🌀 Review each of the plans in the right-hand columns, pause now and commit those plans to the Lord. Don't feel you need to radically change everything instantly. That may be discouraging. Just take a step at a time—that's what spiraling upward is all about. Be sure to talk with the Lord about your desires and plans.

🌀 The memory verse for this unit speaks of the spiral. Commit it to memory if you haven't already and write it out below:

_____

_____

_____

DAY 3

PARTNERING: HOW THE CHURCH FITS THE SPIRAL

We want to be on the upward spiral, growing daily to be more like Christ and experience loving companionship with Him. We've seen how important our personal devotional life is, but we are mistaken if we think private prayer and Bible reading alone can make us all God intends. God has given us the fellowship of believers to support us in our upward spiral. Christ didn't promise to build invincible Christians, but an invincible church. Paul constantly reminds us that a major purpose of the church is spiritual growth—to "build up" believers (Eph. 4:15-16). Church life is an essential ingredient of spiraling upward.

PURPOSES OF THE CHURCH
Any activity done by a group of God's people to honor God can be used to strengthen each member of the body, but Scripture seems to emphasize five major purposes of the church: worship, fellowship, discipleship, ministry, and evangelism. Let's take a closer look at three of them. We'll consider ministry and evangelism in later units.

Worship
Public worship is directed toward God, bringing Him joy, but it also helps each person who truly participates to spiral upward. When we worship, we remind ourselves who God is. We reflect on His nature and purposes, His love and commitment to us.

Instead, speaking the truth in love, we will in all things grow up into him who is the Head, that is, Christ. From him the whole body, joined and held together by every supporting ligament, grows and builds itself up in love, as each part does its work.
—Ephesians 4:15-16

⊚ **List some of your experiences of growth through public worship during the past few months.**

_____

_____

Did you mention the spiritual exhilaration you felt singing a hymn in concert with all God's people or perhaps enlightenment from a Scripture passage you never really understood before? Have you experienced a surge of faith as God's people united in prayer for a special need or been inspired to make an important decision?

Fellowship

Fellowship in the early church was more than standing around after the morning service to visit. It was even more than a "fellowship supper," though they had that every Lord's Day! Fellowship meant a family solidarity in which each member was joined to the others in a caring relationship.

Many of us would list fellowship as a primary way the church meets our needs. Fellowship means what it sounds like: two or more fellows in the same ship. Fellowship means supporting each other as you travel toward a common destination. In the family of God we are on a journey. Along the way we encounter many obstacles. I'm glad to have the companionship of fellow believers on that journey.

⊚ **Can you identify a time when the fellowship of other believers has been particularly important in your life? ❑ Yes ❑ No If so, describe the circumstance.**

_____

_____

Fellowship means more than just company. Fellowship includes elements of accountability and guidance as well.

Discipleship

Discipleship means to spiral up! It means to become more faithful disciples of Jesus, and to do that we need one another. Ways to disciple include preaching, teaching, small-group studies, and one-to-one relationships. The church as a whole also disciples through accountability and guidance.

Small-group discipleship can serve many purposes, both for fellowship and for discipling. Special benefits result from meeting in smaller groups, benefits not available to a large group. Think of your study group for *Life in the Spirit*, for example, or your Bible study class. These groups focus on discipling believers.

⊚ **List below how you felt motivated toward discipleship as a result of your small-group meetings recently.**

_____

_____

Did you list things such as personal encouragement, instruction fitted to my personal circumstances, or seeing that others wrestle with the same problems I do?

Notice that in a small group members reinforce and help each other, and small groups help hold each other accountable.

One-on-one discipleship—"Accountability" is a key element in serious discipleship, and most of us find help in having a relationship with someone for mutual accountability. Perhaps you have a regular prayer buddy or partner with whom you can share freely. I can't get along without mine. A prayer partner is the most common one-to-one relationship in the body. However, many people have chosen to go even deeper by enlisting an accountability partner.

Larry was a college professor and lay preacher who wanted someone to hold him accountable so he could grow spiritually. He asked me to meet with him once a week. I was startled at our first meeting when he gave me a list of very pointed and personal questions he wanted me to ask him every week. Here's his list:

- Ask me about my time each day with God—the content of my prayers, the truths I've learned from Scripture, the amount of time spent.
- Ask me how eating habits have changed and what specific goals I have reached in losing weight.
- Ask me to list the amount of time spent with TV and what specific programs I've watched.
- Ask about how much time I spent with my wife and my sons.
- Ask about what I've done to combat sexual temptation; probe to see if I have done anything to feed an unhealthy sexual appetite. Ask about my relationship with the attractive girl who works with me.
- Ask me about my motives in work: what drives me to accept so many responsibilities, what I have said no to this week, why I said yes to any new responsibilities I accepted.

Larry was serious about "spiraling upward"! Are you serious about it?

⟳ **If you have an accountability partner or would like one, what questions would you want him or her to ask you? Write out questions that would expose every area of your life in which you think God wants you to grow. Be very honest and thorough.**

_____

_____

_____

_____

_____

Discipleship for guidance—The church assists each member to understand what God intends for him or her. I call this *guidance*. The Holy Spirit revealed His missionary purpose for the senior pastor, Barnabas, and one of his assistants, Paul, to the church at Antioch meeting together in prayer. The Spirit didn't speak directly to Paul, but to the church about Paul.

This lesson was difficult for me to learn. Early in my ministry I was responsible for a Christian school. The board did not always agree with me on the direction we should go. Gradually, through painful experience, I began to have more confidence in the leading of the Holy Spirit through our responsible body than through my own independent judgment. Seeking such guidance became a life principle for me.

We need to make our ministry choices in the context of seeking guidance from God's church.

God doesn't save us and put us on a lonely pilgrimage. The Holy Spirit is our constant companion, but He provides touchable companions, too. We neglect those intimate relationships to our own spiritual peril. Paul gives a magnificent description of the role the church plays in Christian growth in his letter to the church at Ephesus.

🌀 **In Ephesians 4:11-16 below, underline every word or phrase that sounds like spiraling.**

> *It was he who gave some to be apostles, some to be prophets, some to be evangelists, and some to be pastors and teachers, to prepare God's people for works of service, so that the body of Christ may be built up until we all reach unity in the faith and in the knowledge of the Son of God and become mature, attaining to the whole measure of the fullness of Christ.*
>
> *Then we will no longer be infants, tossed back and forth by the waves, and blown here and there by every wind of teaching and by the cunning and craftiness of men in their deceitful scheming. Instead, speaking the truth in love, we will in all things grow up into him who is the Head, that is, Christ. From him the whole body, joined and held together by every supporting ligament, grows and builds itself up in love, as each part does its work (Eph. 4:11-16).*

Among others I underlined the words *built up, reach unity,* and *become mature.* You may have selected different phrases, but altogether I counted eight images that fit the spiral.

🌀 **Now circle every word in the passage that tells who helps me spiral toward maturity, toward perfection in Christ.**

🌀 **Did you include your own participation in helping others grow? You are part of "God's people." "Every supporting ligament" and "each part" means we are important to each other. Finally go back and read the passage once more as a prayer of thanksgiving, adding words like, "Thank You Lord that...." Make it personal, "I praise You for giving me...." Or perhaps it would be a petition, like, "Please use me, Holy Spirit, to...."**

DAY 4

ADVERSITY, THE FAST TRACK FOR SPIRALING UP

In day 2 we learned that the Spirit gives us resources to use in "spiraling up." These resources or means of grace include our devotional life (day 2) and the church (day 3). Today we will explore a means of grace we prefer to avoid—adversity. Through stormy weather we learn lessons in discipleship that we would never master if we only experience pleasant breezes and sunshine.

HOW TROUBLE STRENGTHENS US

Colin Green greeted me with a big smile and a cheery "Praise the Lord!" Praise the Lord for what? Here she was, cooped up in the hospital room with that giant of a man she'd lived with for decades, now incoherent, uncooperative, belligerent, far down the terrifying road into Alzheimer's.

"Why so happy?" I asked. She told me how she found a despondent woman in the hospital corridor, a mother who had traveled from a distant city to watch her son die. Colin, forgetting her own woes, became a friend to her and led that distraught mother to find hope in Christ. Both were inundated with unexpected happiness as they embraced and mingled their tears.

The previous week Colin's husband broke down the door of their small home to get out of his "prison." Halfway across the front yard he stumbled to the ground and couldn't get up. Colin couldn't lift him, but she was reluctant to call for help lest they find her beloved in his pitiable condition. He was incontinent, his clothes totally soiled.

Colin pulled off his clothes, cleaned and redressed him as he lay there helplessly. Then she called for help! She spent the night with her husband in the hospital, rescuing the nurses from his irrational behavior. The next morning, Sunday, her son arrived with bad news: "Mom, your house is going up in flames!" A few hours later I entered that bleak scene, received a warm embrace from that courageous little woman who whispered in my ear, "Praise the Lord!"

> ◎ **Not everyone responds to trouble like Colin Green. Some emerge from the storm better people, some bitter. Why? Put a check by each of the following that you think might contribute to differing outcomes. Then circle the one you feel is most important for explaining the differences.**

- ❑ Some people inherit a stronger temperament than others.
- ❑ Some people have traumatic childhoods while others have a nurturing home background.
- ❑ Some people face more tragic events than others.
- ❑ Some people have more faith than others.
- ❑ Some people have a stronger support network of loving people.

Did you check all of them? I did. The crucial difference, however, is not in the circumstances but in our response to them. Lack of faith lets the circumstances put a wedge between God and me. I become a weaker person–less like Jesus than before–perhaps discouraged, despondent, even bitter, or at least a miserable, complaining person. A response of faith in God keeps the circumstances outside, pressing me closer to God; and I become a stronger, better person, more like Jesus.

WHERE TROUBLE COMES FROM

Sometimes when I experience difficulty, I know who or what caused me pain. On other occasions, trying to figure out who's to blame is a frustrating and fruitless task.

Some people forever blame others for their troubles. The perpetrator may be a misguided or evil parent or spouse, a society stacked against them, or the devil himself. Still others tend to blame themselves for everything, guilty or not. Have you ever fallen into the "blame" trap?

Even if my blame-laying is on target, that truth has little power to deliver me from my problems. Indeed, the blame hunt itself may make me a more angry and bitter person, less like Jesus. The effort to fix blame can be self-destructive.

No matter where the problem may seem to come from, I can always recognize one basic truth about trouble. If not even a sparrow can fall to the earth without God knowing and every hair on our heads is numbered, then ultimately God is responsible. Of course, the awful tragedy in your life that is the result of someone's sin is not God's will. He didn't cause it, but no harm can touch the child of God unless it first passes through Jesus' nail-scarred hands. To know that God is aware of every grief of mine and could have supernaturally intervened to stop it may create some anxiety, but at least it simplifies the search for the responsible party!

Once we understand this basic truth concerning suffering, we no longer need devote our energies to determining who is guilty and making him pay for it. We can give our attention to a more important and redemptive truth. Whatever the contributing factors to my suffering, God has my best interests at heart; and He purposes to bring good through it. He can use the most painful of circumstances to shape our lives and our characters. The pain is temporary, but the character He develops in us is eternal. To discover the purpose in the suffering relieves the deepest agony of it, for meaningless suffering is the greatest torment of all. That is the distress of every person who doesn't know God.

THE REASONS FOR PAIN

Why do we experience pain? One or more of the following reasons may contribute to our suffering.

1. **Consequences of sin**—(2 Sam. 12:13-14; Jer. 11:10-11; 1 Cor. 11:31-32; John 5:14). No believer will face punishment for sin in eternity, but while still here on earth Christians may suffer as a result of sin. In former days when tragedy struck, people asked, "For which of my many sins is God judging me?" Nowadays we tend to ask, "What's wrong with God? Why me? I deserve so much better." In searching for the purpose in my grief, it doesn't hurt to ask the old question. God still allows us to suffer the consequences of our sin so both we and others can learn from them.

2. **Chastisement**—This is another word for discipline. God disciplines those He loves (Heb. 12:5-11). Like the shepherd searching for the lost sheep, our Heavenly Father seeks to bring erring children back to the right way (Ps. 119:67,71). The purpose of discipline is correction and restoration.

3. **Warning**—God may discipline an erring child as a warning or example to others (1 Cor. 10:11). The sudden deaths of Ananias and Sapphira certainly served to warn early Christians against dishonesty (Acts 5:1-11).

4. **Guidance**—Sometimes God allows difficult circumstances to direct us to go somewhere or do something we otherwise might not consider (Acts 8:1,4; Matt. 10:23). Jonah refused to go where God said until he had been swallowed by a great fish (Jonah 3:3).

5. **Service**—Suffering prepares a person to help others (2 Cor. 1:3-4). We can be comforted best by one who has suffered in a similar way. Suffering makes us more compassionate toward others.

Although one or more of these five purposes may be in God's design, two purposes are always present in every trial. They are God's glory and my growth.

When I respond to trouble with childlike confidence in God, people see and give God the credit. Sometimes they see His deliverance (John 9:2-3). Sometimes they see Him supply strength in the midst of suffering (2 Cor. 12:7-10), as in the case of Colin Green. Suffering can always bring glory to God (Ezek. 20:9,14,22).

Suffering also has the purpose of growing me up into Christ's own likeness. Trials come to test us and refine us, to purify us as fire purifies gold (1 Pet. 1:7). Every circumstance in life is an opportunity to become more like Jesus (Rom. 8:27-29).

If we judged ourselves, we would not come under judgment. When we are judged by the Lord, we are being disciplined so that we will not be condemned with the world.
—1 Corinthians 11:31-32

It was good for me to be afflicted so that I might learn your decrees.
—Psalm 119:71

The Spirit ... pleads for God's people in God's own way; and in everything, as we know, he co-operates for good with those who love God and are called according to his purpose. For God knew his own before ever they were, and also ordained that they should be shaped to the likeness of his Son.
—Romans 8:27-29, NEB

Talk about a powerful way to spiral upward! The Holy Spirit uses everything in the life of believers for the purpose He had all along: shaping them into the likeness of the Son! That includes the pain (see also 2 Cor. 12:7; Phil. 3:10; Heb. 12:4-13; John 15:2-8; Rom. 5:3-4; Ps. 119:67,71).

How do I make sure adversity actually brings glory to God and growth to me? Watch the spiral carefully.

> *When all kinds of trials and temptations crowd into your lives ... don't resent them as intruders, but welcome them as friends! Realize that they come to test your faith and to produce in you the quality of endurance. But let the process go on until that endurance is fully developed, and you will find you have become men of mature character with the right sort of independence (Jas. 1:2-4, Phillips).*

Faith is the key! When I pass the faith test, I become stronger. Endurance leads to maturity, which produces the character of Christ in me. On the other hand, if I doubt that God is—
- big enough to deal with my problem,
- smart enough to know what's best for me,
- caring enough to see me through,

I spiral downward. I crumple in self-pity and give up, or I grow hard and cynical. I may even become mean-spirited and hostile.

Faith will transform that same trouble from a stumbling block into a stepping stone. Without the testing we would remain spiritually flabby and quite unlike the One who learned obedience through the things He suffered (Heb. 5:8). When we respond with childlike trust in a loving Father, we can join Colin in trusting God. Like her, we can say from the heart that we still have cause to "Praise God!"

Make a list of five major problems, trials, or sources of pain in your life now.

1. _____

2. _____

3. _____

4. _____

5. _____

Now look at the list of your major problems and reflect for a few minutes on how each might turn people to God and how each might develop some Christlike quality in you.

For each of the major problems you identified, below write a response that could cause God to be honored and a response to help you grow.

1. Name of a major problem: _____

Response I could make to cause God to be honored: _____

_____

Response I could make to grow because of this suffering: _____

_____

2. Name of a major problem: _____

Response I could make to cause God to be honored: _____

_____

Response I could make to grow because of this suffering: _____

_____

3. Name of a major problem: _____

Response I could make to cause God to be honored: _____

_____

Response I could make to grow because of this suffering: _____

_____

4. Name of a major problem: _____

Response I could make to cause God to be honored: _____

_____

Response I could make to grow because of this suffering: _____

_____

5. Name of a major problem: _____

Response I could make to cause God to be honored: _____

_____

Response I could make to grow because of this suffering: _____

_____

Are you ready to take the leap of faith? You probably can't thank God for the problem itself, for it may be evil incarnate. But thank Him for how the Spirit can transform each problem into glory to God and growth in you. Write out your prayer of thanks in your journal. Thank Him that He is wise enough, strong enough, and cares about you enough to use that problem for eternal good.

In the margin write this week's Scripture memory verse from memory if you can. Review your other Scripture memory verses.

🌀 Using 2 Peter 1:5-8 as a guide, write the growth pattern on the stair steps below. Begin with "faith" at the bottom.

DAY 5

A STORY OF SPIRALING UPWARD

This week we have looked at how the Holy Spirit enables us to "spiral upward" toward Christlikeness. Let me tell you how God is working to transform my life.

I committed my life to Christ when I was 12 years old, but I didn't automatically begin to grow. I was sincere enough but didn't develop a strong devotional life or learn to follow the direction of the Spirit. I knew nothing of the biblical pattern of mentoring–learning from a more mature Christian. I did not know what I needed to advance up the spiral. Jesus was dear to me, but the Holy Spirit was a stranger. Ignorance blocks progress. I did not understand myself, much less the many aspects of my life I needed to commit to Christ.

🌀 The following Scriptures list aspects of our lives we may find difficult to commit to God. Read each Scripture. Put a check by those items you have difficulty turning over to God.

❏ Reputation–Philippians 2:3-11; Luke 14:11
❏ Future–Matthew 6:33-34
❏ Family, friends–Matthew 10:37
❏ Possessions–Luke 12:33-34
❏ Talents, abilities–1 Corinthians 4:7
❏ Entire self–Romans 12:1-2
❏ Everything you have–Luke 14:33

🌀 List in the margin or your journal any other areas of your thought life, relationships, activities, talk, or habits that you need to yield to God.

At age 18 I became restless about my failures to overcome sin in my life. I had a list of items for daily prayer and on that list I noted "T & T." That was code for tongue and temper. I had the same problem as Matsuyama. In high school, I sometimes settled disagreements with my fists. In college, when I was seeking to be more like Jesus, that never happened, but my tongue hurt people, and I began to feel the pain. That's why "T & T" stayed on my list.

🌀 **Tongue and temper may not be your big temptations. What is your biggest area of defeat?**

_____

To yield to God in biblical terms is not just a passive cry of "uncle"—"I quit, God, you win." Yielding to God is positive, aggressive, an active desire for God and good, an attitude of going for the goal of likeness to Jesus. This desire became an obsession with me. On the spiral I had turned around and was headed up. Still I didn't seem to be making very rapid progress.

My "Ah-Ha!" Moment

I had attempted to live the Christian life in my own strength. Then a preacher said something so simple I wondered how I could have missed it so long. "The key to the victorious Christian life," he said, "is surrender and faith." Suddenly I realized the meaning of Christ living His life through me.

I realized the meaning of the Greek word in 2 Corinthians 3:18. *Transformed* is the word from which we get the word *metamorphosis*—a transformation of nature. God transforms believers. We cannot accomplish the metamorphosis in our own power. I began to replace *try* with *trust*.

In days 2, 3, and 4 we studied the means of grace—the tools God uses to transform Christians into the image of Christ. I began to realize that these means of grace were not part of a self-improvement project. They were the instruments God used to perform needed surgery in my life.

🌀 **Below list the means of grace or tools of the Spirit He puts in our hands to work with Him in this remodeling project.**

_____

_____

_____

_____

Let me illustrate how each of these worked as God began changing me from a short-fused, shoot-from-the-lip person into someone more like Jesus. I had been praying, reading my Bible, and attending church faithfully. But these activities weren't focused on growth, especially growth out of my outbursts of bad temper.

I began to cooperate with God rather than struggle against Him as He used the means of grace—the Word of God, prayer, the church, and adversity.

- The Word preached enlightened me and gave me confidence of what could be.
- My daily prayer focused on a desperate cry for deliverance from my personal quagmire of spiritual failure.
- The church—At that point I didn't know about small-group accountability, and I didn't have a spiritual "buddy." My father modeled the influence of the church for me. He was the most powerful Christian example in my life. I wouldn't have made it on my own. He instructed me, was always available, and demonstrated the life I longed for.

We all, with unveiled face beholding as in a mirror the glory of the Lord, are being transformed into the same image from glory to glory, just as from the Lord, the Spirit.
—2 Corinthians 3:18, NASB

- Adversity—To answer my prayer for mouth-control and a patient spirit, God used the circumstances of life, adversity. Troubles were God's severe mercies, designed to make me more like Jesus. Paul calls suffering a grace—the same word used of salvation, an unearned gift for our welfare, a "means of grace."

God began to use adversity to work on my character when I was a newlywed. Muriel and I had heard all the horror stories of marriage wars and were determined not to follow the pattern. If Jesus were central to both of us, how could we fight? We kept our vows—no controversy for three or four years! If one of us got contrary, the other stayed cool. Remember this is the "T & T" man we're talking about.

Along came our first child and with her something wholly unexpected. We had never discussed child discipline. Now we discovered we differed radically. I began to seethe inside and pulled down the shades. Communication shut down. Oh, I was civil, said "Good morning" and such. But bubbly, outgoing Muriel knew something was wrong. I boiled for three days until finally I could stand it no longer. As I drove down the highway the Holy Spirit made me so miserable that I pulled over to the side of the road, crumpled over the steering wheel and pled with God for two things: forgive me and deliver me.

But it happened three or four times over the next few years. Days of seething anger, finally repentance and restoration. When I was in Christian ministry—a missionary, in fact—I decided this could not go on. I went to the mountains alone for three days of fasting and prayer. With tears I cried to God for deliverance. In desperation, I said, "Lord, if you don't deliver me, I quit. What message do I have for these lost Japanese if it doesn't even redeem me from an evil temper?" I meant it, and so did God. My times of seething anger against my precious one never happened again.

I would like to tell you that God delivered me from all struggles with anger, but that wasn't the end of it. As the children came along, with them came the old temptations—to punish them in anger, to speak harsh words. I remember the day I realized it was OK for a father to apologize to a little person. With tears I knelt by Jan's bed and told her I was sorry for what I had said.

As the children grew older and began to leave home, God brought other circumstances to shape me. I experienced a long-term betrayal in the ministry. By then I wasn't tempted to lash out in anger, but it took me years to truly forgive. Finally, reading Christ's words on the cross, it dawned on me that I should ask God to forgive the person who betrayed me. I was startled to discover the residue of feelings I still carried inside.

I wanted to feel righteous and say that I had forgiven him. "Oh, no, Lord!" I said. "I've forgiven him, never held all that garbage against him anyway, never tried to get back or make him pay for it." But at the same time I thought: *God, I don't want You to forgive him.*

The persistent Holy Spirit worked on me day and night until I was able to pray from my heart, "Father, please forgive him, too. Treat him as if it all never happened."

God continues to use the circumstances of life to shape my character and develop the fruit of the Spirit in my life. In fact, I seem to be in a post-graduate program in patience, caring for a dear wife who suffers from Alzheimer's and whose needs change daily. So far I have been in this school of patience for 18 years.

That's a bit of the story of one man in his spiral up: from physical expressions of anger, to verbal outbursts, to inner seething, to forgiveness, to peace. Whatever growth I have experienced is the grace of God, the work of the Spirit. Part of His grace is to put tangible "tools" in my hand to participate with Him in reconstructing my life. Those tools include prayer, Scripture, the church, and adverse circumstances. Your pilgrimage has been different from mine, but the grace of God is the same!

He has graciously granted you the privilege … of suffering for him.
–Philippians 1:29, NRSV

We … rejoice in our sufferings, because we know that suffering produces perseverance; perseverance character; and character, hope.
—Romans 5:3-4

God disciplines us for our good, that we may share in his holiness. No discipline seems pleasant at the time, but painful. Later on, however, it produces a harvest of righteousness and peace for those who have been trained by it.
—Hebrews 12:10-11

Below rearrange those four means of grace we have studied in this unit. Write them in the order of their strength in changing your life during recent months or years.

1. _____

2. _____

3. _____

4. _____

Have any of the four been under-utilized? We can't pick and choose—we need aggressively to use all the tools God supplies. When we do, the Spirit of God does His transforming work, making us into working models of Jesus to attract people to Himself.

How has He been transforming your life? Matsuyama had only a couple of years to grow before he fell to his death from a utility pole. Or perhaps you count your spiral in decades as I do. How have you changed from impatience toward inner tranquility, from lust toward purity, from gluttony toward self-control, from materialism toward contentment and generosity, from ego-centric thinking toward concern for others, from doubt toward confidence in God's promises? Or maybe it has been something else God has been working on.

List a few key areas in the blanks below.

What I was	*What I am*	*What I want to be*
_____	_____	_____
_____	_____	_____
_____	_____	_____

If you would prefer, write these out in your private journal instead, but be very honest with yourself and the Lord about it. If you can't truthfully see any progress toward Christlikeness, maybe time has come for the great turn-around, the surrender of your will to the will of the Father.

The Spirit makes our spiral-up possible. He works as we participate with Him and utilize the "tools" He provides. Isn't that spiral upward toward God a beautiful plan? The more we know Him, the more we love Him, the more we love Him, the more we trust Him; the more we trust Him, the more we obey Him; the more we obey Him, the more like Him we become; the more like Him we become, the more intimately we companion with Him; the more intimately we companion, the more we know Him, the more we love Him... on and on, upward in a grand spiral toward ever greater likeness to Jesus and closer companionship with Him. If that vision of the Christian life excites you, why not tell God about it right now?

EXPECTATIONS

What can I expect from my life in the Spirit? Total victory over all sin?
Some victory but mostly defeat? Something in between? In this unit we'll consider why
we need realistic expectations of life in the Spirit—biblical expectations.

Marguerite had high expectations. She had been so miserable with her failure to measure up that in desperation she turned to Jesus and invited Him into her life. She thought, "Tomorrow everything will be different. I won't get angry with Robertson anymore."

When she told me her story I responded, "And I gave you plenty of cause to be angry."

Marguerite, my older sister, said, "No, not just you. I was mad at lots of people."

Why did she think her temptation to get angry—and all those other miserable temptations that held her in their grip—would disappear? Because they seemed to have disappeared for her father.

My father preached all over the world about the victorious Christian life. He wrote about it in articles and books read by tens of thousands, but he did more. He lived that life right before us in the home. To outward appearances he lead a flawless life full of love, joy, peace and all the fruit of the Spirit. How was Marguerite to know that she was comparing a babe in Christ to a mature Christian?

Marguerite awoke to great disappointment the morning after her conversion. As she put it, I "smart mouthed" her, and she blew up just as she always had. In addition, none of her other temptations or failures disappeared. "I was so disappointed," she said. "At first I struggled and fought the temptations, just like I always had. Finally, I gave up. For me the Christian life didn't work." For years Marguerite settled for spiritual defeat. She struggled to be good with sometimes modest success, often with failure to be and do what she longed for.

When were Marguerite's expectations of her Christian life too high? When were they too low?

After several years overseas, I returned home to discover a beautiful person, one of the most godly people I've known. Under the bitterest of circumstances, she lived a life of quiet patience and tireless service for others. What had she found?

Is there a balance, a more biblical way? In this unit we'll search out that fundamental puzzle of life in the Spirit. First we will look at the low expectations many settle for, then the high expectations many cling to, and finally the biblical expectations you and I may experience in daily life.

Unit Memory Verse

Thanks be to God! He gives us the victory through our Lord Jesus Christ.
—1 Corinthians 15:57

What can I expect from my Christian life? Will I experience peace or struggle? Can I live above sin and be perfect?

DAY 1

WHAT CAN WE EXPECT?

Before we look at the reality of what we cannot expect of our new life in Christ, let's be encouraged about what we can expect. All Christians agree that the Holy Spirit is in the business of making saints out of sinners. However, many of us disagree about the practical result of His activity in this present life.

> **Read through the following examples. Mark A by those you fully agree with, D by those you disagree with, and U by those you're uncertain about.**
>
> ___ Jason is convinced that both he and all Christians sin consciously and deliberately every day.
> ___ Virginia was baptized by the Spirit last year; her sin nature was eliminated, and she no longer sins.
> ___ Mary has given up on any miracle deliverance from her many woes and relies on her therapist to help her cope.
> ___ Evan is composed of two natures, an old one that can't do right or improve and a new one that can't do wrong. His vote determines which will win out at any moment in time.

Some Christians fervently stick with each of those positions and just as fervently deny others, so how can we know what to expect of ourselves when we have the Spirit living in us? Did you notice that people have a tendency to go to one extreme or its opposite—to expect absolute perfection instantly, or not to expect much of anything? Our temptation is to take a biblical teaching and so emphasize it that we neglect balancing truths. Our lives are then controlled by radical views.

In this lesson we'll see how the Bible cancels out the extremes at both ends of the spectrum. Then we'll look more carefully at the potential of settling for too little (day 2) and the danger in expecting more than God intends (day 3).

Today we want to identify biblically-based views of what we can expect from our life in the Spirit. First, what can we become in the Spirit's power? Second, what means does the Spirit use to transform us into Christlikeness? Third, what is our responsibility in the process? As we search for biblical truth, we will examine the distortions we must guard against.

WHAT IS OUR GOAL?

In answer to the question, What can we become in the Spirit's power? let's look at the two extreme positions. Some people expect one of the following:

Perfection

Bondage and defeat

Emphasizing bondage and defeat places limits on the degree to which the Spirit can overcome our sin nature. This belief causes us to wake up each morning with the expectation of sinning, because we see failure as inevitable. The opposite view expects sinless perfection in this life. If we believe we can or must be absolutely perfect, we either deny that we have a sin nature or we believe that the power of the Spirit makes us incapable of sin.

⟳ **What does the Bible tell us about a life of bondage and defeat? Read the Scriptures below indicating Paul's belief. Circle the words he used to describe the practical experience of the believer.**

In all these things we are more than conquerors through him who loved us (Rom. 8:37).

Thanks be to God, who in Christ always leads us in triumph (2 Cor. 2:14, RSV).

If you live according to the sinful nature, you will die; but if by the Spirit you put to death the misdeeds of the body, you will live (Rom. 8:13).

I circled the words *conquerors, triumph,* and *live.* The Old Testament foreshadowed this good news: "In the Lord is love unfailing, and great is his power to set men free … from all their sins" (Ps. 130:7-8, NEB). The New Testament, both before and after Paul, emphasizes the same theme. Jesus Himself first stated the idea when He commanded us to be perfect (Matt. 5:48). Both Peter and John underscore the same teaching. Peter says that if we aren't godly we are "shortsighted, even to blindness" (2 Pet. 1:9, NKJV), and John assures us that if we live sinful lives we aren't children of God at all (1 John 3:6-10).

No, we're not condemned as human beings to a life of spiritual failure. We must resist those who would push us back into the bog of defeat.

⟳ **What about those who hope for sinless perfection? Anyone who testifies of reaching perfection sure has Paul beat! Below read the words of the apostle and circle the statements that indicate he did not consider himself sinless.**

It is not to be thought that I have already achieved all this. I have not yet reached perfection, but I press on, hoping to take hold of that for which Christ once took hold of me. My friends, I do not reckon myself to have got hold of it yet (Phil. 3:12-14, NEB).

John spells out our imperfection clearly:

If we claim to be without sin, we deceive ourselves and the truth is not in us. If we claim we have not sinned, we make him out to be a liar, and his word has no place in our lives (1 John 1:8,10).

The Bible makes clear that God doesn't expect absolute perfection in this life, though He does promise just that when we reach heaven—"We shall be like him, for we shall see him as he is" (1 John 3:2). In the meantime, what can we expect? What does the Spirit mean by speaking of our being more than conquerors (Rom. 8:37) and always caused to triumph (2 Cor. 2:14)? As we have seen earlier and will see more clearly in this unit, when we live in the Spirit we can expect to:
- consistently win over temptations to choose wrong and
- grow steadily toward greater likeness to Jesus in our attitudes and actions.

WHAT MEANS DOES THE SPIRIT USE?

We may have warped expectations not only about what can be achieved in the Christian life, but also about how we achieve the goal.

HUMAN EFFORT							ALL GOD'S DOING

"It sure is hard being a Christian," moaned our five-year-old Kent after hearing that showing off to the guests wasn't proper. He expressed the sentiments of many grown-ups who try to be good, relying on their own willpower and self-generated effort. Struggling and failing, failing and struggling again. Others, at the opposite pole, see in Scripture the hope of victory by the power of the indwelling Spirit and retire to the grandstands to watch God take over their responsibilities for them.

Read the following descriptions of how some people feel the Spirit makes us successful in our Christian walk and put a ✓ by any you think are true to Scripture and an X by any you think are definitely unbiblical. Don't mark any you're unsure about.

_____ 1. You have a hand and glove relationship. The Spirit is the hand, you're the glove, so "let go and let God" work in and through you.

_____ 2. You are invited to companion with God, and the closer you stay to Him the more He empowers you.

_____ 3. Just as Christ died as your substitute, now let Him live as your substitute.

_____ 4. It's pretty much up to you—your willpower, determination, hard work. God will assist you as you ask His advice.

_____ 5. You'll know when the Spirit comes—you'll experience a surge of spiritual energy like you've never had before and, if you'll let Him, He'll keep you on that high plane, free from struggle and failure.

_____ 6. You have your part in the process—the Holy Spirit puts tools in your hands so you can cooperate with Him in the remodeling of your life.

Though most of those approaches have an element of truth in them, all but the second and last options above have dangerously misleading elements. Approaches 1, 3, and 5 emphasize God's action but neglect our response. They can lead to a passive kind of irresponsibility. God doesn't want you to become the spiritual equivalent of a vegetable. He wants to have a mutual relationship with you. Response 4 clearly goes to the opposite extreme of depending on human effort. By the end of this unit, we'll see more clearly the balance God intends.

THREE FORMS OF UNBALANCE

We can become unbalanced in our Christian lives by having false expectations about our goal—what we can achieve spiritually. We also can get off track by having false expectations about the means—what part God plays in reaching the goal of effective Christian living. But we can also stumble through a misguided understanding of our part in the process.

- **Stoicism**—At one extreme are people who think faith means a kind of fatalism. As a result, they resign themselves to whatever comes along. They stoically settle for a grin-and-bear-it resignation to their fate.

- **Asceticism**–Some go even further–they don't just endure tough times, they create them! True ascetics value the benefits of self-denial so much that they take vows of poverty and chastity–remaining single and owning nothing.
- **Presumption**–At the other end of the "faith" scale are those who presume on God's grace, believing God has promised what, in fact, He hasn't. In that mode of thinking, if I'm not enjoying life free from failure and full of prosperity, it's because my faith is inadequate.

Most of us live somewhere in between those extremes. Examine the following short case studies. Mark each example as either S for stoicism, A for asceticism, P for presumption, or B for biblical faith.

___ When someone commends Mike for his courage in the face of many personal traumas he shrugs and says, "Whatever will be will be," or, "This too shall pass."

___ The TV minister proclaims that if we have faith we will always be healthy and prosperous.

___ Betsy spends years bouncing around from conference to seminar, reading the latest Christian books, searching for a life of tranquility, free from all struggle, and looking for never-failing success in maintaining a Christlike attitude about everything.

___ Hubert is acutely aware of his failure to love as Christ loved, to be as connected to God's will as Jesus was, but he believes the Spirit within him continues His work of growing him daily toward Christlikeness.

___ John is confident God will accept him because he has renounced marriage and personal possessions for the kingdom of God.

I would have marked these examples S,P,P,B,A. Hubert has biblical faith. The other statements point to common teachings of what faith is, but are actually misunderstandings that can lead us far astray. Remember that faith is the uplink to connect us with Holy Spirit power (unit 5). Counterfeit forms of faith–ideas or attitudes that masquerade as faith–will never connect with Holy Spirit power.

Biblical faith keeps us centered between the ditches of self-denying martyrdom and effortless abundance. Biblical faith focuses on continual abiding in the Vine, from which we draw our sustenance.

In this lesson we have examined:

1. Our goal, what we can become
2. The means, how the Spirit changes us
3. Our responsibility, what the faith connection really is.

> **Father, when I hear sincere people fervently pressing on me expectations that contradict what I believe to be Your way, I am easily confused. Guide me as I study to show myself approved of You, a worker who has no need to be ashamed. When I sort through the various options and reach some conclusions, I don't want to become arrogant, boasting that I am right and others are wrong. I do want to have clear light on the pathway before me. Thank You for promising to guide me into all truth. I ask this for my own sake, but in reality it is for Jesus' sake, that He may be pleased by my life. Amen.**

Thanks be to God! He gives us the victory through our Lord Jesus Christ.
—I Corinthians 15:57.

This week's Scripture memory verse appears in the margin. Below rewrite the passage as a prayer thanking God for specific victories in your life.

_____

_____

DAY 2

DON'T AIM TOO LOW

"We confess, Lord," the man in the pulpit prayed, "that we your people turn our backs on you and shake our fists in your face every day of our lives." Would you say amen to that pastoral prayer or do you think he's aiming too low? In a recent book, *Less Than Conquerors*, the author argues that the best we can expect in the Christian life is struggle and failure. He maintains that anyone who claims more is deluded or hypocritical.

Circle the statements below that you think are true.

Nobody's perfect.   God understands when I fail.
God loves me unconditionally.   God accepts me just the way I am.

Did you circle all of them? I did! But I'm a little uneasy and maybe you are, too. Perhaps it's because the thoughts are incomplete. I would worry about what conclusions the reader would draw from these statements.

For example, God is inviting me to come to Him just as I am. But if by saying, "He accepts me just the way I am," we mean, "He approves of me the way I am," or, "God accepts me, so you have no right to expect me to change," we have missed the whole point of salvation. He accepts me as I am to transform me into what He designed me to be. He loves me too much to leave me just the way I am. That would be far too low an expectation.

Some people have expectations for the Christian life that are too low because they have been discouraged by their own lack of progress. Maybe they are frustrated with the level of spiritual immaturity they see in themselves and others. At any rate, they just don't believe God changes human beings all that much in this life.

BROKEN CHOOSERS

I was interviewing Jim, a counselor in a large church. "A counselor friend tells me," I said, "that some people can't respond to God in obedience and faith because their 'chooser' is broken. They can't choose God's way till a therapist helps restore their ability to make choices. What do you think of that idea?" (I didn't tell him my friend's judgment that perhaps five percent of Christians are in that situation.) Jim agreed enthusiastically.

So I asked him, "About what percent of the members of your church are in that category?"

"Oh," he said, "perhaps 80-90 percent."

When I asked Drew, head of a large counseling staff in a megachurch, the same question, he replied: "We operate on the basis that everyone has the ability to make choices, unless a person has mental problems of an organic nature. The Bible assumes that people can, with divine assistance, respond to God's commands and are responsible to do so. We build our therapy on that biblical assumption."

☺ **With whom do you agree?** ❏ Jim ❏ Drew ❏ neither

The church is full of hurting people, some battered more than others. Most of us could use help toward healing, some by a skilled counselor. Perhaps you, like I, have watched with gratitude as a family member was restored with help from such a healer. When a person is—

- blind to his own sinful behavior, or
- her "chooser" is so damaged it can't function, or
- his "truster" is so violated he can't get through to God—

a counselor may be able to help him see himself, others, and God in clearer perspective. Then that person can begin to trust God and choose God's alternative. However, when we begin to use human brokenness as an excuse to disobey God and remain in our patterns of sin, we do ourselves and others a severe disservice.

VASTLY DIFFERING EXPECTATIONS

Jim and Drew have widely different expectations of the Christian life. A lowered expectation of what the Holy Spirit can do may come from treating people as victims like Jim did, rather than as responsible individuals as Drew did.

We can easily see where lowered expectations of Holy Spirit-generated possibilities come from. Americans in general believe less and less in sin and guilt, and more and more in a battered psyche that needs healing. We believe we are no longer guilty sinners needing salvation, but victims of someone else's hurtful behavior and need restoration of a healthy self-image. We could picture the difference in viewpoint this way:

Biblical idea of the human predicament and the way out:

SIN ▶ GUILT ▶ REPENTANCE/FAITH

GROWTH ◀ RESTORATION ◀ FORGIVENESS

FREEDOM AND FULFILLMENT (OF GOD'S PURPOSES)

Victim model of the human predicament and the way out:

INJURY ▶ DAMAGED SELF-IMAGE/ILLNESS

HEALING (RESTORED SELF-IMAGE) ◀ **THERAPY**

FREEDOM AND FULFILLMENT (OF MY PURPOSES)

The victim model contains a critical flaw. We are self-centered rebels against God. We choose to disobey Him and dishonor ourselves in the process. Though the victim/therapy model may get some people part of the way to a life of effectiveness, it can never deliver the spiritual energy for a life of victory.

If we buy into the pattern of viewing ourselves and others as victims, we may block ourselves and others from God. The view of self as a hurting person, damaged by wrongs inflicted by others, may lead persons away from taking responsibility for their feelings or actions. Gradually we descend into denial about our own guilt and personal responsibility to choose right.

In contrast, Scripture bases its promise of salvation and power-filled Christian living on the assumption that we can respond to God in faith. We can choose His way. Some of us may need more help from the outside than others, and the church should provide that help. But let us never underestimate the power of the Holy Spirit to give us the will and the way so that we can indeed "work out our own salvation with fear and trembling" (Phil. 2:12).

The failure syndrome and the victim syndrome are two major paths to expecting less of the Christian life. If I choose to believe that I cannot become an overcomer, that I cannot experience miracle intervention by the Spirit of God, surely my belief will prove self-fulfilling.

To counter low expectations, examine how Paul describes Holy Spirit potential in the life of every believer.

Read the eighth chapter of Romans slowly and let your spirit bathe in the glory of what God promises for your Christian experience. Now go back and skim through, circling every time the Spirit is mentioned.

How many did you find? ____

Now, jot below your five favorite activities of the Spirit in empowering your life, identified in Romans 8. Don't forget to check out verses 28-29 and verses 31-39 which don't mention the Spirit, but which are glorious promises for a victorious Christian life.

1. _____

2. _____

3. _____

4. _____

5. _____

You may have found as many as 21 references to the Spirit in Romans 8. Don't settle for too low an expectation of what your Christian life can be. Listen to Paul's great proclamation of victory: Sin shall not have dominion over you! (Rom. 6:14). He gives thanks to God who always causes us to triumph (2 Cor. 2:14) and exults in the assurance that we are more than conquerors (Rom. 8:37). "Thanks be to God," Paul says. "He gives us the victory through our Lord Jesus Christ" (1 Cor. 15:57). Incredibly, he promises a life filled by the Spirit to "all the fullness of God" (Eph. 3:19). In another passage he describes the Christian life as "attaining to the whole measure of the fullness of Christ" (Eph. 4:13)!

These are not isolated proof texts. They reflect the mood of the entire New Testament. Consider the following examples.
- Jesus Himself offers abundant life (John 10:10) and a bumper crop of Christlike characteristics (John 15)
- Peter promises escape from the world's corruption and the experience of abounding godliness (2 Pet. 1)
- John assures us that we must (and can) live out life in the moral light (1 John 1).

John even draws the curtain on the final act when he writes, "He who overcomes shall inherit all things, and I will be his God and he shall be My son" (Rev. 21:7, NKJV). Such is the destiny of the overcomer. Hallelujah!

Now it's time to write out your prayer response in your journal. Be very honest. If your expectations are quite low, tell Him so. But don't leave it there; ask for wisdom to understand what Scripture really teaches about what you ought to expect. Pray for the gift of faith to believe His promises. If you are excited about the possibilities, tell Him so. He's delighted to see His children liberated and fulfilled!

DAY 3

DON'T AIM TOO HIGH

We've seen some of the dangers of aiming too low in our Christian life. But the opposite can derail us, too, as we'll soon see. If you haven't already started this lesson with a prayer for Holy Spirit illumination, here's a suggested prayer:

> Spirit of God, I need to know Your truth about what I can be in Christ and how I can become the person You plan for me to be. I don't want to aim too low, but neither do I want to have unrealistic expectations. Take my hand and lead me into Your truth that I may experience all You have planned for me. Amen.

Some see the grand promises of Scripture and think they mean we can become sinlessly perfect in this life–perhaps even instantly, through a particular experience. Boris was that way. He enrolled in our graduate program and wanted me to experience what he had experienced years before when God had eliminated his sin nature. Since he was delivered of all sin, he had preached in mighty power all over the world. I'm not altogether sure why he enrolled in a school in which, he assured me, none of the teachers had experienced such a transforming encounter with God.

In contrast, another preacher who turned the world upside down testified that he had not yet attained perfection (Phil. 3:12). Paul struggled with temptation and weakness. He was sometimes filled with fear, for example, and had more than one squabble with his colleagues.

How do we read the same Bible and come up with such different answers? By the way we define *sin* or *perfect*.

DEFINING *SIN*

The following are common definitions of sin. Check the one that you think best represents the biblical definition of sin.

❏ 1. A sin is an action, not a feeling or an attitude, that violates God's law.
❏ 2. Sin is transgression of the law.
❏ 3. Sin is any failure to measure up to the moral character of God.
❏ 4. To sin is to knowingly violate God's revealed will. Involuntary attitudes and misbehavior I don't know to be wrong are part of my finite human nature, not sin.

I checked 3. The biblical standard is to be just like God morally (Matt. 5:48). Yet, all have sinned and fall short of the glorious character of God (Rom. 3:23). You may have checked 2 also because it is a biblical statement (1 John 3:4), but it was not intended as a comprehensive definition of sin. Other attitudes and actions also fail to measure up, such as "sins of omission" (failing to think or do what I ought). I did not check 4. Although to sin knowingly is indeed sin, it is nevertheless sinful to have attitudes or actions that are not Christlike, whether I am aware of them or not. We call them "sins of ignorance," but we are not innocent when we sin in ignorance.

Option #1 is misleading because Christ carefully designated wrong attitudes as sin (Matt. 5:21-30) as well as the outward acts. Some say anger or sexual desire is wrong only if you act them out, that emotions are morally neutral. However, Jesus compared some types of anger to murder and lust to adultery.

If we lower the standard, then it's easier to reach! If I'm guilty of sin only when I deliberately violate what I know to be the will of God, maybe it is possible to live a life relatively free of sin.

DEFINING *PERFECT*

Christians also differ on the definition of perfection because they differ on the definition of sin. How do you define *perfect*?

> Each of the following examples contain a common use of the word *perfect*. Beside each example write the letter(s) that corresponds with one of these synonyms:
>
> RG–really good   M–mature
> H–healthy   WS–without sin
>
> _____ The Smith's new baby is perfect!
> _____ Gifts of ministry enable God's people to grow up into perfection (Eph. 4:13).
> _____ Be perfect as God is perfect.
> _____ This ice cream is perfect.

We would have no problem if people who teach the possibility of perfection in this life meant healthy (like the Smith's new baby) or mature (as in Eph. 4:13) or really good (like the ice cream). The Bible uses the term *perfect* in all these ways. The problem comes when some speak of sinless perfection, meaning without flaw in the moral realm.

Scripture says a person who says he is without sin is self-deceived or, even worse, makes a liar of God. The only way a person can be sinless is to redefine sin, to make it something less than any failure to attain God's moral perfection. Thus when people speak of sinless perfection, the difference is often semantic; they define the term *sin* with limitations. If I promise a life free of deliberately choosing to break the known will of God, for example, maybe perfection is within reach. But if I promise a flawless life, free from all wrong attitudes and actions, full of God's perfection, I am promising more than the Bible teaches.

No doubt to aim too high and fall short is better than to aim too low and hit the target! In fact, Paul prays for the perfection of the Christians in Corinth and tells them to aim for it! (2 Cor. 13:9,11).

> Brainstorm for a moment. In the margin list what might result from a person seeking to live with unrealistic expectations?

Boris said that he alone on our campus was perfect, but don't ask any of the secretaries about that evaluation. They were fearful of his explosive rages. The slightest thing that didn't go his way could ignite his anger. What was his problem? Was he self-deceived? He no doubt considered his anger "righteous indignation" and thus he remained "perfect" through it. Boris' definition seemed to others to result in a life of self-deception.

Some people who believe in perfection aren't like Boris at all. They know they fail; they just talk like they don't. They would be in danger of hypocrisy. For many, however, the danger is discouragement in not being able to achieve or maintain what they expect. Many become so discouraged they drop out altogether. These then, are the hazards of unrealistic expectations:

- Self-deception through rationalization, especially by redefining sin or a particular sin so we no longer acknowledge the attitude or act as sin
- Hypocrisy from knowing they fall short but professing otherwise
- Discouragement from expecting perfection and failing to achieve it.

We've spoken of expectations that are too low and too high, but a strange combination of the two exists. This odd hybrid can't be found in any church's formal teaching, but it is common in Christian practice. People say, "I'm not half as sinful as most people" and think that's good enough (see 2 Cor. 10:12). Another variety of the same syndrome is the Christian who prays, "forgive us of our many sins," but doesn't pause to think of any specific wrong he needs to right. Both may be jealous of a fellow worker or critical in spirit, but quite satisfied with their own level of achievement. Their expectations are too low by biblical standards, but their evaluation of themselves is way too high! They, too, qualify as misguided in expectations; and they, too, may be self-deceived or hypocritical.

We've looked at some of the results of holding unrealistic expectations about our potential for life in the Spirit. Before pressing on to "take hold of that for which Christ Jesus took hold of me" (Phil. 3:12), we need to accept the biblical limitations on our expectations. In this life we'll never be absolutely perfect as God is, without sin, though when we see Jesus we shall be like Him (1 John 3:2).

We praise God for realistic expectations. Here's my response:

> **Thank you, blessed Spirit, for releasing me from the drivenness and disappointments of unrealistic expectations. Help me to accept my own limitations and those of others. And please, please don't let me swing to the other extreme and settle for less than You intend. I want to be all a redeemed human being can be. And that for Jesus' sake—not just for mine. Amen.**

Write this week's Scripture memory verse in the margin. You can check your work on page 115.

We do not dare to classify or compare ourselves with some who commend themselves. When they measure themselves by themselves and compare themselves with themselves, they are not wise.
—2 Corinthians 10:12

DAY 4

TWO KINDS OF VICTORY

If expectations of a Spirit-filled life can be too low or too high, what can we expect? Somehow our expectation of spiritual maturity seems linked to our view of sin, so let's examine sin more closely.

VARIETIES OF SIN

Many of us have far too limited an understanding of sin. The Bible uses several models or concepts to describe sin. When I first saw the biblical distinction among sins, it became a liberating truth that gave birth to hope for my personal life in the Spirit. I want to focus on three different categories of sin.

Notice the distinction between intentional and unintentional sin in Numbers 15:28, 30-31. When a person knew the law and deliberately chose to break it, the sin was intentional. When a person sinned in ignorance, the sin was unintentional.

As Christians we are no longer under the burden of the complex law code, but we can take a lesson from the example in Numbers 15. We can recognize that not all sin fits in the same category. Some sin is willful and deliberate—we know better, and we just choose to do what is wrong. Other sin results from ignorance of God's standard or ignorance of my own heart. Such ignorance comes from failure to study the Word, from insensitivity to the whispers of the Spirit, or from failure to reflect on the holiness of God. It can also come from a warped belief system. Some people's prejudice is an example of this second category of sin. We might call these two types of sin *deliberate sins* and *sins of ignorance*.

We can look at the issue of sin in another way. Galatians 6:1 speaks of someone who is "caught in a sin." The context would seem to be speaking of a fellow believer. Apparently, Christians as well as unbelievers can be caught or trapped in patterns of sin.

Read Ephesians 5:18 in the margin. Circle the big, technical-sounding word in the verse.

To be *debauched* means to be seduced away from duty or virtue. The word implies to be without strength, to be whipped. One form or result of sin is to be so overcome by it that we become slaves. Romans 6:16 says: "Don't you know that when you offer yourselves to someone to obey him as slaves, you are slaves to the one whom you obey—whether you are slaves to sin, which leads to death, or to obedience, which leads to righteousness?"

We can then see three different distinctions of sin:
- deliberate and willful
- result of ignorance
- result of weakness or slavery.

Remember that all types of sin are still just that—sin. While nothing excuses sin, we may be better able to understand ourselves by seeing these distinctions.

Try to write an example of each kind of sin.

sin that is the result of defiance _____

sin that is the result of ignorance _____

sin that is a result of slavery _____

To distinguish isn't always easy, but consider the following examples:
- Deliberate—deceiving people into thinking I have more worthy motives than I do, planning a flirtatious approach to a person I work with, or speeding when I'm late to an appointment.
- Unintentional or unconscious—slipping onto an ego-trip by taking credit for what God has done; impetuously responding to an affront with less than sacrificial love; thinking, "what can you expect of someone of that race?"

- Slavery (want to stop but can't seem to)—a pattern of scolding my child in anger when he forgot my instructions, or rejoicing over the failure of others as a means to make myself feel successful.

This distinction between sins may help solve the mystery of two passages in the New Testament:

- First John 1:8 says: "If we claim to be without sin, we deceive ourselves and the truth is not in us."
- Only a bit later in the same letter John wrote: "No one who lives in him keeps on sinning.... He who does what is sinful is of the devil … No one who is born of God will continue to sin, because God's seed remains in him; he cannot go on sinning, because he has been born of God" (1 John 3:6,8-10).

Those two teachings can't be contradictory; they are by the same author only a few verses apart. The apostle didn't slip up; he meant both basic truths. But how do they fit together?

Recognizing different kinds of sin might help. John chapter 1 is talking about any and all sins, including anything that falls short of God's glorious character, deliberate or not. If you claim to be without any kind of sin you're badly deceived. But in the third chapter he uses a continuous action verb that means: "if anyone keeps on sinning." If you deliberately choose continually to violate the known will of God, John says you're not a Christian at all! And Paul says the same thing (1 Cor. 6:9-10; Gal. 5:19-21). The writer of Hebrews concurs in 12:14.

You will notice these verses apply differently to the three types of sin. Everyone falls short of loving as God loves, of being as humble, selfless, courageous, and holy as Jesus. Everyone is capable of rationalizing to convince themselves that what they want is OK. We may also impetuously do something we know is wrong before we even have time to think about it. Furthermore, the world around us or our background may have blinded us to some teaching of Scripture that condemns an attitude or action we think is right. In these sins of ignorance, we need to study the Word diligently and rely on the Spirit to remodel our minds. When the temptation becomes visible, then we can deal with it—confess and forsake it!

Most Christians struggle with some sins in the third category—patterns like temper, gossip, or gluttony. In these areas we struggle against patterns of sin.

The first category of sin—deliberate and willful—is the key. What do we do when we recognize some thought or action is sin?

🌀 **Mark each of the following examples with either a D for deliberate and willful, an I for based on ignorance, or an S for resulting from slavery. This exercise won't be your easiest!**

_____ 1. Peter decides the only way to get by financially is to cheat a little on his income tax this year.

_____ 2. A co-worker is always hurting Mary. Try as she might, Mary wonders if she'll ever be able to consistently think and behave lovingly toward this co-worker.

_____ 3. Other folks come to church in really nice cars, and Harry is forever fretting about the old clunker he has to drive.

_____ 4. Sandra and Lou aren't married to one another; but they're in love, so they live together.

_____ 5. Dean is an alcoholic, trying hard to be a good Christian. Last night he fell off the wagon again.

_____ 6. Seems like everyone but Helen knows how critical she is. But she's no gossip, she says, she just tells it like it is.

Do you not know that the wicked will not inherit the kingdom of God?
—I Corinthians 6:9

The acts of the sinful nature are obvious: sexual immorality, impurity and debauchery; idolatry and witchcraft; hatred, discord, jealousy, fits of rage, selfish ambition, dissensions, factions and envy; drunkenness, orgies, and the like. I warn you, as I did before, that those who live like this will not inherit the kingdom of God.
—Galatians 5:19-21

Make every effort to live in peace with all men and to be holy; without holiness no one will see the Lord.
—Hebrews 12:14

_____ 7. Yesterday, when someone cut in front of him, Hicks leaned on his horn and muttered imprecations at the person.

_____ 8. Billy's wife is so unreasonable; the only way to keep peace in the family is to deceive her about what he has done, where he has been.

_____ 9. Thelma was wronged by her ex-husband. Try as she might, she can't forgive him.

_____ 10. Ben isn't cruel or abusive, but he is domineering in relation to his wife. After all, Paul said he's supposed to be head of the house.

I know it's difficult to decide on some of those situations because you don't know all the motivations, but I put a D by 1,4, and 8. I put S by 2, 3, 5, 7, and 9. I labeled numbers 6 and 10 as possible examples of ignorance.

TWO KINDS OF VICTORY

A new nature and the indwelling Spirit of God enable a Christian to consistently win over temptations to deliberately choose wrong. Hubert understood that.

In our Sunday School class we were discussing our failures when Hubert finally spoke up: "Well, whenever I was born again I quit sinning." Every head whipped around toward Hubert. We knew he was a godly man, but quit sinning altogether? He continued, "Since I was born again I never deliberately choose to do wrong." Hubert had a limited view of what sin is, but he had the right idea: A Christian ought never deliberately choose to do wrong.

But what does the Bible offer for victory over the other kinds of sin, sins based on ignorance or bondage? Sometimes there is instant deliverance from that kind of sin, too. Like Muriel and her worry. When we find ourselves in any kind of spiritual failure, we should do like Muriel and cry out for total deliverance. But sometimes it doesn't happen that way, like Matsuyama's temper or my impatience. For us there was a pattern of growth.

VICTORY AS GROWTH

The consistent teaching of the New Testament about the Christian life is growth, as we saw in unit 6. We are to grow in all ways, but Peter commands us to grow in two specific ways: grace and knowledge (2 Pet. 3:18).

1. **Grace.** Grace is a gift given to one who hasn't earned it. It's something you can't get no matter how hard you work, like salvation. When we grow "in grace" we receive more and more Holy Spirit power for godly living. The Spirit's bank of grace is infinite, but our capacity to receive His gifts is limited. We need to grow in appropriating more and more the resources the Spirit makes available. For example, Mary, from the previous exercise, needs to grow in her capacity to love her co-worker.

2. **Knowledge.** We must grow in understanding what the will of God is. For example, Ben, in the activity above, seems unaware of his sin, but he needs to learn what a godly husband is. He needs to grow in the knowledge of what it means to love his wife like Christ loves the church—to the point of laying down his life for her (Eph. 5:25).

SIN THAT GROWS FROM WEAKNESS AND IGNORANCE

Sin can be unplanned rather than deliberate for two distinct reasons—weakness or ignorance. I know well enough it's wrong to be impatient, and I don't plan to lose my temper. But suddenly I find myself upset over the way someone speaks to me. I need God's enabling grace. On the other hand, I keep discovering racial prejudices that are buried so deeply I had no idea they were there. I need to correct my belief system with knowledge—of myself and of God's view of right and wrong.

Grow in the grace and knowledge of our Lord and Savior Jesus Christ.
—2 Peter 3:18

⟳ In the margin by each of the examples on pages 127 and 128 mark a G (grace) for those whose primary need is for greater strength or capacity to appropriate God's gracious provision and mark K (knowledge) by those who need to be wiser, to learn what sin is. Since you don't have all the facts about the situation, if you're uncertain, you could put both.

Judging clearly in every example, or even in our own lives, may not always be easy. But usually, we know the difference.

⟳ Are you aware of any sins in your Christian life, things you struggle with, things you need to change? Why not create three lists, either below or in your private journal? Be very honest and thorough. Once you've been honest about it, you can choose to quit or start pleading for God's resources (graces) to overcome.

DEFIANCE	IGNORANCE	SLAVERY
_____	_____	_____
_____	_____	_____
_____	_____	_____
_____	_____	_____
_____	_____	_____
_____	_____	_____

DELIVERANCE FROM UNKNOWN SIN

Did you have trouble with the second column? Of course! How can you change a behavior or attitude if you are not even aware of it? You have three helps available to help you grow: the Bible, prayer, and true friends.

- Stay sensitive in your daily reading of the Word of God. Then you can hear Him when He wants to alert you to something you've been blind to or insensitive about. Stay teachable so you can learn when the Bible is taught by others.
- Through prayer ask the Spirit to reveal your true self to you. You may be surprised how quickly events and people begin to direct your attention to that characteristic the Spirit wants you to acknowledge and change. Stay sensitive to hear His whisper in your heart when your attitude or motive hurts Him.
- A true friend will help you see things you were blind to. That's why an accountability partner is helpful! Periodically I ask family and those who work closely with me, "If you could change one thing about me, what would it be?" Look out! It might hurt. But what a means of growth it has been for me!

⟳ Here's a tough assignment for this lesson: Ask at least one person the above question before your next group meeting. Pray about the answers. If God seems to be speaking to you about change, put it on your permanent prayer list—a list of things you want to be reminded of to pray about daily.

For items in the third column (slavery), consider a stronger, more focused form of accountability. God intends that we overcome areas of spiritual or physical bondage. In addition to all the above, you may need to enlist a "specialist" accountability partner or group. By specialist, I don't necessarily mean a professional but a person or group who have overcome that specific form of slavery. If you are seeking to quit smoking or overcome anger, get a person who has successfully dealt with the problem or a Christ-centered group that focuses on the issue. A person or group that understands can more effectively encourage you and hold you accountable.

Are there any temptations in the first column, things you know are wrong but you keep choosing anyway and trying to rationalize away? If so, now is the time to confess and forsake those sins. You will experience no growth until you choose to obey.

As for those areas of slavery in the third column, why not present each of them in order to the Lord? Tell Him you're truly sorry and thank Him that He is strong enough to give you the victory. Ask Him to give you greater grace (capacity, strength, wisdom) to spiral up. Add a prayer that He will daily give you more understanding of yourself (second column). Begin to make these three areas a regular part of your prayer life.

DAY 5

THE SPIRIT'S ACTIVITY

How can we expect to win consistently over temptations? How can we grow in greater likeness to Jesus? By now we know that the answer has something to do with the Holy Spirit—the quality of our love relationship and how freely we allow Him to work in our lives.

We're more than halfway through our study of *Life in the Spirit*. Pause and review, focusing on the way each of the activities of the Spirit helps us spiral upward toward likeness to Jesus. So far we've looked at five ways the Holy Spirit works in our lives. See if you can name them.

_____   _____

_____   _____

_____

The activities are reflected on the course map. Several of the activities are both past historical actions and present ongoing actions. For example, the first activity of the Spirit is creating (unit 2). The Spirit was instrumental in the creation of the universe (past) and the Spirit created you and me (ongoing). The second activity is revealing (unit 3). The Spirit's work of revelation includes inspiration (past) and illumination (ongoing). The third activity, redeeming (unit 4) included the ministry of Jesus (past) and the work of regeneration (ongoing). The fourth activity is indwelling (unit 5), and the fifth activity is sanctifying believers. We summarized the sanctifying work of the Spirit with the word transforming (unit 6).

For each of the following activities, give your own short explanation of how each relates to Christian living. You could give several good answers for each, but here's a sample possibility:

1. Creation   *We were created as spiritual beings in God's likeness so we can know Him and become like Him.*

2. Revelation: inspiration _____

   _____

   Revelation: illumination _____

   _____

3. Conviction _____

   _____

4. Regeneration _____

   _____

5. Indwelling _____

   _____

6. Sanctification _____

   _____

CREATION

To review some of the important implications of the way the Spirit designed us, answer T for the following statements which are wholly true and F for those you believe false or not wholly true.

___ A person with an interest in the unseen world is therefore a spiritual person by biblical standards.
___ God's ultimate purpose for us is to be like Him in moral character.
___ God's ultimate purpose for us is loving oneness with Him.
___ Though theologians differ on how free our will is, the Bible is clear that God expects us to make choices, to choose Him.

Mere interest in the unseen world will not make us spiritually mature. You may have marked T for the second option, being like God, but God's original purpose in creating us was to have fellowship with Him. The ultimate goal for which God created us is loving oneness with Himself. It's certainly true that our transformation starts when we choose God, trusting Him with our lives. My answers would be F,F,T,T.

REVELATION: INSPIRATION AND ILLUMINATION

Those who know the Spirit trust the Bible He gave. They—
- expect Him to make it plain to them
- study it diligently to know His will
- are prepared to obey it fully.

Is the Bible sitting on the shelf of your life, or is it your actual working guide? In the following list underline the attitudes or activities God expects of every believer.

1. Study the Bible daily, working toward a mastery of its teaching.
2. Be willing to obey every Bible teaching.
3. Know the theme of every book of the Bible.
4. Memorize a verse a day.
5. Be humbly obedient to every church tradition—if a new idea comes along that differs from our way of doing things, reject it.
6. If a new idea comes along, believe in progress and accept it.
7. When people differ on what is right or wrong, eagerly search out all the Bible teaches on the subject.

I underscored the first two and the last. To spiral up into likeness to Christ we have to know what the Bible says, understand it, trust and obey it. What a wonderful gift God has given us to live by!

CONVICTION

People will never turn to God until they feel the need to. No one will feel the need deeply enough to turn unless the Holy Spirit does the work He was sent to do. Jesus promised if He went away He would send the Holy Spirit to "convict the world of ... sin and righteousness and judgment" (John 16:8).

Why do you think some people have been convicted enough to turn and others never seem to be bothered much by their sin?

❑ The person is indifferent.
❑ The sovereign initiative of God convicts some and not others.
❑ Other _____

Circle the word in Christ's promise above (John 16:8) that indicates the convicting work of the Holy Spirit is universal.

In the mysterious connection between God's sovereign initiative and my responsibility, the Bible constantly points to my responsibility. Some people harden their own hearts through resisting the convicting power of the Spirit. In fact, it's possible to close down completely and not even hear the Spirit, but He is still at work. I circled the word *world*. God not only loves the world; as a result of that love the Spirit convicts the world of sin, of righteousness, and of judgment to come. (See also Rom. 1:18-31; 2:14-16.)

REGENERATION

Those who know the Spirit view themselves as new creations, with incredible new potential. The new Christian has been so radically transformed that the Bible uses many word pictures to describe the change.

⊚ In each couplet below, circle the phrase that most closely describes your understanding of the biblical picture of your new life in Christ.

1. **"You were dead, you're now alive" means:**
   a. You were incapable of doing anything good; now you can do good.
   b. You were disconnected from God and His power; now you're connected.

2. **"You died and are now resurrected" means:**
   a. You're "dead" to the old temptations—they no longer even appeal to you.
   b. You have been changed to a new kind of person with new potential you never had before.

3. **"You have been born again" means:**
   a. You have been changed so radically that you could compare the change to physical birth.
   b. Though basically the same, you've changed direction, gotten a new start in life.

4. **"You are a 'new man,' having put off the 'old man' " means:**
   a. "Man" means "nature" and you now have two, an old one that can't improve and a new one that can't sin. Always vote with the new one!
   b. "Man" means "self" and you are recreated, a new person with new capabilities to grow in likeness to Christ.

What a glorious transformation! So radical that Jesus calls it a new birth (John 3). You have been changed from what you were—disconnected from God's life-flow, incapable of consistently choosing the right. You are an altogether new person, connected with Holy Spirit life and capable of being transformed into the likeness of God Himself! Oh, you did good things before you were regenerated, but you couldn't consistently choose right—didn't even want to. You can sin now, but the new you has the power to resist evil influences. Now you can grow in an ever-increasing spiral of love for, companionship with, and obedience to God.

INDWELLING

Those who know the Spirit maintain a close relationship of surrender and faith. Even the new me could never live the Christian life successfully, so God Himself comes to live with me. What an incredible relationship, finite and unholy as I am, the infinite, Holy One becomes my daily companion. Better than that—He becomes my inside Partner! And if I stay faithful to Him, I'll start looking more and more like Him. I can find genuine fulfillment and meaning in life only by developing this intimate love relationship.

⊚ How do we make this connection? And how do we maintain it? One little word in Scripture summarizes it. Do you remember that word?

_____

That's it. The word is *faith*. By faith we enter spiritual life and by faith we grow to maturity. Faith connects with God-power. Of course, there are two sides to faith. We repent, yielding to God's will, and we trust Him to do what He promised. Faith is the key to both salvation and sanctification.

Muriel and I were riding through a tough part of town discussing the problem of evil in the world with our seven-year-old, Kent. A crowd of young ruffians were ganged up on a corner while a small boy played in an open lot across the street. I said, "See that little fellow? Give him a few years and he'll be mean like these guys."

Kent piped up from the back seat, "Not if he says yes to Jesus."

His mother said, "True, Kent, you have to say a big yes to Jesus, but after that...."

Kent interrupted, "I know, I know. Every morning you have to get up and say, 'Well, Lord, here's another day. You'd better take over!'"

And that's just how it is: A big Yes to Jesus connects, and a lifetime of little yeses keeps the relationship growing.

SANCTIFICATION

Those who know the Spirit will faithfully use the tools He provides. They will work with the Spirit to spiral up.

Name the three or four most important tools the Spirit uses to work in our lives.

_____   _____

_____   _____

Prayer and Bible study can be joyous, but there's one tool we would avoid if we could: adversity. When we respond correctly, adversity can be a tremendous opportunity to grow. If I believe God can use suffering to bring honor to Him and growth in me, the pain can press me closer to Him. Faith is the key. Our response to suffering determines if we draw closer to God. Allowing suffering to harden our hearts toward God separates us from God and wastes our opportunity to grow.

Another "tool" the Spirit uses to help us grow is the church. In unit 6 you explored three of the five purposes of the church. Below see if you can name those three. The other two purposes are ministry and evangelism.

_____

_____

In addition to ministry and evangelism, the purposes of the church include worship, fellowship, and discipleship.

The Holy Spirit's activity gives us life and grows us toward Christlikeness. The key to whether we grow is our personal relationship to Christ. The closer we stay to Him, the faster we spiral up!

The more we trust and obey the more He empowers us to grow. The more we grow the more we love Him. The more we love Him the more we trust and obey. The more we trust and obey the more we become like Him. The more like Him we become the greater capacity we have to love and trust. "We ... are being transformed into the same image ... by the Spirit of the Lord" (2 Cor. 3:18, NKJV).

Next time, we'll consider what it means to be "filled with the Spirit." How does the Spirit fill us and how do we remain filled?

Today let's pause and give thanks for the incredible expectation God has given, a confident expectation of transformation into His likeness.

FILLED

FULL

"Do you remember me?" The bright-eyed teen looked at me eagerly. I couldn't bring myself to say no, so I stalled. I asked if she was from Birmingham. I knew a large group from Birmingham was at the youth conference. I heard how God had moved in the local high school. Starting with a couple of girls in a prayer meeting, dozens had come to Christ; the spiritual awakening impacted the whole campus.

Then she helped me recall. "Do you remember last year, the night after that last meeting of the conference when we sat on that stone wall over there?"

The memory came back to me. "Oh yes, Debbie, I remember it well." That night she had talked despondently of a failed Christian life. She said she didn't respond to the invitation to consecrate her life to the Lord, because she was sick and tired of doing it over and over. After a recommitment she said life typically went well for a few days, and then she was back to the same lifestyle of defeat.

"Debbie, who's in the driver's seat of your life?" I asked.

"Jesus is…." She paused, then added, "Most of the time."

"Oh, no," I said. "It doesn't work that way. You don't let Him drive down the road to the first intersection and then grab the wheel. I think this is what you're saying." On a piece of paper I wrote two words: *No* and *Lord*.

"Well, yes, sometimes I do say that."

"But you can't," I said.

Debbie bristled a little, "But I do!"

"But you can't," I insisted. "What does *Lord* mean?"

"Savior?" she queried.

"The Savior is Lord, but what does the word *Lord* mean?" I asked. After a few more guesses she gave up. I tried again, "How about *king*? What does *king* mean?"

"That's easy. A king is the big boss."

"Do you say no to the king?"

"It wouldn't be healthy."

"Right," I said. "And Jesus is King of all kings, Lord of all lords. You can't say no to Him! It's either 'Yes, Lord' or 'No, Jesus.' *No* cancels out the meaning of *Lord*." I tore the paper in half, with *No* on one piece and *Lord* on the other. "Which will it be?" I asked. "*No* or *Lord*?"

She dropped her head and her long hair covered her face as she wrestled with the choice. Minutes passed. Finally she threw her head back, tears streaming down her face. She reached out to take the paper with *Lord* written on it, but I pulled it away. "How long do you want Him to be Lord, Debbie?" I asked.

"I want Him to be Lord forever!" she said. At that moment Debbie experienced something the Bible describes as being filled with the Spirit. Now, a year later, I was hearing the result of Debbie's commitment. Her entire campus had been impacted by her decision.

Unit Memory Verses

Do not get drunk on wine, which leads to debauchery. Instead, be filled with the Spirit.
—*Ephesians 5:18*

The fruit of the Spirit is love, joy, peace, patience, kindness, goodness, faithfulness, gentleness and self-control. —Galatians 5:22-23

INTERNAL RELATIONSHIP: WHO'S IN CONTROL?

Do you sometimes wish the Bible didn't use so much picture language, that it would just tell you what it means? What does it look like to be "filled with the Spirit"? What actually happens? What does it feel like? The Bible never defines it for us. It just points out people who are said to be filled with or full of the Spirit:

- John the Baptist even as a baby (Luke 1:15)
- Stephen in the face of death (Acts 7:55)
- Zacharias when he sang (Luke 1:67)
- Bezaleel for crafting the tabernacle (Ex. 31:3).

We may not be able to describe *full* precisely, but it's a wonderful picture word. There's excitement in it, a completeness, a satisfaction–and a mystery.

🌀 **Below describe what you think "filled with the Spirit" means.**

_____

_____

DEFINITIONS: 3 TYPES OF *FULL*

We use the word *full* in many different ways.

- Bob is full of whiskey.
- That kid is full of mischief.
- Judas was full of the devil.
- John is full of Betsy.
- The Book of Philippians is full of joy.
- He opened the jet full throttle.
- We've got a full tank of gas.
- The people were filled with fear.

🌀 **From the list of uses of the word *full*, can you find any that might be similar to what it means to be *full* of the Spirit?**

_____

Then Satan entered Judas, called Iscariot, one of the Twelve.
—Luke 22:3

Type 1: Full can mean a relationship between two persons where one allows the other to dominate. Luke 22:3 says Satan entered Judas. The chief idea seems to be that he was under the devil's control. Although the devil "entered in" to Judas and the Spirit "indwells" our bodies, the idea of being filled is not physical like a tank of gas. Full control is the first meaning of being filled with the Holy Spirit. We'll look at that meaning in today's lesson.

Type 2: Full also means showing evidence of the Spirit's presence. When a child is said to be full of mischief or John to be full of Betsy, we mean they have characteristics that are highly visible. Everyone is aware of the mischief or the infatuation. Most of the Scripture references to being full of the Spirit indicate some evidence, some outcome of that filling: teaching, acting courageously, preaching, singing, meeting a crisis. To be filled with the Spirit is to have so much of His wisdom or power that things happen and everyone can tell. We'll consider this implication of being filled on days 2 and 3.

Type 3: Being filled also includes a mystery that defies analysis. The mystery has something to do with an inner surge of emotion. For example, joy is often associated with being filled with the Spirit. Though we'll never fully probe the mystery, in day 4 we'll think about feelings associated with being full of the Spirit.

WHAT CAN I CLAIM?

Notice something about these three types of being filled with the Spirit. I am the only one who knows for sure who is in control. You cannot possibly tell whether or not I'm fully yielded to the Spirit. The same is true of any feelings resulting from that relationship. While only I can know about two of these aspects, only others can evaluate the outward evidence, the result of the Spirit's full control.

If you ask me if I am filled with the spirit, I can appropriately say, "Yes, God is in charge here." But if you are asking whether I seem to be a God-intoxicated person in my quality of life and service, it would not be appropriate for me to claim that kind of "fullness." Those who observe my life are the ones who can attest to my fullness. People in the Bible didn't claim to be filled with the Spirit—it was a condition the Bible author said was true of them.

AN OVERVIEW OF FULLNESS

The first option on the list I gave, "Bob is full of whiskey," is an example of fullness as obedience. In our memory passage Paul makes a contrast between being filled with alcohol and being filled with the Spirit: "Do not get drunk on wine, which leads to debauchery. Instead, be filled with the Spirit" (Eph. 5:18).

What happens when a person drinks alcohol? The change of control is clearly evident. The drug takes charge. We even refer to it as "under the influence." Being filled with the Spirit also parallels being intoxicated in another way. Because alcohol is an anesthetic to the brain, it hides a person's awareness of inadequacy and fear. The Holy Spirit also resolves our problems of inadequacy and fear, but unlike alcohol the Spirit does not merely cover them up. The Spirit teaches and empowers us so that we overcome. Thus the Holy Spirit powerfully affects our emotions and attitudes. As a result we begin to solve problems and live effectively.

We might summarize the meaning of being filled with the Spirit like this: 1) You are under the controlling influence of another; 2) that influence is very evident, something everyone is aware of; and 3) it affects your emotions.

CONTROLLING INFLUENCE

Since the first meaning of *full* refers to a relationship between two persons, it's quite possible for the relationship to change. When Debbie refused to let God have the steering wheel of her life, she felt the anguish of a failed relationship. If we can turn control over to God, we can take it back! The Bible says we can quench the Spirit—we can put out the fire.

The Spirit of God won't force His way on you. Saying no will quench the Spirit, put out the fire of passion, stop the flow of power. Whenever I take back control of my life, I'm shutting off His free flow of life.

PUTTING OUT THE FIRE

How can you tell when you are quenching the Spirit? He seems more distant, close companionship seems to have slipped away, service for God lacks power, temptations begin to win out, you begin to spiral down. Here are some ways I can "quench" the Spirit:

- neglect my devotional life;
- allow myself to watch television shows with anti-Christian values;
- rationalize some failure instead of acknowledging it;
- refuse to forgive someone who hurt me;
- flip through a magazine with sexually stimulating pictures;
- say yes to too many people and get overloaded;
- nurse my bruised ego and lapse into self-pity;
- let my mind dwell on envy.

◉ Do you resonate with any of those? Put a check by any that have caused the fire of the Spirit to dwindle in your life. Then list below any other activities or attitudes that have been a problem for you. Refusing to do something you know the Spirit wants you to do, for example, will kill the fire instantly.

_____

_____

MAKING GOD SAD

The Bible uses another expression to describe our relationship to the Spirit. The Holy Spirit is a person with feelings—we can make Him sad. Paul says, "Don't do that!" Earlier in Ephesians Paul gave a detailed list of ways we can grieve the Spirit, quench His fire in us, or drain off the "full-up" relationship.

◉ In your Bible read Ephesians 4:22-32 slowly and add to your list above any attitudes or actions you find that have saddened the Spirit in your life during the past month.

◉ The first meaning of being filled with the Spirit is to yield full control to Him. Are you a Spirit-filled Christian in that sense?
❑ Yes ❑ No ❑ Unsure

You should be able to answer with a resounding yes if, as far as you know your own heart, He is in charge. Let's be sure our unconditional yes to the Spirit is up-to-the-minute current. Here's a suggested prayer:

> Holy Spirit of God, thank You for allowing me to have a personal relationship with You. I really do want You to be the controlling partner in that relationship, and I reaffirm today that You are indeed Lord of my life. I'm truly sorry for the ways I've made You sad. Please forgive me. Give me strength to always say yes to You in the small things as well as the major choices I make. Let me ever be filled with Your presence and power.

DAY 2

EXTERNAL EVIDENCE: WHAT DO PEOPLE SEE?

When I was 12, I was filled with the Spirit in the sense we studied yesterday: As far as I knew my own heart, I yielded my life completely to God. But the results weren't all that visible. I wasn't filled in the sense of being a showcase for Jesus' characteristics. I displayed some fruit—the result and evidence of God's indwelling presence—but it wasn't so abundant that people would say, "That young man is so Christlike!" I went to work for the Lord, too, but no one would have said, "The only way to explain what happens through that boy is that God's Spirit is at work!" Today we'll study about the evidence of Spirit-control.

To be filled with the Spirit means much more than merely turning over control of our lives to Him. It includes bearing fruit. There's another picture word! What does *fruit* mean?

🌀 **What do you think of when you hear of spiritual fruit?**

_____

_____

SEEING THE EVIDENCE: JESUS' DESCRIPTION OF FRUIT

Fruit—the product of a plant or tree—is also the evidence of what kind of plant or tree it is. A peach tree, if living and healthy, will produce a peach. If you see a peach, you know what kind of tree it came from. So it is in your life. If you have become a "Jesus plant," you'll produce Jesus fruit. Everyone in my life is a fruit inspector; they can tell what's on the inside by what comes out. "By their fruit you will recognize them" (Matt. 7:20).

Jesus never intended us to have a few little shriveled fruits, just enough to prove what kind of tree we are. He promises a bumper crop—lots of Jesus characteristics. You might call it *full*, a full crop. He told us about it Himself.

🌀 **In your Bible read John 15:1-17 (Jesus' description of fruit) and list everything that looks like a characteristic that only the Holy Spirit can produce.**

_____

_____

_____

You discovered lots of love fruit, right? (vv. 9-10, 12-13, 17). And joy! (v. 11). There's that word *full* again (KJV) —He's teaching us about fruit-bearing for the specific purpose that our joy will fill to the brim. And did you find "obedience"? He speaks in many different ways of obeying His commandments—all of them! (For example, see vv. 10, 14.)

Jesus says we must allow His words to take up residence inside us (v. 7). Do you get the image of a vine or tree so heavily loaded that the fruit becomes the dominant characteristic of the plant? Everyone can tell, except possibly the person him- or herself. The person will yield so much Jesus fruit that people will be drawn to Jesus, either to embrace Him or to crucify Him.

SEEING THE EVIDENCE: PAUL'S DESCRIPTION OF FRUIT

🌀 **Another way to inspect fruit is to use our memory verse as a checklist. Below write Galatians 5:22-23 (Paul's description of fruit).**

_____

_____

_____

These characteristics are the product of the Spirit's activity. They can't be explained by the influence of a person's early environment or present circumstances. The kind of love, joy, or peace that can be explained by genetics and conditioning—though desirable and beautiful – is natural, not supernatural.

From the people you have known or heard about, write a short illustration of someone who is an example of one of these qualities when there was no human reason to have it. Choose three characteristics to illustrate. I'll do the first "fruit" as an example.

love: Pastor Kim attended the trial of the young man accused of killing his two sons in a communist insurrection. He asked the judge to pardon the murderer and turn the young man over to him. He hoped to lead him to Christ and train him to take the place of his sons in serving God.

joy: _____

_____

_____

peace: _____

_____

_____

patience: _____

_____

_____

kindness: _____

_____

_____

goodness: _____

_____

_____

faithfulness: _____

_____

_____

gentleness: _____

_____

_____

self-control:_____

_____

_____

SEEING THE EVIDENCE: TITLES OF THE SPIRIT

Another way to identify the evidence of the Spirit's activity is to examine the titles given Him. He is called the Spirit of truth (John 14:17; 16:13). He is also called the Spirit of grace (Zech. 12:10) because He is the dispenser of all God's free gifts. A marvelous passage in Isaiah describes many characteristics of the Spirit that He will produce in the coming Messiah: "The Spirit of the Lord will rest on him—the Spirit of wisdom and of understanding, the Spirit of counsel and of power, the Spirit of knowledge and of the fear of the Lord" (Isa. 11:2).

Count all the characteristics of the Spirit in the paragraph above. How many did you find? I found eight but the most important of all I left out!

(◎) **His title throughout Scripture is the _____ Spirit.**

Above all He is holy, set apart from all moral pollution, clean and pure. And His objective is to make holy people.

Notice that the picture word, *fruit*, in the sense of Jesus-like attitudes and behavior is what we've been thinking about most of the time as we've studied life in the Spirit. In Romans 6:22 Paul describes what we become. He connects the two key words *fruit* and *holiness*. The ultimate fruit of the Holy Spirit is a holy people (1 Pet. 1:15; 2:9).

(◎) **On the list of fruit above, put a check by any of the nine characteristics you feel God is developing in your life. Remember His job is to conform us to the image of Christ (Rom. 8:29). Put a star by any characteristic you sense that God wants to cultivate in your life.**

Below name at least one way you can encourage the trait you chose to grow and blossom.

_____

_____

SEEING THE EVIDENCE: A FRIEND'S EVALUATION

One sure-fire way exists to know what your crop looks like. Do you have an accountability partner? Remember, Christlikeness is the one meaning of *full* only others know for sure. You need a fruit inspector! Show your partner, or someone you can trust to be honest about it, the work you have done in this unit. Ask the person for an evaluation—"Is my life obviously full of any of these characteristics? Are there others you have to search for to find?" Write down your partner's answers in your journal.

Now being made free from sin, and become servants to God, ye have your fruit unto holiness, and the end everlasting life.
—Romans 6:22, KJV

What attitudes, actions, or responses do you desire to have more consistently? In your prayer time, reflect slowly on the four areas you studied in this unit (Jesus' description of fruit, Paul's description of fruit, the titles given the Spirit, and your friend's evaluation). In the margin write three characteristics you most need to develop. Choose traits that don't come right out of your circumstances and temperament–characteristics that you will have to cultivate to grow. Now ask the Holy Spirit to grow you in each of those qualities.

DAY 3

POWER-FILLED MINISTRY

Another evidence of being filled with the Spirit is some result in our work for God that we can't account for by human explanation. Every believer has at least one God-given ability to serve Him.

> "There are different kinds of gifts, but the same Spirit. Now to each one the manifestation [visible evidence] of the Spirit is given for the common good. All these are the work of one and the same Spirit, and he gives them to each one" (1 Cor. 12:4,7,11).

The gifts are so important that we'll devote an entire unit to studying the gift-giving activity of the Spirit. Today we'll focus on how a Spirit-given ability can be evidence of being Spirit-filled. In units 10 and 11 we'll look at all the gifts, but now we'll look at a few of the gifts Paul lists (Rom. 12; 1 Cor. 12; Eph. 4). Being filled with the Spirit can be the difference between merely having a Spirit-given ability and having maximum impact with that ability.

MINIMUM EVIDENCE
The Bible doesn't tell us how to distinguish spiritual gifts from natural gifts. One key distinguishing mark is the fruit the gift produces. Is the outcome supernatural? The Corinthians said Paul was an unpolished speaker, but when Paul taught the Bible lives were transformed. There's the touch of the Spirit!

The Bible leaves us in the dark on how natural abilities and Spirit-giftedness relate. Maybe we should look rather at the tasks that need to be done and trust God to give us the right combination of natural and supernatural ability to fulfill the tasks He calls us to do.

For example, what is your current role in the church or serving God?

_____

_____

How can you tell if you have the touch of the Spirit to accomplish the task or ministry involved?

_____

_____

🌀 **Here are some abilities the Holy Spirit gives. After each example describe what a supernatural outcome that indicates the touch of God might look like.**

To teach the Bible _____

To preach _____

To "practice hospitality" _____

To evangelize _____

To do pioneer missionary work _____

To counsel hurting people _____

To lead in the church _____

To help the poor _____

To encourage _____

Other? _____

The possible answers are almost limitless. Here are some examples that would show the power of the Spirit at work:
- teaching: in response, someone yields her life to God
- preaching: after the sermon, someone trusts God to change his life
- hospitality: people are drawn to the church and then to Christ because you served them and made them feel welcome
- evangelizing: someone is saved
- missionizing: new churches come into being
- counseling: someone begins to become more like Jesus
- leading: the church begins to move together toward biblical goals
- helping the poor: someone is drawn to Christ through assistance received
- encouraging: someone begins to draw strength from God.

MAXIMUM IMPACT

The apostles were filled with the Spirit on the day of Pentecost and 3,000 people were converted (Acts 2:41). I'd call 3,000 responses *really* full. Yet a few weeks later they had a special need–their leaders had been arrested and threatened. They did the only thing to do; they called a prayer meeting and prayed for courage to witness in the face of persecution.

Once again they were filled with the Spirit (Acts 4:31) and as a result proclaimed the word with boldness. Amazing! Spirit-filled people were filled! The same pattern is common throughout Acts—Spirit-filled people are said to be filled again. How can that be?

Remember, *filled* is a picture word. I get the picture of a great schooner plowing through the ocean with sails full of wind when suddenly a gust of wind sweeps down and the schooner surges ahead under really full sail. So it is with the wind of the Spirit. (In both the Hebrew and Greek the word *spirit* means "breath" or "wind.")

Those who accepted his message were baptized, and about three thousand were added to their number that day.
—Acts 2:41

After they prayed, the place where they were meeting was shaken. And they were all filled with the Holy Spirit and spoke the word of God boldly.
—Acts 4:31

> ◎ **Have you experienced the "wind of the Spirit" at a critical time in your life? Check any of the following experiences you can relate to.**

❑ Your boss wants you to lie, threatens you if you don't; you ask God for help and suddenly have a surge of courage to do right.

❑ Someone makes fun of the church. You don't know where the ideas came from, but scriptural truth just flowed as you spoke and the attack failed.

❑ You haven't been able to give a clear explanation of the gospel to your neighbor, you plead with God for help, and you're astounded to hear yourself give an engaging and well-spoken presentation.

❑ As you taught your Sunday School class, you were aware of God's presence. Later someone told you about a life-changing insight.

❑ The meeting was deadlocked, no solution could be found, so you suggested a time-out for prayer. The Spirit moved, brought unity, and a clear vision of what to do emerged.

❑ You are naturally a timid person, so ushering isn't easy; but you pray about it ahead of time, and your wife is astounded at the way you are so out-going and helpful with new people.

When we practice surrendered, obedient faith, we will experience the movement of the Spirit. The Spirit moves in with wisdom, courage, and words that just weren't naturally there. You know God is at work and others can tell, too.

Before I preach I always ask the Spirit to move with power. I've been at it a long time. If I rely on myself I can explain Scripture and tell stories. People will listen and say nice things, but nothing of eternal value will happen if the Spirit doesn't act. When the Spirit works, I watch in wonder as God transforms lives.

When I write, I'm always grateful to note any small amount of "fruit" God gives. But once in a while the words flow almost uninvited out of my computer like they're on fire. When published, the work seems to take on a life of its own. When I read it later I say, "Where'd that come from? Did I write that?" The Spirit had been working that day, and the result wasn't just my work.

I wish it happened always. I wish every time I write or speak lives would be changed. I do not want to glorify myself. Rather I long to be filled permanently with the Spirit, so people will know for sure God is at work and give Him the credit.

> ◎ **Do you have some gift working at a minimal level? Can you tell God is at work through you, but it's not full throttle so that other people can tell? Ask Him to fill you. Open your heart to the wind of the Spirit and trust Him to empower and use you. Begin the habit of asking Him, at the time of special opportunity or challenge, to completely empower you so that He may get the glory.**

DAY 4

THOSE ELUSIVE FEELINGS

As we've seen, the picture word *full* seems to have three different emphases. A person is full when, in his or her relationship with the Spirit, the Spirit is in full control. Second, a person is full when plenty of evidence shows the Spirit at work—a miracle quality of life (fruit) or a miracle impact in ministry (gifts). People can see it. The third emphasis is more elusive, as feelings always are. Do I feel full?

A MYSTERY, LIKE A GOOD MARRIAGE

Full can also speak of a personal relationship—the kind of thing that defies scientific analysis. How do you analyze a relationship? Like a good marriage, the outward evidence, such as a home and children, may be obvious, but the feelings are more mysterious. A relationship includes moments of shared ecstacy and shared agony, a deep and constant sense of well-being and surges of passionate love. So it is living in a deep relationship with the Spirit.

If I'm filled with the Spirit I'll have joy, confidence, or peace when there's no earthly reason to have any peace at all. My affection for God will be filled with passion—an excited sense of anticipation when I worship Him, a rush of pleasure when I think about His love for me. I may not sustain an emotional high; but I will have moments of uninhibited ecstacy, especially in devotional times alone with Him. But also, unexpectedly in the midst of a busy day the wind of the Spirit may blow in gale strength. I can't explain it, but I can feel it.

Have you recently had such a surge of affection or some other emotional response to God's presence? Below write out a brief description of the experience.

_____

_____

_____

If you can't remember anything out of the ordinary in your relationship with God and you are thirsty for a full surge of awareness of God's presence, why not pause right now and tell Him so? But don't leave it there. Tell Him how much you love Him, how grateful you are for Him, for His constant companionship, and for all the wonderful blessings He floods into your life. Ask Him to fill you up with Himself. Pause now and write out in your journal either the description of your experience of fullness, the prayer for fullness, or both.

DOWNERS AND UPPERS

Write your memory verse from Galatians.

_____

_____

_____

Now in the verse circle all the fruits that are emotional words to you.

You may have circled some or all. Several of the fruits involve our emotions, but even the ones that seem mostly matters of feeling have practical results. To love, for example, is to act lovingly no matter how you feel. Maybe that's why God seems to expect us to have these qualities as a steady state in our lives—all the fruit, all the time. Their presence is evidence of the Spirit at work. But the emotions that accompany them may not be surging all the time.

For when we came into Macedonia, this body of ours had no rest, but we were harassed at every turn —conflicts on the outside, fears within.
—2 Corinthians 7:5

Pray also for me, that whenever I open my mouth, words may be given me so that I will fearlessly make known the mystery of the gospel, for which I am an ambassador in chains. Pray that I may declare it fearlessly, as I should.
—Ephesians 6:19,20

Perhaps God intends the fruit to be constant and the surges of feelings to be special outpourings?

- Jesus was a man of sorrows and acquainted with grief. He agonized in the garden of Gethsemane, but he also experienced times of surging joy–"At that time Jesus, full of joy through the Holy Spirit" (Luke 10:21).
- David, the joy-filled singer for the ages, experienced dry times. When God seemed distant, David cried out in alarm, "Do not … take your Holy Spirit from me" (Ps. 51:11).
- Paul had times of fear and called on friends to pray for the Spirit-gift of boldness (2 Cor. 7:5; Eph. 6:19-20).

For these Bible characters, the inner sense of fullness seems not to be "steady state."

In my own life, I can count on having a truly exalted experience of God when I go away for my annual time of fasting and prayer. So much so, I can remember most of those occasions, even decades later. But only occasionally do I have that rushing sense of God's presence in my daily quiet time; even less often do I have it unexpectedly in the midst of a busy day. How I long, sometimes ache, to have those experiences daily, but I don't.

I'd say, "It's OK. No one does." But I'm not so sure. Christian mystics through the ages give testimony of such a walk with God. My son, Kent, is an example. He lives among the slum dwellers of Calcutta, surely the nearest place to hell on earth. Kent keeps so in step with the Spirit that those highs seem to come daily, right in the midst of agonizing squalor. He is so pained when he doesn't experience God on a daily basis. I wonder if the rest of the time he joins the mystics in a daily flood-tide of the Spirit. For myself, I'll keep praising God for the sporadic winds that blow and stay on the alert for a more constant walk on the highest plane–however God defines that for me.

Fullness, then, in the sense of an inner feeling is not subject to analysis; but it can be a glorious experience. The Holy Spirit will give it to those who love and stay close to Him.

MEASURING THREE KINDS OF FULLNESS

If full feelings are elusive, the other meanings of "full" are not. By each of the following examples of being full of the Spirit, mark an O by those which emphasize obedience to the Spirit's control in a personal relationship, S for evidence of Spirit empowered service, and F for a feeling or subjective sense of fullness. Mark more than one if several meanings seem present.

_____ 1. Billy Graham preaches and thousands respond to Christ.
_____ 2. Paul was not gifted as a public speaker, but when he taught lives were transformed.
_____ 3. Hubert said, "If I knew it was wrong, I'd never deliberately choose to do it."
_____ 4. Only I know for sure if I'm "full."
_____ 5. Many in that church are spiritually gifted.
_____ 6. Widow Smith is dying of cancer, but she's always so joyful.
_____ 7. I had a glorious sense of God's presence in church Sunday.
_____ 8. Debbie chose to say "Lord" rather than "no."

My answers would be 1,S; 2,S; 3,O; 4,O; 5,S; 6,F; 7,F; 8,O.

⊙ The following are most of the examples in the New Testament where the context indicates the meaning of being filled with the Spirit. Check each example where the evidence of the Spirit's fullness seems to be subjective awareness or feeling. Underline the feeling described in the examples you check.

❏ "All of them were filled with the Holy Spirit and began to speak in other tongues" (Acts 2:4).
❏ "The disciples were filled with joy and with the Holy Spirit" (Acts 13:52).
❏ "Then Peter, filled with the Holy Spirit, said, ... 'Enable your servants to speak your word with great boldness.' And they were all filled with the Holy Spirit and spoke the word of God boldly" (Acts 4:8,29,31).
❏ "Choose seven men from among you who are known to be full of the Spirit and wisdom" (Acts 6:3).
❏ "He was a good man, full of the Holy Spirit and faith, and a great number of people were brought to the Lord" (Acts 11:24).
❏ "Then ... Paul, filled with the Holy Spirit, looked straight at Elymas and said" (Acts 13:9).

Most of the examples have to do with power in ministry, but some subjective evidences appear. I found joy, boldness, and faith. However, both the boldness and faith are related directly to ministry! So, in the biblical examples, the subjective element of feelings, which we so emphasize today, is not prominent.

My obedience to the Spirit or lack of it should be clear to me. If I have a full crop of fruit and ministry effectiveness, that should be clear to others. But the inner sense of fullness may not be all that apparent—it may defy analysis. But that is OK. Think about it: in filling us with Himself God promises to give us a love beyond comprehension (Eph. 3:19) and He speaks of a peace that is unfathomable (Phil. 4:7). How exciting to feel the mysterious surge of the Spirit!

EPHESIANS 5:18—STEADY-STATE FULLNESS

One of our memory verses in a subtle way ties together the three different aspects of being filled with the Spirit. The verb *be filled* is unusual in that it is a command—something I must do—but it's in the passive form, something the Spirit does to me. "Be being filled" would be an awkward translation, but gets at the meaning. So how do I obey if He is the one who does it? I take the initiative and deliberately yield control. Then I keep on praying and expecting Him to produce the fruit of godliness and power for ministry. If He chooses to surge through with a flood of some special emotion, how blessed!

The command *be filled* is also a continuous action verb: "Keep on being filled with the Spirit." Being filled is a constant in that sense, an abiding relationship. Steady-state filled, you might call it. If the Holy Spirit has control of my life, He'll continuously fill me with power to live and serve.

In Ephesians 5:18-20, Paul also identifies some of the inner feelings associated with being filled: singing, praise, and prayer. Paul says to let the Spirit fill you always as a way of life. Then, from time to time out of His grace, He'll blow into your life with gale force and fan the embers into an all-consuming fire of His own making. When that happens simultaneously to a lot of people, we call the result revival—our topic for day 5.

(I pray that you may) know this love that surpasses knowledge — that you may be filled to the measure of all the fullness of God.
—Ephesians 3:19

The peace of God, which transcends all understanding, will guard your hearts and your minds in Christ Jesus.
—Philippians 4:7

REVIVAL

Until now we've talked of being filled with the Spirit on a very personal level, but we do not live as individuals only. We are part of a larger community of believers. Can you imagine the power unleashed when a group of Christians simultaneously surrender to the Spirit? What would a worship service be like with such a group? How would their prayer meetings be? What kind of impact would they make on unbelievers? Do you ever long to be part of such a Holy Spirit outpouring? We call it revival.

Since the Bible doesn't use the term "revival," why have Christian people always used the term? The Bible repeatedly describes great movings of the Spirit; and the church has experienced such movings periodically through its history. We've called those times revival– "re" means *again* and "vival" means *life*. So when I speak of revival I mean a renewal of life that once was, or ought to have been.

Even with the examples from the Bible and church history coupled with the plain meaning of the term itself, however, *revival* doesn't seem to mean the same thing to everyone. People use the term to describe a great variety of different events and experiences.

⟳ **Put a check by each of the stories below which you think could be a Spirit-sent revival.**

❑ In the midst of the speaker's message students began to stand all across the college chapel and confess their sins, often with tears. The meeting went on till midnight, and the movement continued for days in the dorms and across the campus. The results included changed lives and spontaneous eruptions of joyful singing.

❑ At the revival meetings at Bent Creek Church last week an alcoholic, a business man and his wife, three teens, and an adult were saved.

❑ The "Evangelical Awakening," powerfully advanced by John Wesley, transformed the entire British social structure. It lead directly to the abolition of slavery and revitalized the Christian community so that the modern Protestant missionary movement was launched.

❑ When the invitation was given, the leading deacon in the church tearfully confessed that his opposition to the pastor had caused grief in the church. He asked the pastor and church to forgive him. Then a stream of people came forward or went to others in the congregation, asking forgiveness, embracing, weeping, and laughing. They began to experience healing of old wounds.

❑ Jan studied about life in the Spirit, sensed that something in her life was lacking and turned her life over unconditionally to the Spirit's control. She experienced such a surge of His life-force that she found herself spiraling up toward greater likeness to Christ. She began to see spiritual results from her work for God and sensed God's own loving companionship. She was puzzled that not everyone in the church seemed interested in her great discovery.

Did you check all of them? I did. But they are so different! Instead of helping us understand the term, the exercise may confuse. So let's try a few definitions I've gleaned from various sources.

From the following list, check the descriptions of revival you think best define the term.

❑ 1. Revival is a powerful activity of the Spirit in large numbers of people at the same time.
❑ 2. Revival is a quickening of believers to extraordinary levels of praise and prayer, powerful witness, and loving concern for others.
❑ 3. Revival is a renewal of God's people in which lives are reclaimed, and the dying embers of spiritual life are fanned back into a flame. It's a visitation of life where there had been signs of death.
❑ 4. Revival is an evangelistic campaign.
❑ 5. Revival is an outpouring of miraculous signs and extraordinary emotional upheaval.
❑ 6. Revival is a time when spiritual concern becomes the pressing and absorbing concern of many.
❑ 7. Revival is a time Christians are restored to their first love for Christ. Sham and hypocrisy are exposed; bitterness and strife in the body of Christ are revealed and repented of with the result that sinners are brought to Christ in great numbers.
❑ 8. Revival is a sovereign act of God that cannot be anticipated or brought about by human effort.

Among these "definitions" I like #7 best, though each touches on some aspect of what has been called "revival." The Bible doesn't use the term *revival*, but does report movements of spiritual renewal of various kinds. Perhaps we are safest not to prescribe the details of what must happen to qualify as true revival. We can, however, discern some common features among these examples and definitions:

1. Revival is the work of the Holy Spirit.
2. He revitalizes or renews those He has already given life.
3. Others see the renewed vitality, resulting in change in them also. Revival spreads among believers and unbelievers turn to Christ.

This last characteristic would seem to rule out the idea of a "personal revival," which some use to describe a fresh encounter with God. Anyone can experience personal renewal at any time he or she is prepared to acknowledge a need, yield to God's control, and trust Him to give renewed life. Personal renewal may best be referred to by terms like the theme of this unit—being filled with the Spirit. I can experience the fullness of God's blessing whether or not others participate.

Check the following signs of revival that sound like your church.

❑ Both young and old experience excitement in our times of worship.
❑ People often find Christ through our church.
❑ We feel a family closeness and loving spirit of care for one another.
❑ The people in our community who don't join us still know something is going on and have to admit we're alive.
❑ When one member fails, the others reach out in love and restore the person; repentance, confession, reconciliation are common.
❑ Prayer meetings are vital. God is answering prayer and changing lives, and people are spontaneously clustering with others to pray.
❑ We have a heart to reach the whole world for Christ; most members could be called "world Christians." Concern for missions is a powerful factor in our praying, giving, and sending our sons and daughters into missionary service.

Do you easily identify spiritual needs in your church? Are evidences of spiritual vitality hard to find? Are you satisfied with the way things are, or do you hope for revival in your church?

Vern Strom was a wheat farmer in Western Canada who tells of the "dirty thirties" when they planted 1,000 bushels of precious seed and reaped barely 1,000 bushels in return. On 1,000 acres, that's a bushel an acre! Like many a church—hard, hard work for a "survival" harvest. But in 1942 the rains came, and they averaged a crop of 55 bushels an acre on 1,500 acres! The silos, barns, and garages wouldn't hold it all; so they stored it in piles outside, 12,000 bushels to a pile. That's the kind of harvest when God sends rain.

Wouldn't such an abundant spiritual harvest be great for your church? If you are experiencing a drought, you can do two things—

1. Be sure that you personally are experiencing the fullness of the Spirit as a continuing pattern of life; and

2. Pray diligently for revival, recruiting others to join you in prayer.

G. Campbell Morgan said, "We cannot legislate spiritual awakening, but we can set our sails to catch the wind." My son Bob and I were trying to cross a large lake on the boundary between the United States and Canada, but the wind kept driving us toward the shore long before we reached the end of the lake. We paddled our canoe with all the energy we could muster, like the poor remnant in a church that stays faithful and tries to move things forward. Also, like that remnant, we wore out, went with the wind and beached our canoe.

After a rest we started out again, but made little progress. Then Bob, the veteran canoer, told me to tie his poncho between two paddles, sit in the prow and hoist my "sail" to the wind while he relaxed in the stern and navigated. Amazing! We began to skim across the lake under full sail, much to the astonishment of other canoeists struggling vainly to make progress. So it is when the mighty Wind of God blows through His people with renewing power.

So let us set our sails, covenant to pray, and keep on praying till revival comes. In the meantime, until God chooses to unleash a widespread renewal, you can make very sure that you personally are eligible for revival and thus no barrier to what God would do. That's the first meaning of being filled with the Spirit—unconditional yieldedness to His will, making sure each day that He is in charge.

In this unit we've seen that by keeping a close connection with the Spirit we can be sure of a full harvest of godly characteristics and powerful service, and at least a periodic inner sense of God-intoxication. We can do what Paul says in Ephesians 5:18 and keep on being filled with the Spirit! As He "pours in," we will be truly filled full, or we could say fulfilled.

On top of that—as if that were not exciting enough—by daily obeying the command to keep on being filled, we open the door for the Holy Spirit to do His work. We do our part to set up the whole church for joining in that filling. We pray that the entire church will experience a "chain revival," leaping on from one degree of glory to another.

> Stop now and tell God how you feel about all this good news of Spirit fullness. Begin your own revival prayer watch, too, committing to keep at it till God's Spirit renews His church.

UNIT 9

BATTLE

PLAN

Diane had been a Christian for two years, spiraling upward, open and eager for all the Spirit was teaching. Then she made a discovery. She took a class I taught on the Christian life. The assignment was to write a paper on developing a battle plan for overcoming temptation. The paper wasn't just about how to overcome temptation. The assignment was very personal: "A Strategy for Overcoming My Own Strongest Temptation." Diane should have known about temptation–even Jesus had to slug it out with the devil! But in the exuberance of her new found faith, she missed the issue of dealing with temptation. She added a note to her paper:

> As a "toddler" Christian, I had had very little knowledge about Satan and his tactics. I never felt plagued by temptation. Consequently, when you gave the assignment, I did not feel a need to devise a plan to overcome temptation.

> After researching this paper, life isn't as comfortable. I now realize the devil is working in my life, and I see the temptations that beset me. This discovery is both terrible and wonderful. I've already defeated Satan in one way, because I'm no longer ignorant of and oblivious to his attacks in my life.

Students really got into the project, some writing almost book-length theses, many testifying that the project was life-transforming. "My life has been radically changed. For the first time I'm beginning to see progress toward victory."

Once in a while I get a letter from a former student, "Remember the assignment on developing a strategy to overcome temptation? That was the turning point in my Christian experience." Each of these students discovered that being filled with the Spirit doesn't lift one beyond temptation. In fact, the battle will escalate! Unfortunately, this battle catches too many sincere, growing Christians off guard–faltering before they know what hit them. Others know they are being tempted; but they don't know how to defend themselves, so they go down in defeat.

In this unit you will develop a personal battle strategy for partnering with the Spirit in winning the victory over temptations that assault you daily. Give particular attention to your memory verses because they provide an outline for the unit.

Unit Memory Verse

I beseech you therefore, brethren, by the mercies of God, that you present your bodies a living sacrifice, holy, acceptable to God, which is your reasonable service. And do not be conformed to this world, but be transformed by the renewing of your mind, that you may prove what is that good and acceptable and perfect will of God. –Romans 12:1-2, NKJV

> **After I have been filled with the Spirit, what can I do to maintain that relationship with Him? How can I consistently overcome temptation?**

DAY 1

PREPARATION FOR BATTLE

The Scripture memory verse for this unit is Romans 12:1-2. The passage is so familiar, we're tempted to let the words run through our minds without engaging their powerful meaning.

🌀 **Before we begin our study, rewrite Romans 12:1-2 in your own words. Briefly explain the meaning as you see it. Try to capture the essence of what Paul is saying in these verses.**

_____

_____

_____

Each of the papers I received from students was unique. Each student offered a different approach to overcoming temptation, but the temptations were similar. Men most often wrote of sexual temptation. "How can I control my lustful thoughts and even my eyes?"

Often the women spoke of emotional struggles. Sandra is 38, single, and worried she'll never get married. An unsaved guy keeps asking her out and she knows she can't marry an unbeliever, but… Maribelle has lots going for her and she knows it. It's hard not to feel a little smug when she sees someone else who isn't as well-dressed, attractive, or intelligent. Even weak Christians are fair game for her condescension. She hates herself when these attitudes erupt.

REST OR WRESTLE?

Everyone needs a workable battle strategy to conquer temptations. Apparently some seek to deal with temptation in a different way. Once or twice in every batch of papers I found a "paper" that was one-sentence long: "I have no strategy; the Holy Spirit lives in me and that's all the strategy I need." Which will it be? Do I get out of the way and let God do it all, or do I personally slug it out with the enemy? We may be tempted to go to one extreme or the other–to opt for a spectator role and leave it up to God, or develop a do-it-yourself mind-set.

Put a check where you find yourself in your present attitude toward your main temptation(s).

God does it all– rest in Him								It's up to me– wrestle it out
ı	ı	ı	ı	ı	ı	ı	ı	ı

The Bible teaches both a faith that rests and a faith that wrestles. We trust the Spirit to do the work of remaking us. But we must also use the weapons He provides to fight the evil in our lives. If we concentrate solely on what He does, we may slip into complacency or presumption and get ambushed by the enemy. If we concentrate exclusively on our responsibility to fight the good fight, we may become battle weary and discouraged–even give up the battle.

Since we've examined the Spirit's role in some detail in previous units, let's examine our role in the spiritual battle. We've got to develop a war mentality. We need to take the following specific steps. We must approach spiritual battles as seriously as a commander planning a military campaign.

THE FIRST STEP—SURRENDER

The spiritual war differs from all other battles. In this battle, surrender is victory. The first step in winning spiritual war is surrendering ourselves to the Lord.

Surrender seems a strange way to win a victory, doesn't it? When faced with temptation, the only way to win is to give up! However, we do not surrender to the enemy or temptation but to the Victor. "I plead with you," says Paul, "to make a grand presentation of yourself to God. Present yourself as if you were a carefully prepared sacrifice at the temple. Surrender yourself, your rights, even your life. That's where victory begins" [my paraphrase].

Sacrifice can be painful. Sometimes you must give up:
- a friend who deflects you from God's highest and best
- the ambition that is really an ego trip
- that fun thing that eats up time you should be spending on God's business
- a purchase so that the hungry of the world may eat.

Those sacrifices can hurt. But the grand presentation God demands is more than those little particulars. God wants all of you—a living sacrifice. That alone starts you on the way to holiness and is acceptable to God, but in the light of all God has done for you this living sacrifice is only reasonable.

STEP 2—IDENTIFY THE SOURCE OF TEMPTATION

Presenting yourself unconditionally to God is only the beginning. The next step is to identify the source of temptation. You must be clear about the battle you are waging. In our memory passage, Paul identifies the pressure of "the world"—other people, things, and circumstances can cause us to stumble (Matt. 18:6-7). The world presents us with occasions to become angry. It makes sin look attractive. Circumstances like poverty or riches (Prov. 30:8-9) can also put pressure on us.

Paul also identifies minds that need renovation—our inner desires and impulses. Ultimately our source of temptation isn't the people or circumstances, it's our response to them. We've given ground already in our minds—"Each one is tempted when, by his own evil desire, he is dragged away and enticed" (Jas. 1:14).

Satan is the original source of all temptation; and he still is on the prowl, ready to pounce on the unwary (1 Pet. 5:8). We should be on guard at all times (Eph. 6:11), never give ground (Eph. 4:27), always fight back (Jas. 4:7), and stay alert to his tricks and deceptions (2 Cor. 2:11).

From where do your greatest temptations come? On the line beside the source, write your most frequent temptations. Number them in order of their strength.

Source	Example
___ Satan	_____
___ inner desires, impulses	_____
___ other people	_____
___ things, circumstances	_____
___ God	_____

Steps to winning over temptation
1. Surrender

Steps to winning over temptation
1. Surrender
2. Identify the source

153

When tempted, no one should say, "God is tempting me." For God cannot be tempted by evil, nor does he tempt anyone; but each one is tempted when, by his own evil desire, he is dragged away and enticed.
—James 1:13-14

Steps to winning over temptation
1. Surrender
2. Identify the source
3. Recognize the root sin

All the sources of temptation in the activity can be sources of temptation except one—God. James 1:13-14 clearly states that God tempts no one. How then does the Bible sometimes credit the same tempting circumstances as coming from both Satan and God? (See 2 Sam. 24:1 and 1 Chr. 21:1.) The motive is the key. Satan uses people or circumstances to bring us down. God uses those same circumstances to test or prove our allegiance and make us stronger.

STEP 3: RECOGNIZE THE ROOT SIN

Have you ever stopped to analyze just what temptation is? It doesn't look bad, it looks good; otherwise it wouldn't tempt. Actually, God designed our desires in the first place. He purposely gave us the ability to experience desire. Enticement to sin is the temptation to abuse a God-given desire. God created us to enjoy our bodies, acquire possessions, and accomplish worthwhile goals. But when we try to fulfill those desires in the wrong way, we sin.

The next step in our strategy is to discriminate between God-given drives and our destructive responses to those desires. God has given us the ability to enjoy many things, but we can easily twist the ability to enjoy into sinful responses that become destructive life patterns. When we recognize the legitimate desires we can identify the root sin behind our temptations.

In the following lists, match items in the three columns by drawing a line connecting the God-given desire, the sinful response, and the end result of a lifestyle of sinful response.

God-given desire	Sinful response	End result
desire to enjoy food sex, rest	covetousness	egotist
desire to own things	pride	materialist
desire to be somebody, have significance	lust	sensualist

Some people believe that all sin can be placed under one of these categories—
- lust (abuse of our desire to enjoy food or sex)
- covetousness (desire to possess something that is not mine or not in God's will for me)
- pride (taking credit for something God has achieved).

If I give in to any impulse long enough, I will become that type of person. Lust yielded to creates a sensual person. Covetousness too often indulged ends in a materialistic outlook. Pride may so often prevail that I become egotistical. To win the battle against temptation, we sometimes need to recognize the root sin, not just the outward result. We especially need such understanding when a sinful attitude becomes entrenched as a disposition.

For example, outbursts of anger may actually be rooted in some unresolved bitterness. From where did the bitterness come? What caused it? To root out the basic problem, we must identify both the problem and the source.

STEP 4: ACKNOWLEDGE THE TAPROOT

So far in this lesson we have looked at three root temptations. We might picture temptation as a tree with three roots: lust, pride, and covetousness. However, some scholars point to an underlying taproot—unbelief. Some say unbelief is the source of the other three! Eve fell before temptations to lust, covet, and act arrogantly because she doubted God's word. The taproot is the single root that grows deepest into the ground. We can picture the taproot of unbelief like this:

Steps to winning over temptation
1. Surrender
2. Identify the source
3. Recognize the root sin
4. Acknowledge the taproot

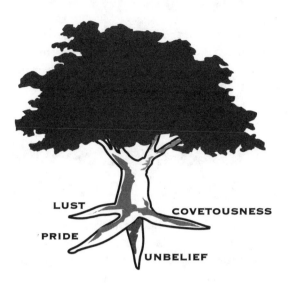

Other scholars say the fundamental flaw in human nature is self-love. A problem exists with that idea. Self-love is more like the innocent drives God built into us—the desires to enjoy, possess, and exist. However, like those innocent drives, rightful concern about one's own interests can run out of control. When I act in my self-interest at the expense of God or someone else, I've sinned. Perhaps I have committed the most fundamental sin of all, since the first and great commandment is to love God supremely. If self-love is the source of my sin, I'm not going to win the battle till I obey God's first commandment.

We must identify as best we can the roots of the temptations we face. Unbelief and love skewed toward self-interest seem almost always to be present, but they are so general that it may be more helpful in our battle strategy to look at the root sins more easily identified: lust, covetousness, and pride.

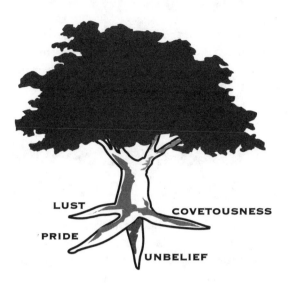 **What current temptation is enticing you to enjoy what God doesn't intend for you or to enjoy it in wrong ways (lust)?**

_____

What, specifically, are you tempted to covet? _____

_____

What are you tempted to be proud about? _____

_____

Temptation always masquerades—it looks so appealing, promises so much good. That's why it's a temptation. If it wore its own face, it would be so ugly we'd run! The first task, then, is to unmask the temptation—identify it for exactly what it is: lust, covetousness, pride, unbelief, or just plain self-love. These enemies take away the power or filling of the Holy Spirit in our lives, and they grieve Him. Our sins of unbelief and self-love reveal themselves in the temptations of lust, covetousness, and pride.

In developing your "war mentality" and battle plan you began with unconditional surrender to the will of God. That propelled you out of a dangerous no-man's land or out from behind enemy lines and solidly on God's side. Thus you became ready for the next step—to identify the enemy. The underlying source of the temptation may not be that easy to spot, so you may have bypassed that step and identified the temptation itself. That isn't always easy either, since temptation fights dirty; but you can spot any disguised temptation by focusing Scripture on your situation. Finally, make your choice about that temptation. Choose right and grow stronger, choose wrong and grow weaker.

DAY 2

DEFENSIVE STRATEGY

Every battle plan needs defensive and offensive strategies. Today we'll study ways to defend, to ward off temptation even before it strikes. On day 3 we'll take the offensive, developing strategies to defeat the enemy at the time of temptation.

LEGITIMATE DESIRE OR SINFUL DESIRE?
Sometimes distinguishing between legitimate desire and sinful desire is difficult. Is this new TV a legitimate need or coveting what God doesn't intend? Is my reaction to this situation righteous indignation or sinful anger? Is the pain I feel justifiable, or am I so unhappy because my ego took a heavy hit?

🌀 **How do you most often decide between legitimate need and temptation to sin?**

❑ I trust the Holy Spirit to show me what's right.
❑ I recall Bible teaching on the subject.
❑ I quote a Bible command I've memorized.
❑ I listen to my conscience.

All of those answers do help us know right from wrong, but the first and last are tricky. None of them will work without the Holy Spirit. But we must not run to the extreme and assume that the Holy Spirit within is all we need. He deliberately provided other means of knowing His will, so we are sure to go down in defeat if we neglect any of them. The Spirit is no substitute for the other means of understanding; He's their energizer.

What about depending on our conscience? "Let your conscience be your guide," we say. But natural conscience is a very unreliable guide since it is no more than our judgment in the realm of right versus wrong. That judgment has been programmed by home, school, and society, not to mention our own sinful inclinations. As a result, we seem to have infinite capacity to con ourselves into believing what we want to believe.

For conscience to be a reliable guide we must constantly—
_____ be transformed into a new creation by the Holy Spirit
_____ use Scripture as a guide for the decision-making process
_____ keep in tune with the Spirit
_____ develop judgment by consistent, obedient practice.

🌀 **Go back and number the four essentials needed to have a "true" conscience in the order of the priority you place on each.**

CONFORMED OR TRANSFORMED?
I had just returned from a 12-year TV famine. In Japan we rarely watched TV and understood little of what we did see. Besides, Japanese TV was very tame by Amer-

ican standards. I was astounded to hear friends guffawing over sexual innuendos in a popular show. "They put garbage like that on television?" I remonstrated.

Twenty years passed. I hadn't watched TV much, but enough to get a feel for the programming. Suddenly I woke up to an astonishing change in me. For a year or more I had been periodically watching reruns of the same show I had criticized previously, and feeling grateful for an oasis of good family fare in the moral badlands of network television. What had happened? I had been molded by my world into its way of thinking. And Paul says, "Stop!" Our memory verse might be literally translated: "Resist the conforming influences of your environment and keep on resisting." Who will deny that popular media is hell-bent (literally) on cultivating lust, covetousness, and pride? And I was letting it happen to me. In fact, I recently made a covenant with myself to stop surfing the channels. When I finally got honest with myself and God, I had to admit what I was actually looking for—and it wasn't purity, contentment, and humility!

> Have you ever come to a similar realization? Have you found yourself watching, doing, or buying something that you previously considered destructive or off-limits? ❏ Yes ❏ No. If so, describe.

_____

_____

Sometimes I watched TV just to relax and unwind after a difficult day, but doing so ate up priceless time. Even worse, it was subtly molding me into a different kind of person. Paul says to resist and keep resisting—eternal vigilance is the price of spiritual freedom.

To take this proactive stance we must do four things:
- be involved with a warfare mentality
- decide firmly on whose side we belong
- identify our major enemies
- take hold of or use our weapons.

In the fight for our spiritual freedom the Bible, prayer, and the church are our frontline weapons. The Spirit uses them in combination to create an effective defensive strategy. Let's examine each of these weapons.

THE BIBLE: STOCKPILING YOUR AMMUNITION

Scan the war stories recorded in Genesis 3:1-6 and Matthew 4:1-11. Here we have deadly battles. First is the battle between Satan and Eve, then between Satan and Jesus—the welfare of billions depending on the outcome of each battle. Eve met the enemy with a background of perfect heredity and a perfect environment while Jesus' heritage on His mother's side was a fallen humanity and His environment was a sin-cursed world. But Eve lost, Jesus won.

> Did you find any clues as to why? In the previous paragraph circle the names of those who quoted God's Word.

Eve quoted God's Word, but she wasn't all that committed to its authority. She quickly abandoned her only defense and accepted the enemy's word over God's. Satan cynically used Scripture to push his ungodly ends. Only Jesus used the Word of God as His weapon. He won! You will, too. But you must stockpile your ammunition or you won't have it available at the time of testing. Jesus knew His Bible.

How can a young man keep his way pure?
By living according to your word.
I seek you with all my heart;
do not let me stray from your commands.
I have hidden you word in my heart that I might not sin against you.
—Psalm 119:9-11

157

We can stockpile ammunition in two ways: regularly reading the Bible and selectively studying it. For example, I may be blind to the discontent in my life that is choking out the growth of joy and peace. As I read the Word daily, I see how great God is and how greatly He cares about me. Then I realize how sinful my discontent really is, how foolish it is in the light of His greatness. The Word has spotlighted a temptation I didn't even know existed. God's Word alerted me to a hidden enemy.

Selective study, on the other hand, is to search out all the Bible teaches about a specific issue. As I deal with a particular temptation, I study all the Scripture has to say about that temptation. The passages I find can then be used as a weapon in the moment of temptation, like Jesus did.

For example, my desire for material things may be choking out my spiritual growth. If regular reading of Scripture doesn't raise my consciousness about a materialistic lifestyle, a study of what the Bible says about covetousness may help. I find that covetousness is a slick con artist, it beguiles (Mark 4:19). If I really want something or want to hang on to something, covetousness provides the rationale. Further, I'd find the Bible calls covetousness "idolatry" (Eph. 5:5; Col. 3:5). When I covet I'm no better than the savage bowing before his little stone god! When I find that covetous people are classified along with adulterers and murderers, having no part in God's kingdom (1 Cor. 6:9-10), I might just be prepared to recognize covetousness as a mortal foe and face this temptation the next time it strikes.

List again your major temptations that you listed in day 1.

1. _____

2. _____

3. _____

4. _____

After each one write one or two Scripture references that refer to that sin. If you don't know any, maybe it's time to start stock-piling your ammunition! Check your Bible concordance or cross-references in your Bible. See if you can spot a good reference or two that would help with the temptations you listed. Later, you'll probably want to do a more thorough study of what the Bible says about your special enemies. Begin to stockpile your ammunition, even if it's just beginning a list of key passages you discover in your regular Bible reading.

PRAYER: STRATEGIC BOMBARDMENT

Remember the story of how I put in my prayer notebook "T & T"? Every day I pinpointed the enemies of a renegade tongue and an explosive temper. I didn't wait until the enemy loomed on the horizon and started his barrage of temptations. I started every day with a plea for the Holy Spirit to send in His troops and knock out the enemy in my life.

The Spirit knew in advance what I'd face that day. I asked Him to prepare me, to give me strength to win, to alert me to ambushes I wouldn't even see. I didn't pray: "Lord, help me be good today" or, "Lord, make me victorious today." I prayed about the specific sins that were winning in my life. I targeted my big enemies, and I prayed daily for victory over them.

Watch and pray so that you will not fall into temptation.
—Matthew 26:41

Lead us not into temptation, but deliver us from the evil one.
—Matthew 6:13

From your list of personal temptations choose the one that brings you down most and write a model prayer you might use on a daily basis until God gives consistent victory.

_____

_____

_____

_____

THE CHURCH: BUILDING A DEFENSIVE TEAM

The defensive use of the local congregation is primarily to build a support network of people who grow strong together in studying the Word, uniting in prayer, exhorting one another, and setting the example for one another. Together we build spiritual muscle in preparation for the battle in a way we never could on our own.

A high-ranking Air Force officer sat by me on the plane. He had been a pilot during the Vietnam war. Though American planes over North Vietnam took an average of one hit every 12 missions, he came through more than 300 flights unscathed. "What a great pilot!" I exclaimed.

"No," he responded, "what a great partner! You always go in pairs and you're responsible to watch the tail of your partner. Your job is to warn him when a missile is coming. If you fail, there's no hope for your partner." So it is in spiritual warfare—you need a faithful partner to watch out for you!

An accountability partner is someone you can share with openly about your temptations, your victories, and your defeats. A word of caution: to share with a partner who is vulnerable to the same temptation you are fighting is usually unwise. A drowning man doesn't need another drowning man to come to the rescue! But one of the greatest defenses against temptation is a buddy in the battle, an accountability partner to pray with you about your besetting temptation.

If you have a prayer buddy or accountability partner and haven't shared your struggle with temptation, why not do it this week? If you don't have an accountability partner, have you prayed about who to enlist? Take time to pray now. Ask God to show you who you can join forces with to help each other overcome temptation. As you go about your activities this week, keep asking God for the person and the courage to enlist such an accountability partner. When God answers your prayer, write below the name of the person you will ask.

_____

We've considered a defensive strategy that uses the weapons of the Spirit to prepare for battle. Only this way can we build a defensive wall around our minds to block out the ideas of the world and counter the onslaughts of the enemy. "Reject and keep on resisting the conforming influences of your environment," says Paul. This we will do with the Word, with prayer, and with our fellow soldiers. On day 3 we'll take the offensive.

All of you stand shoulder to shoulder, becoming one in heart ... put together your strength and fight.
—Philippians 1:27-28, translated from the Japanese

OFFENSIVE STRATEGY

We use the same weapons at the time of encounter with the enemy that we used in building up our defenses: the Bible, prayer, and the church. But we use them differently.

🌀 **Let's start with our memory passage. Write Romans 12:2.**

_____

_____

_____

The mind is the battleground where spiritual battles are won or lost. I use the term *mind* as a comprehensive category–it includes all of you, what you think, how you feel, what you choose. You need all the activities of your mind renewed.

Notice several things about Paul's command. First, the word for *renew* in Greek is *metamorphosis*. Consider how we use that term. The little earth-bound fuzzy worm metamorphosed into a gorgeous creature of the skies! That's what Paul says we're to work at–"be totally renovated in your entire outlook and response."

Second, the form of the Greek verb is passive–meaning to have this done to you by the Holy Spirit. But that passive verb is contained in a positive command. The command calls for some initiative on your part. You must participate with the Spirit.

Third, though the grand presentation (v. 1) is a "point action" verb–speaking of a decisive turning point, the transformation (v. 2) is a "continuous action" verb, speaking of a process. You have to keep working at it.

The mind is the battlefield where a deadly war is in progress. You either win or lose the battle in your mind. In the war against the conforming influences of your environment you must take the initiative to have your entire mind-set transformed. To do that we use the Bible, prayer, and the church as offensive weapons of the Spirit at the time of confrontation.

THE BIBLE: OFFENSIVE WEAPON

Last night I felt an excitement about today–I was looking forward to writing this lesson on winning the victory over temptation! About 4:00 a.m. I woke to the persistent ringing of the phone. My heart jumped–I immediately thought, *which of my children is in an emergency?*

The voice said, "Is this Mr. McQuilkin?"

"Yes," I responded. A dread settled in as I realized it was a police officer on the phone.

Oh, no, not again, I thought. Three months ago my car had been stolen from my backyard. While the police officer talked, I looked out the back window and, sure enough, my car was gone again. And once again, the police had found it, torn up as before.

I was angry. *I'd like to put a booby trap on that car. Guess what would happen to the next person who touches it!* I said to myself. And I was afraid. Was it the same people? Will our house be next? Maybe we should move out of this inner city neighborhood we deliberately chose to live in ...

No temptation has seized you except what is common to man. And God is faithful; he will not let you be tempted beyond what you can bear. But when you are tempted, he will also provide a way out so that you can stand up under it.
–1 Corinthians 10:13

🌀 **Here are some of the emotions and thoughts I had this morning. Check those you think are unacceptable to God.**

    ❑ 1. I'm angry.
    ❑ 2. I'll booby trap that car!
    ❑ 3. I'm afraid of what will happen next.
    ❑ 4. I'm outta here—forget this evil neighborhood!
    ❑ 5. Why did God let this happen? I asked Him only last night to protect my car.

A couple of those are clearly bad. The booby-trap strategy is vengeful, and I would be disobedient if I left my calling to live for God in this neighborhood. Anger and fear are not necessarily sinful (#1 & 3); it depends on who they're directed at and why. The last item could become sinful depending on how I respond to the emotions. I lapse into unbelief if I conclude God won't care for me (#5).

No use to go back to bed—I was too agitated. So I turned to Scripture for an earlier-than-usual devotional time. I was reading Hebrews 10, but I couldn't concentrate. This chapter seemed irrelevant to my crisis, so I decided to quit halfway through. *I'll pick it up here tomorrow,* I told myself. Then, listlessly, I decided to read on. The next words hit me like a bolt from heaven:

> *You cheerfully accepted the seizure of your possessions, knowing that you possessed something better and more lasting (Heb. 10:34, NEB).*

The Word of God was a sword to annihilate those evil temptations that had been winning out in my mind. Cheerful? Hardly. Better and more lasting? Definitely. A couple of chapters later the Spirit gave me more reassurance about my situation:

> *Be content with what you have; for God himself has said, "I will never leave you or desert you"; and so we can take courage and say, "The Lord is my helper, I will not fear; what can man do to me?" (Heb. 13:5-6, NEB).*

God is my better and lasting possession!

Notice that the Spirit used the Scripture in a way that was legitimate and in context. Remember when I tried to find guidance from Deuteronomy 1:6 "You have stayed long enough at this mountain"? At that time I was making the verse speak to me in a way different than its original meaning. In the case of Hebrews 10:34 God showed me Christians who were faithful when they faced a trial worse than my own. Their response challenged me to be faithful.

The Bible is not only our defensive weapon as we stockpile its truth against the hour of temptation, it's our offensive weapon at the moment of temptation. Like Jesus in the wilderness, we wield the sword of the Spirit against temptation and rout the enemy.

My agitated mind settled down in a miraculous calm, and cheerfulness actually began to bubble up as I focused on the positive things God is doing in my life.
    • Though it was all the transportation I had, it wasn't much.
    • They broke into my car, not my house.
    • They took my car, not my life.
    • They were the thieves, not I.
    • They can take my possessions, but they can't take my God.
I was tempted, but the Spirit delivered me—through the Word. Hallelujah!

⊚ **Put yourself in each of the following situations, then match the Scripture verse that could help you fight the temptation described.**

___ 1. Your boss didn't give you the raise you deserved; you're tempted not to work as diligently as you used to.

___ 2. You just heard an unbelievable story about your pastor; you reach for the phone to call your best friend about it.

___ 3. Jerome didn't speak to you in church Sunday. "He must be mad at me," you concluded. "Wouldn't be surprised, he's such a moody person."

___ 4. You have your rights; you're not going to give in to your spouse one more time.

___ 5. The guys at work are going golfing Sunday. Maybe you'll just skip church this time.

A. "Remember the Sabbath day by keeping it holy" (Ex. 20:8). Don't skip church as some do (Heb. 10:25, paraphrase).

B. "Be kind and compassionate to one another, forgiving each other, just as in Christ God forgave you" (Eph. 4:32).

C. "Do not judge, or you too will be judged" (Matt. 7:1).

D. "Do not entertain an accusation against an elder" (1 Tim. 5:19).

E. "Submit to one another out of reverence for Christ" (Eph. 5:21).

What mighty firepower we have right in our hands! I would have answered 1-B; 2-D; 3-C; 4-E; 5-A.

PRAYER: OFFENSIVE WEAPON

Not only do we pray about our besetting temptation as the day begins in preparation for the battle, but we also use prayer as a mighty weapon at the time of temptation. Many men have talked with me about their sexual temptations with movies, magazines, TV, co-worker, or a friend's wife. I always ask, "Do you ask God to help at the moment of temptation?"

So far I've never encountered an exception. If they called on God for help, they won the battle. Those who did not call on God for help were never victorious in overcoming the temptation. When men tell me: "At that point, I didn't want deliverance," or, "When the temptation comes, it's too late"–they are telling me something about their spiritual state. Do they really want the will of God? It's not enough to love the good, we must hate evil. We will hate it if we think about what it will do to us in the end, and what it does to Jesus at the time. Only when we hate evil will we cry out for help in the moment of temptation.

⊚ **Review the major temptations you noted in day 1. Check below whether or not you prayed at the moment of the last temptation and then check the outcome.**

My Besetting Temptation	Most recent encounter: Did you pray? Yes No		Outcome Success/Failure	
_____	❑	❑	❑	❑
_____	❑	❑	❑	❑
_____	❑	❑	❑	❑

They cried out to him during the battle. He answered their prayers.
—1 Chronicles 5:20

"Call upon me in the day of trouble; I will deliver you."
—Psalm 50:15

Another key to victory through prayer is to confess sin immediately. That is a great test of where my heart is. If I'm yielded and truly want only God's will in my life, the moment I realize I've failed I'll eagerly repent. I'll tell Him how sorry I am and ask for deliverance and strength. When I feel the enemy overpowering me, if I'll only admit it's sin and ask God for help, the Spirit intervenes and delivers.

If we confess our sins, he is faithful and just and will forgive us our sins and purify us from all unrighteousness.
—1 John 1:9

Do you have any unconfessed sin in your life? Flee to Jesus! Make it right! Don't continue this lesson until you have, because that sin breaks contact with the Spirit. It's worse than useless to study about the Christian life and not obey what you know.

THE CHURCH: OFFENSIVE WEAPON

My brother-in-law died two weeks ago. The church stood by through the painful weeks of dying and through the long good-byes. And they stand by us still. It wasn't just the theology of dying and eternal life the church had taught us through the years, important as that preparation is for the crisis time. At the time of testing God's people came to the rescue.

In the longer dying of my beloved—18 years now under the hammer blows of Alzheimer's—what would I do without God's people? The temptations they deliver me from include: discouragement, self-pity, worry, loneliness, and fear. Don't ever hesitate to call on your brothers and sisters for help in the time of need! That's what they're there for! "A brother is born for adversity" (Prov. 17:17).

Before we were married I wrote Muriel about how we wanted to be one in every sense. "Let's not have any secrets," I wrote.

She responded, "Yes, let's be completely one and share everything. But let's not make our home a garbage dump."

We covenanted before marriage that we would never say anything that would harm another person. We didn't want a dump of foul-smelling garbage in our home. We haven't kept that vow perfectly, but we worked at it by keeping watch on one another. She became my accountability partner. When the enemy launched a rocket, my buddy warned me!

I'd start to say, "Honey, I probably shouldn't say this about Holly, but ..."

"Then don't!" she'd interrupt and head off the enemy attack.

At times I'd go ahead and say things I shouldn't. She'd quietly respond, "We really shouldn't be talking like this, should we?"

She would gently lead me to repentance. A spiritual buddy will help us win in the hour of attack.

In this lesson we have examined two overlapping weapons: the church in general and an accountability partner in particular. Many times Muriel served both functions. She was an expression of the body of Christ, and she was a partner to help me be accountable to Him. That's part of "church," a powerful weapon when facing temptation.

We've studied a defensive strategy of preparation for battle and an offensive strategy for the moment of attack. We need both. To build up your defenses against the hour of temptation, use the Bible and prayer every day, the church at least every week. Then, when the enemy strikes, reach for those same weapons to fend him off. You'll win the victory!

Review your memory verses from all 9 units you have studied so far. Use each memory verse as the basis for prayer.

I beseech you therefore, brethren, by the mercies of God, that you present your bodies a living sacrifice, holy, acceptable to God, which is your reasonable service. And do not be conformed to this world, but be transformed by the renewing of your mind, that you may prove what is that good and acceptable and perfect will of God.

—Romans 12:1-2, NKJV

DAY 4

VICTORY CELEBRATION

We've examined our defensive and offensive weapons for overcoming temptation. Since God's purpose for us is to be like Him, no wonder Paul calls His will "good and acceptable and perfect" (Rom. 12:2). But what does he mean by proving it? As we "prove" His will, we will experience a distinct result of obedience to God's will. Just as His will is "good, acceptable, and perfect," we will grow to more closely resemble those aspects of His will.

The following 7 steps describe the process from temptation to character development. When we resist the conforming influences of the world and work with the Spirit in the renovation of our thinking, we will increasingly prove by our experience those excellent qualities of God's will. We will become a showcase for all to see, conclusive evidence that God's will really is good, pleasing, and perfect. When we ignore the Spirit and surrender to temptation, we become a showcase for defeat, sin, and hypocrisy. Here is my description of the 7-step process:

Step 1. Temptation comes, either from without or within. Remember that temptation itself is no sin, it's just enticement to sin.

Step 2. We have an emotional response to temptation: like or dislike, love or hate.

Step 3. We make a decision of the will: to reject or consent to temptation.

Step 4. If we reject temptation, we experience victory; if we give in to the temptation, sin follows.

Step 5. Our responses give birth to a pattern. Success strengthens us to win future battles; sinful failure leads to weakness and susceptibility to further failure.

Step 6. Habit is formed; we develop a pattern of success or failure.

Step 7. Character is formed; we spiral up or down.

To translate the process from general theory to a practical beginning for developing our battle plan, take the personal temptations you listed earlier and describe your responses for the past week.

Step 1. My temptation _____

Step 2. My emotional response _____

Step 3. My decision at the time _____

Step 4. The short-term result _____

Step 5. The pattern in my life _____

Step 6. The habit I am forming_____

Step 7. The character result _____

Using separate paper, or in your journal, write the 7 steps for each of the temptations you identified earlier.

When in battle you make godly choices, you put on display—or prove—for all to see how good, acceptable, and perfect the will of God is by exhibiting God's character. Let's take a look at those three words Paul uses to describe what you'll look like: good, acceptable, perfect.

GOOD

In week 6, day 4 we learned about the two purposes God always has for allowing suffering in our lives. Those two purposes are—

_____ and _____.

The purpose of suffering is always growth and glory: our growth, God's glory. Would He have those same purposes for allowing temptation to assault us? Yes and no. Yes, both suffering and temptation are tests (often intertwined) and His purpose in allowing either kind of test is always our growth and His glory. But a big difference exists between suffering and temptation. Sometimes we are to accept suffering as God's will for us, but we can never accept temptation—we fight it!

God's good will is to overcome temptation. If we don't, we neither bring credit to Him nor growth to ourselves.

When a prominent Christian falls to sexual temptation, what bad things happen to God's reputation?

_____

When you yield to temptation and throw a "pity party," what happens to you?

_____

When we yield, we grow weaker, less like Jesus, and that's not God's good will. We demonstrate God's good will when we do His will. Victory is His good will, defeat is certainly not His will.

Dennis and Brad came to me with a theory they found liberating. They were forever defeated by lustful temptations. "We've decided lust is the cross Jesus is calling us to bear," they said.

Put yourself in my place as a counselor/advisor. How would you respond to their theory?

_____

_____

I explained that God's good will is to nail our evil desires to the cross, not excuse them. God purposes to give victory over temptation, not that we give up in defeat. Dennis and Brad were demonstrating what the will of God is not. They brought dishonor to the Lord and more rapid descent down the spiral for themselves.

On the other hand, Cubby saw a positive demonstration of God's good will. His business partner, Det, found Christ and was radically changed. Cubby said he'd never seen anything like this. Det was a big-time political operator and hard-driving businessman, but Cubby watched in amazement as a transformation took place.

One day in a particularly difficult confrontation with competitors, Det responded calmly and graciously, not like the old Det. Cubby returned to his office, shut the door, fell to his knees and prayed, "Lord, whatever Det has, I want it!" Cubby had seen God's good will on display in Det, and as a result something very good happened. Cubby was born again.

ACCEPTABLE

Another word Paul uses to describe God's will is *acceptable,* or as some translations have it, *pleasing.* Success in overcoming temptation is pleasing all right, but to whom?

> **Who do you think Paul had in mind as being pleased?**
>
> ❏ God   ❏ Yourself   ❏ Others

Bible scholars may debate which of those Paul had in mind, but I would say, all the above! To overcome temptation brings joy all around. It's a victory celebration! To fail and not do the good will of God is pleasing only to unholy men and unholy spirits. To you, God, and all good people surrender to temptation is distressing.

PERFECT

> **Following are some of the meanings for the term *perfect* in Scripture. Check the one(s) you think fits best Paul's meaning here in describing God's will worked out in your life.**
>
> ❏ flawless, without defect
> ❏ mature, adult, full-grown
> ❏ loyal, sincere, whole-hearted obedience to the known will of God
> ❏ ability and readiness to meet all demands, outfitted
> ❏ having reached appropriate or appointed end, goal, purpose

I checked all but the first and last. Those are indeed our ultimate goal, that we will one day be flawless, just like Jesus. The other three are more appropriate to describe what we can fulfill in this life—His will is that we demonstrate maturity and obedience. When we demonstrate that, what a celebration of the glorious will of God! It's perfect! And that's very pleasing and very good!

DAY 5

MY PERSONAL BATTLE PLAN

In this unit I've shared with you my personal strategy for overcoming the enemies that have most successfully assaulted me. Every battle plan needs to be custom designed for the individual. It may change for each stage of life, whether the temptations and uncertainties of youth, the frustrations and failed dreams of middle years, or the regrets and anxieties of age.

Where are you today in your spiral up toward likeness to Jesus? It's time now for the big assignment: write out your own battle plan for overcoming the failure that most grieves the Holy Spirit and embarrasses you. This is for real, not just an assignment to be fulfilled. Create your own strategic plan to battle temptation.

To begin, pause and ask the Holy Spirit for wisdom. Ask Him to enlighten your mind and bring to mind both Scriptures and principles you have been studying.

1. For what temptation do you need to develop a battle plan? _____

_____

2. Do you really want victory over this temptation? ❏ Yes ❏ No
   Are you yielded unconditionally to the Spirit about it? ❏ Yes ❏ No
   ❏ Not sure

When you can say yes from your heart, Holy Spirit power is released and you're on your way to victory. Go ahead with your plan! But if you couldn't answer yes to that question, no need to proceed. First you must become willing to obey.

How do you become willing to obey? Read the following words from Luke 11. Jesus was speaking specifically about persisting in prayer.

Then he said to them, "Suppose one of you has a friend, and he goes to him at midnight and says, 'Friend, lend me three loaves of bread, because a friend of mine on a journey has come to me, and I have nothing to set before him.'

"Then the one inside answers, 'Don't bother me. The door is already locked, and my children are with me in bed. I can't get up and give you anything.' I tell you, though he will not get up and give him the bread because he is his friend, yet because of the man's boldness he will get up and give him as much as he needs.

"So I say to you: Ask and it will be given to you; seek and you will find; knock and the door will be opened to you. For everyone who asks receives; he who seeks finds; and to him who knocks, the door will be opened" (Luke 11:5-10).

Pause and ask God to make you willing to obey. Ask Him to give you a desire to overcome. Don't ask and give up. Keep asking, knocking, and seeking until God gives you the desire to obey Him.

3. Skim through days 1-3 and put an asterisk in the margin by any of the points in my strategy that you think may work for you.

4. Using those points you've chosen, plus others you may have heard about, discovered in Scripture, or learned through experience, make a broad outline of your own personal strategy for overcoming temptation. The following is an outline of how you might proceed:

   1. Who or what most often causes this temptation? _____

   _____

   2. What are the camouflages this enemy uses—how do I tend to

   rationalize the attitude or behavior? _____

   _____

167

3. Among lust, covetousness, pride, and unbelief, which is most likely

the root cause(s) of my temptation? _____

4. What is my defensive strategy—how do I plan to use the Bible, prayer, and the church to build up strength to face this particular temptation

when it comes? _____

_____

_____

_____

5. What is my offensive strategy—how do I intend to use the Bible,

prayer, and the church at the time of temptation? _____

_____

_____

_____

How did it go? Are you pleased with the outcome? Time and space may not have permitted you to finish your plan to your own satisfaction. Your strategy will need revision as you put it into action. Let it be a developing plan. No matter how satisfied you are with your strategy, remember: success in the Christian life does not ultimately depend on a technique, a strategy, or your own activity.

Ultimately, the Holy Spirit within is the overcomer. But the indwelling powerful One does not displace your personality with His. Rather, He is a personal companion, living in you to:

- strengthen you when you falter
- remind you of truth from His Word when your focus is blurred
- point out the enemy when you're under attack
- comfort you
- lift you up when you fall
- forgive you when you fail
- guide you when you're confused
- sensitize your moral judgment
- strengthen your will when you waver.

Glorious as those activities of the Spirit are, it's not all He does. He prays for us when we don't know how to pray (Rom. 8:26-27); and as we rely on Him, He enables us to pray effectively. God the Spirit gave us His Word and enables us to understand and appropriate that Word in the face of testing. He enables us to live in the kind of relationship with other Christians that will make us overcomers together. What a great God we serve!

THE SPIRIT'S GIFTS

I asked a group of high school students, "Are all occupations of equal importance?" They unanimously agreed that all are equal.

"That's an interesting concept," I said, and told them the story of my flight to Norfolk. "On the way here I sat by a man who wanted to sell me stock in his company. He said it was the fastest growing industry in the country."

"What's the industry?" I asked him.

"Cosmetics," he answered.

"In your industry is there some segment that is growing faster than others?"

"Oh, yes. Male cosmetics."

"Like—what? Deodorant? After-shave lotion?"

"Oh, no," he said. "Last year we sold a quarter million dollars worth of false eyelashes for men."

"There's an occupation," I told the students, "selling false eyelashes for men. Here's another one. My nephew is a skilled surgeon who could make a bundle of money in the United States. Instead, he chose to care for a forgotten people in the heart of Africa. He barely escaped one country as the communist insurgents swept to power. Now, in Kenya, he tells me he does more surgery in a week than he used to do in a year at a renowned hospital in Pennsylvania. Then he adds with a wry smile, 'and none of it is cosmetic!' "

"There you have it," I said,"selling false eyelashes for men or healing the bodies and souls of thousands for whom you're the only hope? Let's vote again: Are all vocations of equal importance?"

That split the crowd and about half wavered. On the front row sat a 12-year-old girl who didn't vote either way.

"Not going to vote?" I asked her.

"No. It's a bad question."

"What's bad about it?"

"You didn't say important for what."

She caught me! Which is more important: a knife, a fork, or a spoon? The answer might depend on whether you had a bowl of bullion or a steak. Vocations need to be considered likewise—important to whom? For what?

Unit Memory Verses

To each is given the manifestation of the Spirit for the common good.
—1 Corinthians 12:7, RSV

Eagerly desire the greater gifts.—1 Corinthians 12:31

> **How do I know what God is calling and equipping me to do?**
> **What spiritual gift(s) does God want me to have?**

DEFINITIONS: WHAT THE GIFT IS NOT

A spiritual gift is a Spirit-given ability to serve God. So much confusion reigns in the church over the subject of spiritual gifts that many give up and avoid the whole subject. That's a big mistake. The only way the church will be effective, and the only way we'll spiral up into likeness to Jesus, is through each believer using the abilities the Spirit gives.

We won't try to settle all the controversy about spiritual gifts. Instead, we'll focus on the basic teaching on which we all can agree. Some Christians believe the gifts—or at least some of them—are no longer given. However, even they must agree that unless the Holy Spirit empowers us we can never accomplish the tasks He gives us to do. Other Christians distinguish "sign" gifts and "ministry" gifts, but a little reflection will make clear that the sign gifts were also for ministry, to build up the body of Christ. So we will concentrate on the common ground, the all-important ways the Spirit enables His people to accomplish His work. Today we'll look at three things the Spirit's gifts are not. They are not fruit, talents, or offices.

GIFTS AND FRUIT

You may have wondered, "Why no chapter on the fruit of the Spirit?" The reason is that so far in our study we have concentrated on the fruit of the Spirit throughout all these units. Our focus has been on how the Holy Spirit produces Christlike characteristics in us, and that is the nature of "fruit." Now we need to ask another question: "How do the fruit and gifts relate?"

Check all the answers you think are true. I will share my answers with you throughout today's study.

❑ 1. The more fruit in a Christian's life (the more Christlike the character), the greater the gift he/she will be given (the more results in ministry).
❑ 2. A person could have a godly life without a conspicuous spiritual gift.
❑ 3. It's more important to have lots of fruit in our lives than to have a great gift.
❑ 4. All Christians should have all the fruit.
❑ 5. All Christians should have all the gifts.

In the most thorough discussion of gifts in the Bible, 1 Corinthians 12–14, fruit is said to be more important than gifts (3 above). Right in the middle of Paul's discussion of gifts, immediately following our memory verse, he says, "Now I'm going to describe something far more important than all these gifts combined" (my paraphrase). Then he gives the magnificent love chapter, 1 Corinthians 13. Love is a fruit. In fact, some say it is the summation of all the fruit of the Spirit.

In the following mixed list of gifts and fruit circle the ones you think all Christians should have:

love	pastoring	evangelism	patience	
goodness	teaching	helping	administration	peace
joy	missionizing	preaching	humility	

God intends for all His children to be like Him—to bear all the fruit of the Spirit (4). Yet, 1 Corinthians 12–14 demonstrates clearly that the Spirit does not give all the gifts to any one person (5). In the list of gifts and fruit, love, patience, goodness, peace, joy, and humility are fruit. I hope you circled all the fruit and none of the gifts.

It's just as well He doesn't give all the gifts to one person. God wants everyone to be completely like Him in character, but not like Him in His abilities. He never intended anyone have infinite wisdom or power. However, He does want His church to have wisdom and power, so He distributed abilities (gifts) among the members to enable the church to accomplish His purposes. No one member can be Godlike in power lest he or she be tempted to use the gifts in accumulating personal authority and prestige. In summary, fruit is for everyone, always; gifts, some to one, some to another. The exciting fact is that every member is given at least one ability to serve God. That includes you!

How the gifts and fruit relate is a mystery. The Bible does not spell it out for us. God sometimes mightily uses a person who is egotistical or quick-tempered. We see another who is very godly in character but is not gifted to serve in any conspicuous way (2 in the previous exercise). How can that be?

🌀 **Of the possible reasons listed below check those you believe help explain the puzzle of why God sometimes gifts those who have major character flaws and gives inconspicuous gifts to those who are godly.**

❑ a. God doesn't necessarily evaluate giftedness as we do.
❑ b. "Fruit" is a more certain measure of spirituality than giftedness.
❑ c. Rewards will be based on how great a gift you had and how prominently you used it.
❑ d. Rewards will be based on faithfulness, a fruit of the Spirit, not on the kind or effectiveness of one's gift.
❑ e. Some giftedness can be natural rather than spiritual.

I would have checked all but c. A person may have great natural ability to lead, sing, preach, teach, or manage money (e). We might be unable to tell if the ability were natural or Spirit-powered. God is the judge (a). He will judge us on the basis of faithfulness, not giftedness (d). Faithfulness will include our use of the gifts the Spirit gives, to be sure, but faithfulness implies our Christlike choices (b).

So, before we explore the contrast between Spirit giftedness and natural talent, go back and check your answers to the first exercise in this lesson. I agreed with statements 2, 3, and 4; not 1 and 5.

Gifts and Talents

First note that both natural ability and spiritual ability are gifts from God. We must use both natural and supernatural gifts for His glory, not our own. To use either natural or spiritual gifts for our own glory is sin. We are responsible to use all that we are to glorify Him. The second thing to note is that the Bible doesn't explain the relationship between natural and spiritual giftedness.

🌀 **In the following list of church activities circle those that people might be successful at without Spirit-enabling if they had great natural ability.**

singing   witnessing   ushering   preaching   teaching

counseling   leading a group   hospitality   managing finances

To one there is given through the Spirit ... to another ... to another ... and to still another.... Are all apostles? Are all prophets? Are all teachers?
—1 Corinthians 12:8-11, 29

171

No two people would have exactly the same answers, perhaps, but I circled all except witnessing. However, even witnessing can be faked if the person has enough personal charisma; but we're talking here of those who truly lead people to Christ. If my opinion is anywhere near correct, the conclusion is scary! Most of the work of the church could be carried on by gifted people without the Spirit of God doing anything.

Some people refer to ministry as either "in the flesh" or "in the Spirit." A difference does exist between the two, but the difference may not be between spiritual gifts and natural abilities. The difference is between depending on self or depending on the Spirit. Evidence of a supernatural touch is one indication that a ministry is accomplished in the Spirit.

For example, Paul wasn't a world-class public speaker–he agreed with the Corinthians in that judgment (1 Cor. 2:1). But when he taught the Bible, lives were transformed. Whether the Spirit merely lifts a natural ability to a higher power we may not know; but if it's a Spirit-gift, there will be the Spirit's miracle touch.

> **Below write your own paraphrase of 1 Corinthians 12:4-7. Give special attention to the term *manifestation*.**

_____

_____

_____

_____

Though the word "manifestation" in our memory verse means "visible evidence" and that is the ultimate proof, we need to exercise two cautions.

- some may have "visible evidence" resulting from strong natural ability, not really the work of the Spirit. For example, the magicians in Pharaoh's court managed to duplicate some of the signs Moses performed (Ex. 7:11), but they certainly did not do them through the power of the Spirit.
- a person may have been given a gift and still experience a lack of evidence because of adverse circumstances. For example, Ezekiel was God's own prophet, but the people were rebels and wouldn't listen (Ezek. 3). Paul was no doubt the greatest of evangelists, but in Lystra they stoned him out of town (Acts 14).

In general, however, if no evidence shows the Spirit at work, if the ministry makes no spiritual impact, we need to ask if the ministry is God's. When I fail to see evidence in my own ministry, I ask myself the following diagnostic questions:

1. Am I Harboring Unconfessed Sin? When I've preached my heart out and lives aren't changed, I first examine myself to see if something in me blocked the flow of the Spirit. Do I have some unconfessed sin, a wrong motivation (wanting "success" for human praise), unbelief (not trusting God to do what only He can do), or lack of prayer preparation? I don't immediately conclude that I don't have the gift or that He hasn't called me after all.

2. Do I Need to Be Persistent? When I felt called to do missionary work, I kept asking God for the gift of evangelism. People came to Christ through my ministry only sporadically, and I longed for the ability to consistently win people to Christ. I'll tell you the outcome in the next unit, but I'll give you the principle here. The principle is to keep asking until you see one of two things: "visible evidence" of the gift you long for, or the assurance that God doesn't intend that gift for you. Stop

When I came to you, brothers, I did not come with eloquence or superior wisdom as I proclaimed to you the testimony about God.
—1 Corinthians 2:1

There are different kinds of gifts, but the same Spirit. There are different kinds of service, but the same Lord. There are different kinds of working, but the same God works all of them in all men.
Now to each one the manifestation of the Spirit is given for the common good.
—1 Corinthians 12:4-7

asking only when God shows you that the gift is not for you.

3. Am I in the Right Place? In Japan, we discovered that we were ministering in a very unresponsive area. We asked God if there should be a change of location to a place or people who would respond. This is what Paul did more than once. (See Acts 13:46 for example.)

4. Is God Vindicating Himself? Perhaps, on the other hand, God intends a gifted person to stand firm when there is no "fruit" or outward result, as His vindication among an unresponsive people (as in Ezekiel's case).

You can see from the above examples that a legitimate gift may be without "visible evidence" in some situations. But in general we distinguish between natural ability and supernatural ability by the outcome of the ministry.

GIFTS AND OFFICES

Just because a person is appointed or elected to an office is no guarantee he or she has the Spirit-given abilities needed for that office.

> Read the list of qualifications for office in 1 Timothy 3:2-10 that appears in the margin. Below list qualifications that seem to be fruit of the Spirit and those which seem to require gifts of the Spirit.

Fruit of the Spirit   *Gifts of the Spirit*

_____   _____

_____   _____

_____   _____

_____   _____

_____   _____

You probably came up with a short list on gifts required to serve. Actually, the only one definite ability is to teach the Bible with faithfulness. A couple of others might require a spiritual gift: to be hospitable and a good manager. The focus seems to be more on character than giftedness. To have Paul's designated gifts does not mean a person must be chosen for office, but no one should be given an office without the gifts Paul lists as qualifications.

> The most exciting thing about the gifts of the Spirit is that He has given some ability to serve God to every Christian. List the gift(s) you have or you believe you may have. If you aren't sure, then list any job(s) you do reasonably well.

_____

_____

Are there any additional gifts you would like to have, any role in the church you aspire to? If so, in our next lessons we'll find out how to discover and develop those gifts.

Then Paul and Barnabas answered them boldly: "We had to speak the word of God to you first. Since you reject it and do not consider yourselves worthy of eternal life, we now turn to the Gentiles."
—Acts 13:46

Now the overseer must be above reproach, the husband of but one wife, temperate, self-controlled, respectable, hospitable, able to teach, not given to drunkenness, not violent but gentle, not quarrelsome, not a lover of money. He must manage his own family well and see that his children obey him with proper respect. (If anyone does not know how to manage his own family, how can he take care of God's church?) He must not be a recent convert, or he may become conceited and fall under the same judgment as the devil. He must also have a good reputation with outsiders, so that he will not fall into disgrace and into the devil's trap.

Deacons, likewise, are to be men worthy of respect, sincere, not indulging in much wine, and not pursuing dishonest gain. They must keep hold of the deep truths of the faith with a clear conscience. They must first be tested; and then if there is nothing against them, let them serve as deacons.
—1 Timothy 3:2-10

DEFINITIONS: WHAT IS A GIFT?

The New Testament contains several lists of gifts or abilities given by the Spirit to do some work for God in the church or in the world.

Romans 12:6-8	*1 Corinthians 12*	*Ephesians 4*	*1 Peter 4:10-11*
prophesy	wisdom	apostleship	various unnamed
service	knowledge	prophecy	speaking
teaching	faith	evangelism	serving
encouraging	healing	pastoring	
giving	miracles	teaching	
leading	prophecy		
showing mercy	discernment of spirits		
	tongues		
	interpretation of tongues		
	apostleship		
	teaching		
	helping others		
	administration		

Some gifts clearly reveal themselves by the results of their use. The name explains the meaning. Others are not that clear, so it's difficult to decide whether or not you have that gift.

> In the gift lists you just read, check the words you think represent gifts that are easily recognized. Beside the gifts you check, state the outcome you would expect if a person had the gift.

DEFINING THE GIFTS

The following gifts seem to have clear outcomes:

1. Teaching may be clear, but only if we define the outcome as we did in the last lesson: a person explains the Bible and spiritual truth in such a way that lives are changed.

2. Healing would seem clear since a sick person would have to get well. I've personally experienced healing. What the doctors described as an incurable disease kept me from becoming a missionary. A friend came and prayed for me, and that night my pain left me forever! To my knowledge, that's the only time that friend saw such dramatic results from his prayers. He could hardly be said to have the gift of healing. Jesus healed everyone who came to Him. No contemporary healer can match that. Still, if people are consistently healed through the prayers of a particular person, I would be comfortable in saying that person has a gift of healing.

3. Evangelism also seems clear. If people routinely come to Christ through a person's witness, that would be the sign of God at work. Such a person could surely be said to have the gift of evangelism.

These three are the only gifts I believe have clear outcomes: teaching, healing, and evangelism. You may have put others, such as tongues or interpretation. Godly people disagree on exactly what those gifts are and how you can tell if you or some-one else has them. I put on my list only those spiritual gifts in which the meaning is evident by the word used to identify the gift.

You may have included prophecy. If by prophecy you mean prediction, that would be clear and the person with such a gift could be easily spotted–predictions would come true. But prediction is only one use of the term in Scripture and, in fact, other uses are more prominent. Basically, a prophet was a Spirit-directed spokesperson for God. Sometimes prophets foretold future events, but that was not the defining activity.

In the Old Testament, musicians–even instrumentalists–were in the order of the prophets (1 Chron. 25:1-3). How could that be? No prediction there, not even words! But if they officially represented God in leading His people in worship, that was considered prophecy. The Scripture does not clearly define what is and what is not included in the gift of prophecy.

Spirit-anointed preaching might be one kind of prophecy, for example. I'm sure many in our day are authoritative spokespersons for God. But since Scripture is not clear, I'll not be dogmatic about all that prophecy might mean.

IMPORTANCE OF EACH GIFT

Are all the gifts of equal importance, or are some more important than others? Remember how the young lady asked, "Important for what?"

1. First consider how the gifts are important for you.

> **Which of those gifts listed at the beginning of day 2–and especially those that are fairly clear in their meaning–are most important to you personally?**

_____

Let me guess. You listed those you have or those you would like to have, right? For you personally, the most important gift is the one God has for you; and the most important thing for you is to find that gift or pattern of gifts and develop them to the maximum.

2. The gifts are also important for the church.

> **Which of the gifts from the lists do you consider the most important for your church?**

_____

_____

You may have given any number of good answers. You could even have answered *all the above*! Paul seems to be saying the Spirit puts into each church all the gifts (or gifted people) needed to accomplish His purposes in and through that church. Members should function in the way He designs. In most churches about 15 percent of the members try to fulfill the functions of the whole body. No wonder the body is handicapped!

The Spirit's will for the church is for every member to function as designed, because every member is needed to accomplish His purposes. All members can function effectively only when they are fully using their gifts.

David... set apart for the service certain of the sons of Asaph, and of Heman, and of Jeduthum, who should prophesy with harps, with stringed instruments, and with cymbals... who prophesied in giving thanks and praising Jehovah.
—1 Chronicles 25:1, 3 (ASV)

In the church God has appointed first of all apostles, second prophets, third teachers, then workers of miracles, also those having gifts of healing, those able to help others, those with gifts of administration, and those speaking in different kinds of tongues.
—1 Corinthians 12:28

Eagerly desire the greater gifts. And now I will show you the most excellent way.
—1 Corinthians 12:31

3. The gifts are important to God.

Surely all gifts are of equal importance to Him? Careful! The central purpose of 1 Corinthians 12–14 is to get the church to understand that gifts are not all of equal importance for accomplishing God's will. Some gifts are less important. The church at Corinth was focusing on one of those less-important gifts (speaking in tongues).

Furthermore, the church at Corinth should have focused on some very important gifts, but they didn't—gifts like apostle, prophet, teacher. Paul even numbered them 1, 2, and 3 (1 Cor. 12:28), so they wouldn't miss the point. He doesn't continue his numbering system beyond those three, so they may just be representative. But these three give a hint as to what Paul considers more important—roles which seem to have the greatest impact for God's purposes in the church and in the world. My personal definition of his top three would be pioneer missionary evangelist (apostle), power-filled preaching (prophesy), and spirit-anointed teaching. These three represent important tasks indeed.

If you read chapters 12–14 of 1 Corinthians in a hurry, you may conclude that Paul is contrasting lower gifts with the highest gift, love. If you draw that conclusion, you will miss the point.

Paul is teaching the people at Corinth about spiritual gifts, and having exhorted them to seek the higher ones, he pauses for a mid-course correction. "Don't get me wrong," he says. "These gifts, even the more important ones, aren't the most important thing. Love is most important." Love isn't a "gift" in the sense Paul is talking about; he calls it a "way." "I'll show you an even better way"—better than the best gift (see 1 Cor. 12:31 in the margin).

Elsewhere Paul describes love as the fruit of the Spirit. So let's not confuse fruit with gifts. Gifts are Spirit-given abilities; fruit represents Spirit-developed character. Paul's command in verse 31 is to desire Spirit-given abilities to serve God, but his teaching in all of chapter 13 is that love is more important than any gift.

The importance of a gift does not imply that one gift is more spiritual than another. Spiritual has to do with fruit of the Spirit, likeness to Jesus, as Paul concludes in 1 Corinthians 13. Also, importance does not equal greater reward. Reward is based on faithfulness, not outward results.

To accomplish God's mission on earth, however, some gifts are of greater importance than others. For 12 years I was a pioneer missionary evangelist. My job was starting churches, a very high calling according to Paul.

Today I'm primarily a homemaker, which calls more for fruit than for gifts. My Spirit-given gifts have a limited outlet through some writing and speaking. But I'm not claiming that my role in life is as important as anyone else's. My calling cannot compare with that of others in terms of eternal impact. God only expects that we be faithful to our own calling. Then the whole body can function smoothly. In turn, we will find personal fulfillment, and God will be pleased.

Although we've learned something about what the gifts are by examining the biblical lists of gifts, apparently the Holy Spirit didn't intend to give a clear-cut list of specific job descriptions. Perhaps He intended for us to see what needs doing and trust Him to provide people with the abilities needed to do it. We'll examine that possibility in tomorrow's lesson.

Use the two memory verses for this unit as the basis for a time of prayer. Thank God for making the body fit together—each member with the appropriate gift(s). Ask the Spirit to help you rejoice in the gifts of others. Express to Him your desire to serve with maximum impact through the gifts He supplies.

DAY 3

FINDING MY ROLE IN THE CHURCH

We had just finished a faculty workshop on helping students identify their gifts when Kenneth Kantzer, distinguished theologian, seminary leader, and former editor of *Christianity Today*, came to the microphone. "I've never known what my gift is," he said, to our astonishment. "All my life I've seen a need, been asked to fill it, and trusted the Holy Spirit to enable me to do it."

Maybe Kenneth is on to something. As we've worked through possible definitions of spiritual gifts you may have been frustrated that they are not more precise, especially if I questioned your favorite gift definition. I felt that way for years. I read books filled with precise definitions and self-evaluating check-lists, searching for my personal gift. Could I ever really know my specific gift for sure?

I finally understood that the Scripture did not define the gifts precisely, and that imprecision was not by accident. I suddenly felt truly liberated. I recognized that I should focus on the tasks that needed to be done rather than worrying about my gifts or lack of them.

We should ask God for the abilities necessary to accomplish what He has clearly told us are His purposes for the church. We can leave the combination of abilities, natural and supernatural, to the Holy Spirit to decide—"as he determines" (1 Cor. 12:11). We can tell when that custom-designed pattern of gifts is from Him: the outcome will demonstrate the supernatural power of God.

TASK-RELATED GIFT DEFINITIONS

I conclude that we should focus more on roles for another reason. Each of the biblical gift lists are different. No one particular gift appears in all of them. Teaching and prophesy appear in three, apostle shows up in two, and the others occur only once. None of the lists is exhaustive; they're just representative or suggestive.

Perhaps other gifts are not listed. Tasks may need to be done in your church which Paul didn't include in any of his lists. Can you think of any?

_____

_____

You probably listed music, a major ministry of the church. If your church uses drama, you surely listed that; you don't want your dramatic efforts to be purely human talent. You want the strong anointing of the Spirit to produce eternal outcomes. You may have listed other activities that don't clearly fit under any of Paul's categories, for example, children's work. Many other activities might either be listed as separate gifts or be combined as forms of "teaching" or "prophetic proclamation." Writing, for example, might fit under one of those.

You may have listed counseling. I would consider that the activity of one gifted to "pastor," which literally means "shepherd." The Bible doesn't define "pastor." Today we use it as the over-arching identification of the chief church leader, and certainly the shepherd was called to lead the flock. But the original idea was more like what today we call discipling, counseling, or nurturing. "Encouragement" in the Romans list of gifts might fit here, too.

All these are the work of one and the same Spirit, and he gives them to each one, just as he determines.
—1 Corinthians 12:11

177

Many Christians are like Barnabas, good at "coming alongside" and helping others through the tough times. The ancients called counseling the "cure of souls." Professional counselors who have the gift of curing the whole soul, who see supernatural results in the counseling process, might be said to have the gift of pastoring. If the Spirit anoints the professional's natural talent and training, he or she can be especially effective in healing the soul.

Other possibilities exist for linking contemporary tasks with biblical gifts. Leading, administration, wisdom, discernment, or helps, for example, are capable of wide application. Just be sure not to be too dogmatic in claiming that your understanding of a gift name is the only meaning it could have. Always identify the touch of the Spirit by spiritual outcomes.

DEFINING GIFT BY PURPOSE OF THE CHURCH

Remember the purposes of the church you studied in unit 6? The 5 purposes are united worship, fellowship, discipleship, ministry, and evangelism. Let's think about how these five purposes of the church can help you identify and use your spiritual giftedness.

The Holy Spirit gives gifts or abilities so that the purposes of the church may be fulfilled. Think about how the spiritual gifts empower the church to fulfill its purposes. Rather than using the extensive lists as they appear in the Bible, unexplained, let me consolidate and describe some of the key gifts Scripture points toward—abilities clearly needed to fulfill the purposes of the church.

My description of eight key spiritual gifts includes the abilities to:
1. teach the Bible in such a way that lives are changed
2. win people to faith
3. help the physical and social needs of the community in such a way that people are drawn to God
4. discern a person's spiritual need and give wise counsel in such a way that he grows spiritually.
5. lead people to worship in spirit and in truth
6. proclaim (preach) God's truth with life-changing authority
7. understand the way God wants the church to go and get people to go that direction
8. help in practical ways like financial management, feeding people, seeing needs and meeting them

On the following chart, write the number of the Spirit-given ability that could help fulfill each of the purposes of the church after the appropriate purpose. You may use a gift (Spirit-given ability) in more than one place on the chart.

Purposes of the Church		Gifts That Contribute to the Purpose
worship	(united praise, adoration, thanksgiving)	_____
fellowship	(caring for one another, family solidarity)	_____
discipleship	(teaching, accountability/discipline)	_____
ministry	(to a hurting community outside the church)	_____
evangelism	(bringing people to a conversion decision)	_____

Not everyone will connect the same gifts with a given purpose of the church, but here are my choices. I put the gifts of preaching, leadership, and administration (6,7,8) by all the purposes since those are gifts needed to accomplish the over-all purposes of the church. The worship purpose of the church obviously fits gift number 5–this could include all the music ministry of the church, for example.

I left fellowship off the list. Though some people seem to be more gifted at caring than others, the whole family shares the responsibility to care lovingly for the emotional, physical, material, and spiritual needs of the other members. Fellowship seems to be fulfilled more by people bearing the fruit of the Spirit than by any special giftedness.

I included teaching (1) and counseling (biblical pastoring) (4) as gifts that especially advance personal discipleship. Ministry in the way we use it here refers to those who are called to minister to the needs of the surrounding community (3). Though all participate in evangelism through faithful witness, some are effective in "closing," consistently winning others to faith (2).

Look back to the list. Put an asterisk (*) by each of the gifts you think you have or might have.

Which of the purposes are most strongly fulfilled in your church?

_____

_____

_____

Which purposes are not fulfilled as well as you feel they should be?

_____

_____

How might your gift help with the fulfillment of any of the purposes of the church, especially those you identified as in need of strengthening?

_____

_____

Is God calling you to seek some gift to help fulfill the purposes of the church? There may be other roles in your church that don't easily fit into the above categories. If you have a gift or desire a gift that could be used in that way, be sure to add it to your lists above.

If you have a strong desire to see some of the gifts used more in your church, this would be an excellent topic to discuss in your next group meeting.

Do you have a strong desire to be used more than you have been? Paul says to "earnestly desire" the higher gifts. That's a command! So if you don't feel strongly about something you'd like to accomplish for God, now is the time to pause and ask God to give you such a holy desire. If you already have a longing for a particular gift, pause now and ask God for it! Write out your petition in your journal.

On day 2 we looked at the gifts of the Spirit as listed in Scripture, and in this lesson we looked at the gifts needed to fulfill the purposes of the church. You might call the latter "definition by job description." Another essential way to identify your gift is to try it out! Since that is also the basic way to develop your gift, we'll consider using your gift in the next lesson.

DAY 4

DEVELOPING MY GIFT

Using the ability God gives you has a dual purpose: to prove what the gift is and then to develop it. Though most of today's lesson is devoted to developing your gift, we look first at getting to work—a way of confirming your gift.

DISCERNING YOUR GIFT BY INVOLVEMENT

The churches we started in Japan were composed of people who had known nothing of the gospel and, of course, nothing of what a church is supposed to be. We assumed that these newborn Christians would be given abilities to serve God, just as the Spirit promised.

We gave everyone a job. We even gave unconverted regular attenders a job—like cleaning up before and after services or serving tea and rice crackers. From the outset they felt part of us, and people were born into the family serving. They assumed that to be a Christian meant to participate in God's work. At first the assignments were housekeeping, nothing that would test one's spiritual giftedness, but would test one's availability and heart for serving the rest of the family.

Here is a list of jobs we gave. Number them 1-10 in order of spiritual responsibility, beginning with the task requiring the least supernatural enabling.

____ straighten shoes in the vestibule where they were left when entering
____ preach to Christians
____ teach a Sunday School class
____ serve rice crackers and tea
____ give a testimony at an evangelistic meeting
____ preach to non-Christians
____ teach Sunday School teachers
____ lead the meeting
____ play the electronic organ
____ greet and seat guests

Your order might be different from mine, but here's the way we did it: first, the tasks not requiring a supernatural touch, like cleaning and serving; then, greeting and seating guests; next, a prepared testimony; after that, leading a meeting or playing the organ; then, teaching Sunday School; next, preaching to non-Christians; then, preaching to Christians; and finally, teaching other teachers. We trained and coached each believer until he or she seemed ready for the next assignment, stopping when one wanted to stop or the leaders in the church felt one was not yet gifted for the next assignment.

There are two reasons for this approach. First, how do you know whether you have a gift or would be given a gift till you try it out? Second, giftedness should be confirmed by the church. A man once wrote me from across the continent, asking for help. He was an evangelist, he said, but the church wouldn't recognize him. Could I write a letter of endorsement so that he could get meetings? I had two problems with his request. If a person is truly gifted in evangelism, that is self-evident. But there's a deeper problem. I didn't know the man, his character, how he went about evangelizing, what the results were. He is accountable to his church, not to me. The church must confirm a person's gifts.

Does your church have a systematic plan for helping people discover their gifts? ❑ Yes ❑ No

Is every member expected to serve in some capacity? ❑ Yes ❑ No

Are people encouraged to try out new roles and use their abilities to the maximum? ❑ Yes ❑ No

If the answer to any of these questions is no, what changes need to be made?

_____

_____

Not only must the gift be confirmed by the church, it ought to be sought in the context of the church to begin with. If God doesn't intend for me the gift I aim for, the church leadership should help me reach that conclusion.

Once I've identified the gift I have or the gift I'd like to have, or once I've identified the job I'd like to do, I must get to work. I must develop the abilities necessary to do that job effectively. The church's role is to help me identify the role I should pursue, free me to do it, and help me grow in it.

DEVELOPING MY GIFT

Paul told Timothy, "Do not neglect your gift.... Be diligent in these matters; give yourself wholly to them, so that everyone may see your progress" (1 Tim. 4:14-15). In our churches in Tsuchiura, Japan, we used all the training methods we'll study in this lesson and the result was that we started five churches in five years. We could never have done that if the "professional," in this case the missionary, had to do all the important functions of the church. Because the people were freed up to use their Spirit-distributed abilities, I concentrated my energies on equipping them for their ministries (Eph. 4:11-12). We could move forward simultaneously in every outlying community. Here's the strategy we used—

1. Practice. We've seen how getting to work on a job is the way to confirm as well as develop your gift. If pupils throw spitwads the first day in class, don't conclude you're not called to teach! Work at it. The beauty of getting involved is that working in a job not only helps identify a gift, it's the only way to develop that gift.

Contrary to the proverb, however, practice doesn't always make perfect. In fact, it can make very imperfect—consolidating all the bad habits we practice. We need someone who has gone on before and knows how the job should be done to come alongside and help us grow. Therefore, in addition to practice we need to move to the next step.

2. Apprentice/Mentor. Dan was a handsome people-person with a gifted wife. He had just been called to his first assignment after graduation— associate pastor of a prestigious old church. He was excited because the senior pastor was a remarkably successful leader, and Dan intended to learn all he could.

Dan soon approached his boss, requesting this distinguished senior pastor to help him discover and develop his gifts. The pastor—a self-starting, can-do man who never asked anyone for help—said, "Who do you think I am? The Holy Spirit?" Crushed, Dan limped along for a few months, dropped out, and has been in construction work for the last 25 years. I've often wondered: if Dan had encountered a true mentor, would he have been building the church all these years?

If your church has a structure where everyone has a mentor, or if someone has reached out to help you grow in your ministry, how blessed you are! But if not, you can do the reaching out. Ask for feedback on your performance, for example. Have the best teacher you know sit in on the class you teach and talk with you informally afterwards. You have to really want candid responses, and you have to let them know that; or the exercise will be a waste of your time and theirs.

Another way to get feedback is to distribute questionnaires to those who see you in action; the one to whom you are responsible, the students in your class, anyone whose judgment might be helpful.

> Is there someone you would like to mentor you? Why not talk over the possibilities with him or her?

> If you don't feel competent to develop an evaluation checklist for a job you're doing, could someone in the church help you develop such a questionnaire or checklist? Why not give him or her a call today?

You can take the initiative and recruit your own mentor, but the best way is for the church to provide mentors to apprentice everyone who begins a new ministry.

> You are not alone in needing a mentor. Is there someone you could help in developing his or her gift? Pause now and pray for wisdom as to the best way to feel that person out and see whether he or she would like such a relationship.

> Perhaps God would use you in an even larger role. If you are in a leadership role in the church, what steps could you take to get the church into a mentoring mode?

_____

_____

_____

_____

3. Literature and Media. In Japan we gave everyone, along with the job, a page of simple instructions on how to do that job. Today churches are rich in resources: teachers' manuals or how-to books on virtually every job in the church. For some of the key roles of service, videotapes or a series of audiotapes are produced by people who are experts in that role.

> Do you know how to find these resources? If not, who is the most likely person in your church to know about such things?

_____

Consider checking with your church media-librarian, a pastor, or other church leader. Make an appointment to learn more about available resources. If resources aren't available in your church, contact your local Christian bookstore.

4. Special Training Classes. In Japan we opened a mini-Bible college on Tuesday nights to train people who were serving or wanted to serve in spiritual ministry. We taught new believers teaching methods, preaching, principles of Bible interpretation, Bible survey, church history, theology, various Bible book studies, principles of Christian ministry, and evangelism.

Circle any of the courses above that would be helpful in your church. Add any others you think are needed.

---

5. Inter-church Seminars. Our mini-Bible college was an inter-church project and people came from a distance to attend. Today one of the most popular means of learning is through special training events. In many areas churches or groups of churches sponsor seminars on Christian education, counseling, witnessing, apologetics, family life, political action, preaching, prayer, missions—you name it. World famous teachers lecture; specialists offer workshops on every conceivable related topic.

Does your church budget include funds for key people to attend such conferences? ❑ Yes ❑ No

Have individuals or groups from your church attended such, either as a representative of your church or independently? ❑ Yes ❑ No

Which kinds of seminars could you encourage your church leadership to consider making a major part of the church program?

---

6. Formal Training. Formal training is available for those who have grown beyond what the local church offers or who feel the need of intensive study. From our fledgling churches in Japan more than half a dozen went away to prepare for full-time ministry and three have become pastors with a nationwide impact. They came from churches which at the time totaled less than 100 members!

In America today increasing numbers of mature adults are choosing to enroll in formal Christian education. Some Bible colleges (undergraduate) and seminaries (for college graduates) have one-year introductory courses to give a broad overview of biblical studies. The full program is available for those who feel the Spirit's drawing toward vocational Christian ministry. Furthermore, seminaries and Bible colleges offer studies in locations away from their home campus—perhaps near you—and a few have a highly developed home-study curriculum.

You may have already known about most or all these possibilities for developing your gift. I've outlined briefly the possibilities for a specific purpose. Earlier this week you identified the gift or gifts you already are using and the gift or pattern of abilities you'd like to have. Do you have a desire to serve God in a particular way beyond what you are now doing?

⊚ It's time to develop a personal plan for developing your gift. Would you like to try any of the strategies I've suggested? Or maybe you know of other methods? In the list below, write out an action plan for any you choose:

Method to develop my gift	*Action plan*
1. Practice: try a new job	_____
2. Apprentice-mentor	_____
3. Literature/media	_____
4. Training classes	_____
5. Inter-church seminars	_____
6. Formal training	_____
7. Other: _____	_____

⊚ Thank God that the Spirit has a particular calling custom designed just for you. Then commit yourself to Him for serious action toward maximizing your potential, and ask Him for wisdom and fortitude in carrying out that plan.

DAY 5

DESIRING THE BEST

⊚ Write out your memory verses below. Underline the words that encourage you to seek a gift you may not now have.

_____

_____

_____

First Corinthians 12:31 says, "Eagerly desire the greater gifts." Today we'll examine three important things about this crucial command. It is an active command, a continuous action command, and a command for the whole church.

1. AN ACTIVE VERB

The command to "eagerly desire" is not a description of the feeling you have when you see a luscious slice of pizza on a television commercial. The word Paul used carries the concept of action. We would say "get with it!" If you pick up the phone and order that pizza, then you've "eagerly desired."

My mother wanted me to eagerly desire service for God, but I didn't. I yielded my life to God, but it was a passive yielding. I wasn't excited about it. "God, you shove and I'll move," was my mode. I didn't add: "but I won't like it, I'm sure," even though that's the way I felt most of the time.

I wasn't obeying the command, I wasn't eagerly desiring any gift. But I was involved. Mother saw to that. That's what Sunday afternoons were for. She arranged (I later learned) to have college students invite me to go with them in their ministry to housing developments, for example. Flattered by the attention, I went with them. I even helped start a little country church one year–I hauled wood for the pot-bellied stove in that one-room schoolhouse. Mother was my secret mentor, helping me discover my spiritual gifts! But I still wasn't desiring anything.

When I was 18, however, the desire began to stir. In fact, I began to desire most earnestly that my life should count to the maximum for what God is up to in this world. That meant getting involved. I joined other young men in preaching on the street corner. Folks didn't stop much, so we took up preaching in jail. No one walked away! I began to obey the command to "get with it."

You may not have desired earnestly the jobs you've held in church. You may have been drafted, in fact, like my mother drafted me. But whether you volunteered or were recruited, in the margin list every job you've held in the church or in ministry outside the church.

Now go back and circle any jobs that have really excited you. Does your effectiveness or excitement about any of those point to the possibility of your being used in a larger way, maybe even some other more important role? If so, name the larger ministry to which you aspire.

_____

2. SEEK AND KEEP ON SEEKING
The command to seek earnestly is not only an active verb. It also describes a continuous action. It means, "seek and keep on seeking."

Reflect again on your church and list below some purpose of the church that's not being strongly fulfilled. Is something lacking that burdens you greatly?

_____

_____

Paul says to eagerly desire those gifts–for your church and, perhaps, for yourself. Are you obeying the command? Are you praying for those needs to be met? Is the church praying?

Some say of spiritual gifts: "It's a gift, so don't ask for it." That's a strange way of thinking. What of salvation—is that a gift? Did you ask for it? Paul commands us to seek the greater gifts! To obey that command we will ask God for the gift. We may ask for ourselves or for someone in the church. We will do so eagerly, and we will keep asking. The form of the verb Paul uses is not a one-time request; it means to keep on desiring. Continue in persistent prayer until God gives the answer!

Ministry jobs I have held:

_____

_____

_____

_____

_____

For example, is your church growing in numbers, at least 5 percent a year in baptisms of adult converts? If not, what gift does the church need?

_____

Is the church pleading with God for the gift of evangelism?

Or perhaps your concern is the lack of spiritual growth. Once a person joins the church, nothing much seems to happen. Church members aren't spiraling up. What gifts are needed?

_____

Many gifts would help, no doubt, but how about Spirit-anointed teachers or counselors?

Is the church harassed with gossip, squabbles, or in danger of splitting? Is it stuck in the rut of some worn-out tradition? What Spirit-gifted person is needed?

_____

You may need a courageous prophet or the dynamism of Spirit-anointed leadership. Are you asking God for that? Eagerly? Persistently?

3. UNITED PRAYER

To obey the command to "eagerly desire," we must commit ourselves to prayer for the gifts needed to meet the needs of our church. But solo praying won't do. The church as a whole must obey the command. The verb Paul uses is in the plural—"you all eagerly desire."

If you can't inspire the church as a whole to focus on this kind of praying, some smaller prayer group could include this request on a regular basis. If not, perhaps you and your prayer partner could begin to focus on asking for the gifts the Spirit wants to give. Such a prayer meeting must not be a thinly veiled invitation to criticism. Don't dwell on the negative aspects of the church. The prayer must spring from eager desire for God's highest and best.

What is your action plan to involve others in desiring earnestly the needed gifts?

Group	*Action plan*
The church as a whole	_____
	_____
A small group within the church	_____
	_____
You and a prayer partner	_____

HEART TROUBLE

Translators have chosen various expressions in English to translate *eagerly desire*–
- "covet earnestly" (KJV)
- "set your hearts on" (GNB)
- "try your best" (TLB)
- "try to have" (Beck)
- "earnestly desire" (RSV).

This emotional desire for a gift to serve embodies a deep longing that moves us to action. I began to experience such a desire in my late teens. I started to feel a compelling desire to count for God. I wanted every possible gift and opportunity the Spirit would give to advance the cause of the gospel. Until then I didn't see the needs or opportunities or, even if I did see them, I didn't care that much.

Notice that Paul doesn't say, "wait around till the desire hits you." Paul gives a command: set your heart on that gift that is so desperately needed by your church or by a dying world. "Take the initiative," says Paul. Go for it! The place to begin may be with your desire. Instead of asking for a particular ability, as I have often suggested in this unit, perhaps the request should be for the Spirit to ignite a great flame of desire in your heart. Ask Him to give you a passion for Him and a passion for people to know Him.

◎ **Stop now and tell God your heart's desire. If you lack a passion to serve Him, commit to keep on asking every day until He lights the fire or gives the gift.**

◎ **Review your Scripture memory verses for this week and for the previous weeks of your study.**

◎ **By way of review, let's try a true/false quiz on the gifts of the Spirit:**

_____ 1. It's OK to be ambitious for greater usefulness.
_____ 2. Only the church as a whole should seek gifts, not an individual.
_____ 3. Gifts of the Spirit are just as important as fruit of the Spirit.
_____ 4. Natural abilities can be used by God to accomplish spiritual good.
_____ 5. No connection exists between a gift and an office.
_____ 6. Every Christian is given at least one ability.
_____ 7. The Bible lists all the gifts available.
_____ 8. What the Bible means by some gifts is unclear.
_____ 9. The purposes of the church may give a hint of some gifts needed which aren't listed in the Bible.
_____ 10. Trying out a job can help you identify your gift and develop it.
_____ 11. A church should help identify each member's gift and provide opportunity for him or her to fully use it, but primary responsiblity for developing the gift is up to the individual.
_____ 12. To "eagerly desire" means to deeply care about the matter, to persistently pray for, get involved.

How exciting! The Spirit plans to use you in God's service more than you ever dreamed possible. And what a treasure hunt–to discover the gifts He has for you! What a privilege, too. Do you ever feel the wonder of God's amazing plan–to accomplish His purposes in the world through mere mortals like you and me? And what about the exhilaration of cooperating with the Spirit in developing and using your gifts to the maximum? Isn't it time to tell God how much you appreciate Him? Do it now!

My answers to the activity are 1-T; 2-F; 3-F; 4-T; 5-F; 6-T; 7-F; 8-T; 9-T; 10-T; 11-T; 12-T. If you missed any, review that section of unit 10 until you understand the issue involved.

Giftedness is great, but never forget something greater—fruit. How do the two relate? Both are the work of the Spirit. Both represent a part of His intentions for every believer. But a difference between fruit and gifts exists; the Spirit longs to give all the fruit to all believers in maximum measure, while the gifts He distributes among believers. Some receive greater gifts, some lesser. Great fruit without great gifts can bring great glory to God, but great gifts without great fruit clouds, perhaps even eclipses, His glory. When a godly person is also gifted, however, what glory to God! And that's why we devote two units (10 and 11) to the Spirit's supernatural touch in our ability to serve God and His church.

Conclude this week's study with a time of prayer. You may want to spend more time than usual in prayer. One way to pray about what we've been studying is to divide your prayer time into short segments.

1. Tell God how thrilled you are with the incredible plan He has to use you to accomplish His purposes.

2. If you know what role He has for you in the church, or you're aware of some ability the Spirit has given you, thank Him for that and offer it back to Him to use exclusively for His glory.

3. If you have the desire for greater usefulness in the abilities you do have or for some gift you don't have, spend some time asking God for the gift (1 Cor. 12:31). Remember the verb in 1 Corinthians 12:31 means to ask and keep on asking. If your heart is burdened to serve, don't stop with a single request. Make the request a matter of regular prayer until God answers yes or no.

4. If you don't feel any burning desire to do something important for His kingdom, ask Him to ignite a fire in your spirit.

5. Ask God to protect you from ever taking credit for what He accomplishes through you. Tell Him how you long for godliness above any gift, that He is your greatest joy. "Delight yourself in the Lord and he will give you the desires of your heart" (Ps. 37:4).

6. Pray for your church, appealing to God especially for gifted people to meet the specific needs you sense.

Be sure to conclude your prayer time with thanksgiving for the great plan the Spirit has to distribute His power among all believers so they may accomplish His purposes.

UNIT 11
POWER TO CHANGE THE WORLD

The students at a leading evangelical seminary wanted to examine the question: What is the place of world evangelism in the life of a Christian and in the life of a church? They wanted to determine what the Bible says about the issue. Being seminarians, they staged a debate. They invited the most influential man in world missions at that time, Donald McGavran.

McGavran said, "Missions is a most important purpose of the church." After the meeting I approached him, "Dr. McGavran, the last time I heard you speak you said it was the most important task of the church. Which is it, 'a' or 'the'?"

"Well," he said, "if it's 'the' purpose, that includes 'a'; and some audiences aren't ready to call it the purpose of the church." He obviously ranked world evangelism near the top of his agenda of what the church is about.

On the other side of the debate was a leading evangelical theologian. The task of a theologian is to organize biblical truth in logical order. Most theologians consider missions part of the church history department or the practical theology division along with subjects like Christian education. They usually do not consider missions a proper subject for theology.

Before the debate began, the theologian said, "Dr. McGavran, before we begin I just want you to know that I believe in missions. It's even in my theological system. It's point number D-12 in my theology." By the designation D-12 he meant that missions was a part of the outline but not a central part. It was simply lost in the list.

The theologian's statement set the stage, because missions was clearly A-1 in McGavran's theology. After the debate the theologian said, "Dr. McGavran, you're very persuasive and I admire you and your work. But I want you to know that missions is still point number D-12 in my theological system."

For most evangelical churches in America, world missions is point D-12 in the church program or off their agenda altogether. What about the handful that are committed to world evangelism? Are they misguided, or are they merely obedient to the Lord of the church? Finding an answer to that critical question is the goal of this unit.

Our memory verse gives us a hint. When the Holy Spirit was given, nothing was said of all the glorious truths we've been studying about. The initial emphasis in Scripture was not how He enables us to spiral up into likeness to Christ. The focus was not about teaching us to be free and fulfilled. The arrival of the Holy Spirit stressed reaching a lost world.

Unit Memory Verse
You will receive power when the Holy Spirit comes on you;
and you will be my witnesses in Jerusalem, and in all Judea and Samaria,
and to the ends of the earth.—Acts 1:8

> **How important to God is world evangelization?**
> **How will living in the Spirit impact my concern for missions?**
> **What can I use as a measure of my concern and commitment?**

SEEING IT GOD'S WAY

More important than where we stand in a debate on world evangelism is to discover where God stands! When we examine Scripture, we find that—

- God's character makes world evangelism inevitable.
- God's activity proves His heart is passionate for the world to know Him.
- God's promises assure a successful conclusion to His plan.
- God's command means we must think as He thinks and act as He acts.

In this lesson we want to get the big picture, reviewing Scripture from beginning to end to see what God considers most important.

GOD'S CHARACTER

What characteristic of God do you like best? _____

You may agree with John the apostle. He says that a certain characteristic of God is so central to His nature that you could even say He is that attribute (1 John 4:8). John so wanted to get the point across that he repeated the same words a few verses later: "God is love" (1 John 4:16). God didn't create love to give His creatures something to aim at. He is love by nature. As a result the Spirit created humans in the image of God, so that He could love them and be loved by them.

Creating humans with the power to choose was a risky proposition. We might not return His love. People might choose to walk away from a loving relationship. They might even defy that love—which is just what our first parents did, and every son and daughter of Adam since. But that didn't change God's character. He continued to so love the world that He gave His own Son to buy us back (John 3:16). That's the express purpose for His invasion of our humanity—to seek and to save the lost (Matt. 18:11).

If love was the the reason for Jesus' first coming, love is also the reason He has not come again. People keep resisting God's loving advances to them; and it breaks His heart. The broken-hearted God delays His coming because He doesn't want anyone to perish (2 Pet. 3:9). Consider the tension in the loving heart of God: longing to return to embrace His bride, the church; but at the same time, distressed over the many who are lost.

How many? Just a number doesn't reach our hearts, since we don't have the capacity to love each one as God does. But here's a statistic that should snap into focus what distresses God: the population explosion is so great that one demographer concluded more people now live than all who have lived and already died.

The Lord is not slow in keeping his promise, as some understand slowness. He is patient with you, not wanting anyone to perish, but everyone to come to repentance.
—2 Peter 3:9

How many people need Jesus today? World population is approaching six billion. What is your guess as to the number of lost people?
- ❏ one billion
- ❏ two billion
- ❏ three billion
- ❏ four billion
- ❏ five billion
- ❏ more than five billion

Although almost two billion people are called Christians, the vast majority are Christian in name only. For example, Europe would be counted almost wholly Christian because people are born into state or dominant churches, but in many nations no more than two percent attend church. The most generous estimates are that evangelical or born again believers number no more than 600 million. This means that more than 5 billion people today are lost. It's difficult to grasp such numbers and even harder to love those faceless multitudes. But God does love each one—they aren't faceless to Him.

The situation is more difficult than numbers alone can tell. Half those lost people are out of reach of any witnessing church. That must break God's heart. Because God is love, world evangelism is central in His thinking. Is it central in yours?

🌀 **Take this little quiz to check yourself. In the list below check the one that most nearly reflects your own feeling about lost people:**

❑ It's too bad, but I don't think about it much.
❑ I really grieve about the lost people I know, especially in my family. But how could I be expected to care a lot about people I don't know, especially those across the ocean?
❑ Frankly, I don't care; they'll get what's coming to them.
❑ I think a lot about the lost people I know.
❑ It bothers me that many people have had no chance to hear the gospel.
❑ Other: _____

🌀 **That's an evaluation of your feelings, but what about your actions? What would people who know you best say is most important to you?**

_____

If what is central in God's thinking turns out to be peripheral in mine, perhaps I have heart trouble. But God doesn't. God is love, so much so that He gave His one and only Son that no one might perish.

GOD'S ACTIVITY

God's activity demonstrates His love for the entire world. He does not care only for His chosen people.

🌀 **Several major acts of God in history appear below. Evaluate each example. If the act clearly is a part of God's love for the whole world, underline it. If the act is an expression of love for Israel only, scratch it out. If you're not sure, leave it.**

1. The call of Abraham
2. The exodus when the people of Israel escaped slavery in Egypt
3. The captivity when Jews were taken from Palestine into Babylon
4. The incarnation
5. Pentecost when the Spirit was given to a small group of Jewish disciples

1. Abraham wasn't called by God to shower all His loving attention on his descendants and let the rest of the world be doomed. He favored Abraham in order to bless the whole world though him (Gen. 12:1-2). God created a people isolated from the moral pollution of the nations, so they could receive a revelation of Himself without distortion.

2. The exodus seems to be just for Israel—it meant the destruction of Egypt's military power and the subjugation of the people of Palestine. But God had a larger purpose. He was reestablishing His missionary task force which had been in danger of extinction in Egypt.

The Lord had said to Abram, "Leave your country, your people and your father's household and go to the land I will show you.
I will make you into a great nation
and I will bless you;
I will make your name great,
and you will be a blessing."
—Genesis 12:1-2

191

3. God's missionary task force itself became corrupted, running after other loves, other gods. So God disciplined Israel, sending them into captivity to purify them. God was creating the spiritual and social context into which He could come and find a foothold.

4. The next major event was the greatest missionary act in all history. God's only Son left His homeland to become one of us in order to save us (Matt 18:11; John 1:14).

5. The Spirit came at Pentecost for the express purpose of establishing a new method to carry out His saving purpose for the whole world: the New Testament church (Acts 1:8).

So in the activity above I underlined every example. Some of them seem at first glance to be for Israel only, but God was always at work to save the entire world. God's activity proves what His heart is like. Perhaps our activity proves what our hearts are really like, too.

GOD'S PROMISES

God demonstrates His commitment to reaching the entire world through more than just His actions. God's promises assure a successful conclusion to His plan of world evangelization.

In the following Scriptures, underline the reason God blessed Abraham, the reason He blesses us today.

"I will make you into a great nation and I will bless you; I will make your name great, and you will be a blessing ... and all peoples on earth will be blessed through you" (Gen. 12:2-3).

May God be gracious to us and bless us and make his face shine upon us, that your ways may be known on earth, your salvation among all nations. God will bless us, and all the ends of the earth will fear him (Ps. 67:1-2,7).

Remarkable! Abraham's blessings and ours are for the same purpose: that God's salvation may reach all people. God promises both Abraham and us that His purpose will be accomplished.

Here are some promises of a coming Messiah. The Israelites in Jesus' day, including His disciples, expected Messiah to deliver them from Roman bondage and set up a Jewish state. In these two ancient promises of a coming Messiah underline the part that shows that their expectation was too narrow:

The Father promises the Son: *"Ask of me, and I will make the nations your inheritance, the ends of the earth your possession" (Ps. 2:8).*

The Father promises the Son: *"It is too small a thing for you to be my servant to restore the tribes of Jacob. ... I will also make you a light for the Gentiles, that you may bring my salvation to the ends of the earth" (Isa. 49:6).*

The Old Testament prophesies repeatedly predicted the coming of the Messiah, but He was not for Israel only. He was coming for all peoples.

What does the New Testament predict about Christ's second coming? Jesus Himself said: "This gospel of the kingdom will be preached in the whole world as a testimony to all nations, and then the end will come" (Matt. 24:14).

Finally, John pulls the curtain on the last act of earth's drama: "After this I looked and there before me was a great multitude that no one could count, from every nation, tribe, people and language, standing before the throne and in front of the Lamb" (Rev. 7:9).

From Genesis to Revelation, the Bible is full of promises about God's plan of world evangelization. The Spirit has a global plan, and He is bringing it to pass in our day as never before. I told you the downside of the population explosion—more people are lost today than ever before. Now let me tell you the positive side. God is bringing in a harvest greater than any since the world began. In fact, more people have been born into God's family in the last 25 years than in all the centuries of church history from the apostles' day until 1975! God's promises assure us His salvation purpose will be accomplished.

CHRIST'S COMMAND

We often call Christ's command to preach the gospel in all the world the Great Commission.

> On how many different occasions after the resurrection do you think Christ gave what might be called the Great Commission?
> ❏ 1   ❏ 2   ❏ 5
> ❏ 8   ❏ 10

1. On the night of the resurrection, Christ appeared among the disciples and said, "As the Father has sent me, I am sending you" (John 20:21). The same heart of love that sent Jesus must send us also.

2. Next we meet them up north in Galilee where Jesus announced, "All authority in heaven and on earth has been given to me. Therefore go and make disciples of all nations" (Matt. 28:18-19).

3. Then we find them back in Jerusalem. Jesus explained to them about His intention of world evangelism. He showed them from the Old Testament how "Repentance and forgiveness of sins will be preached in his name to all nations, beginning at Jerusalem. You are witnesses of these things" (Luke 24:47-48).

4. From there, Jesus led them out toward Mount Olivet where He was to leave them; they were still thinking about Kingdom restoration. He said that wasn't their concern and they should wait in Jerusalem till the Holy Spirit came on them. When that happens, He said, "You will receive power ... and you will be my witnesses in Jerusalem, and in all Judea and Samaria, and to the ends of the earth" (Acts 1:8).

5. The most comprehensive Great Commission of all is found in Mark 16:15, but the writer doesn't give us enough context to know if it was on one of the other four occasions or on yet a fifth: "Go into all the world and preach the good news to all creation."

Thus Jesus gave the command four or five times! Can there be any doubt about the priority Jesus would have for my life?

If God's program of world evangelism seems pretty far down the list of important things in your life, why not tell Him so now at the beginning of this unit. Ask Him to move you toward likeness to Him in His passion for the lost.

> Take time to copy Acts 1:8, this week's Scripture verse, onto a card. Practice memorizing it. Review your previous Scripture memory verses. If you already know Acts 1:8, choose another verse to memorize.

BEGINNING AT JERUSALEM

When God commissioned the church to reach the world, He told them to start at home—in Jerusalem. He's concerned about the lost people in your world: where you live, work, and play. If God's passion is the salvation of people and His method for reaching them is other people, surely the Spirit-given ability to win people to Christ is very important. But what does the gift of evangelism look like?

My ambition was to be a pioneer church-starting missionary among those who had never heard the gospel, but I was a schoolteacher. So I prayed earnestly for the gift of evangelism. And I went to work, preaching on weekends and during vacation. Sometimes many would come to Christ, sometimes no one would respond. I pled with God, sometimes with tears, to give me the gift of evangelism. After all, the Spirit had told me through Paul to do that: "Eagerly desire the greater gifts" (1 Cor. 12:31). My problem was, I had the wrong idea of what the gift looked like. I thought of "evangelism" as a public meeting in which the gospel is proclaimed, an invitation given, and people respond. That is one type of evangelism, but it isn't the only form.

WITNESS OR EVANGELIST?

To help distinguish between an evangelistic gift and a witnessing responsibility, mark each of the following T if you think the statement biblical, F if you question its validity:

___ 1. Every true Christian will win people to faith in Christ.
___ 2. Every true Christian will tell others about Christ.
___ 3. Every Spirit-filled Christian has the gift of evangelism.
___ 4. Some show, others tell. It's OK just to witness by living a godly life, since I'm timid and don't like to talk about religion.
___ 5. Every church should be baptizing new believers.

A witness is someone who has a personal experience and talks about it. Think of the term *witness* as used in a court of law. If I've only heard about the crime but haven't seen it, I'm no witness. If I've seen it, but won't talk, I'm no witness. In the last of the great commissions (Acts 1:8), all disciples are commissioned as witnesses. Disciples have experienced God and are to tell others the good news. So number 2 is true, number 4, false. But not all are given the gift of evangelism (1 Cor. 12:29-30), so 1 and 3 are false.

All believers are part of a "team" that brings people to faith. In that way the church grows. And God does expect His church to grow—"I will build my church," said Jesus (Matt. 16:18). The Book of Acts records how He did it: the Spirit won large numbers to Christ and started local congregations all over the Roman Empire through many witnessing Christians and a handful of pioneer evangelists. Number 5 is true—every church should be baptizing new believers unless there are special circumstances, which we shall consider later.

When I agonized over not having the gift of evangelism, my definition of "evangelism" was too limited. Perhaps God heard my prayer, was giving me the gift, and I just wasn't smart enough to recognize it. When we got to Japan, we found we could live in a community and love people in Jesus' name and many would come to faith. In a land where the average church has 25 members, even after decades of existence, we were baptizing 20 new converts a year. God had answered my prayer for the gift!

Or had He? I rarely prayed with someone to receive Christ, and we never gave a public invitation. Then how did they come? I call it body-life reproduction. We discovered that the Spirit-led or Spirit-filled church as a body can bring new believers to God's family. If church members are living authentic, Spirit-filled lives, and talking about it, people will come to faith.

BODY-LIFE REPRODUCTION

Ordinarily, every church should be baptizing new believers. Church-growth experts say that in the typical American community a church should be growing at 5 percent a year. This 5 percent should not be through baptizing its own children or from believers coming from other churches. New converts should account for a 5 percent increase. If a church isn't reaching new believers, something is wrong. Here are some possible reasons:

- The church may be spiritually ill, incapable of reproducing, in need of revival (as we saw in unit 8). Members may not be modeling an authentic Christian lifestyle that's attractive to unbelievers. The passion for lost people may have died out, or united prayer for the lost may be weak.
- Not many members may be sharing the gospel—too few faithful witnesses.
- Too few members have the gift of evangelism. Analysts say that in most churches that are growing through new believers coming to faith, about 10 percent of the members have the gift of evangelism.
- In some cases the people to be evangelized may be especially unresponsive. For example, a missionary working among Muslims in New York City would not likely get this kind of growth. The problem is that we often use unresponsive people as an excuse. Wherever I am, if people are not being saved, I'm tempted to proclaim it to be "hard soil." Assuming that we aren't rationalizing, unusual hardness in a given community can be a cause of little fruit.

How is the "birth rate" in your church? Do you think God is pleased? We don't want to be judgmental, but as spiritual "fruit inspectors" it wouldn't hurt to make a general estimate. In fact, I think it's important to be honest in evaluating our own church life as best we can.

To be a little more objective in your evaluation, here's a checklist. Some items are statistical and you may not know the answer. You could do one of three things: make an estimate, call the church office, or ask your group leader. Other items are subjective evaluations.

1. Total active membership _____
2. How many were baptized last year?_____
3. What percentage of church membership is that? _____
4. What percentage of members talk about spiritual things with non-Christians, even seeking opportunity to do so?_____
5. What percentage of members consistently win people to faith? _____
6. Does a specific group pray for the lost? ❑ Yes ❑ No
7. What percentage of members attend church regularly?_____

This evaluation is a basis for interaction in your next group meeting. If you see needs in your church, why not lay plans together on how to become more effective in doing what Christ commissioned us to do—reach our own "Jerusalem"?

GETTING PERSONAL

How about you? Are you a faithful witness, letting people know what Jesus means to you? Name here the people you want to talk to about spiritual things in the next month. Note what might be a good approach:

Name of person   Possible approach

_____   _____

_____   _____

_____   _____

_____   _____

Pause now and pray for each person and for yourself that God will give you (1) opportunity, (2) wisdom, (3) boldness, (4) sensitivity, and (5) Holy Spirit power. Do you have a growing desire to be more than a faithful witness, to have the gift of evangelism? Why not boldly ask the Spirit for that gift? Start today and keep on praying until He gives an answer, one way or another.

DAY 3

TO THE ENDS OF THE EARTH

Repeat Acts 1:8, your Scripture memory verse for this week. The verse contains a "snapshot" version of God's plan to evangelize the world. The Holy Spirit empowers all Christians to be witnesses. He gifts some as evangelists to reach their home community, their "Jerusalem." The church also has a responsibility for the surrounding area, its "Judea."

The following chart represents your community (Jerusalem and Judea) and your church—everyone a witness, some gifted in evangelism. Put the percentage of members who witness and the percentage who are gifted in evangelism (from your last lesson) on this diagram:

Church   Jerusalem   Judea

Percent of church members who witness _____

Percent of church members who have gift of evangelism _____

Not all can travel to begin a new work, so a few are chosen by the Spirit to reach out to places without a witness to start congregations. That kind of evangelist is given a special name in Scripture, *apostle*. The word means "one who is sent." We would probably call them home missionaries if they are in evangelistic church starting. Paul ranks apostle number 1 in God's plan to evangelize the world (1 Cor. 12:28). He isn't talking about the 12 apostles in this chapter, but the gift of pioneer missionary evangelist. The extension of the Kingdom depends on such gifted people. No wonder Paul says, "first, apostles."

🌀 **On the diagram below, after "Apostles," put the number of your church members or former members who have gone away from home to start churches elsewhere. If you don't know, your group leader or church office can no doubt give you the information.**

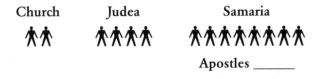

Church   Judea   Samaria

Apostles _____

If the apostolic missionary crosses cultural barriers into another ethnic group, we might call that our church's "Samaria." Samaritans lived near the early Christians, but they were a different cultural and ethnic group. Ethnically or culturally different people near us are our responsibility. Finally, Acts 1:8 mentions the "uttermost parts" or those peoples who live out of reach of present gospel witness.

THE ENDS OF THE EARTH

🌀 **Put on the diagram below the number of those from your church who have gone into "foreign missionary" work, cross-cultural evangelism, whether in the United States or overseas.**

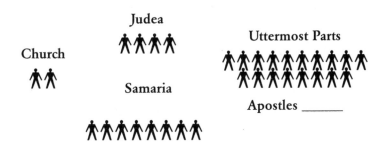

Judea

Church   Uttermost Parts

Samaria

Apostles _____

A TALE OF TWO CHURCHES

I spoke in two church missions conferences in the same state, the same month. The churches shared many similarities. Both were widely recognized for their missions interest; in fact, one was the anchor church for the eastern end of the state, the other for the west.

Both were large, vibrant, growing churches. Both had very large budgets for missions, perhaps half their total giving. "East" had 1,800 members and gave enough money to missions to support 180 missionaries. "West" was half the size and gave enough money to support about 75 missionaries. There the similarities ended.

"East" was only 30 years old, but 180 missionaries had come from this church. They were their own sons and daughters. "West" was 150 years old, but only one of their own had ever gone to the mission field. She was now retired and present in the conference. "West" paid for the sons and daughters of others to go.

In the church God has appointed first of all apostles, second prophets, third teachers, then workers of miracles, also those having gifts of healing, those able to help others, those with gifts of administration, and those speaking in different kinds of tongues.
—1 Corinthians 12:28

Where would your church fit on a continuum between "West" and "East" so far as sending your own members into missionary service?

West (0 % of members who are missionaries)									East (10% of members who are missionaries)

"BUT THE NEED AT HOME IS SO GREAT."

Whenever we begin to talk about the needs of the world, someone always chimes in with: "But the need at home is so great." The need at home is great. Our first responsibility is for those nearby. The question is not either/or but both/and. Jesus' command was Jerusalem, Judea, Samaria, and the ends of the earth.

To get a feel for the relative needs of our world, look at three places: the slums of Calcutta, where my son Kent lives; Columbia, South Carolina, where I live; and your city or county. Fill in the blanks with your best estimates about your city.

	Columbia, SC	Your Home City	Calcutta Slum Dwellers
Population	300,000	_____	5,000,000
Number of churches	600	_____	5
Number of evangelical Christians	100,000[1]	_____	approx. 1,000
Christian radio stations	2	_____	0
Christian TV stations	1	_____	0
Christian bookstores	15	_____	0

In America 1 out of 5 people with whom you do business or associate will be Bible-believing Christians, in Calcutta 1 of 10,000. How many Bibles are in Columbia, South Carolina? A million? Calcutta may have a few hundred Bibles, while many of the languages in that great city have none at all. I use Calcutta merely as an example of the spiritually dark half of the world where people don't have access to the gospel. If someone doesn't go in from the outside—if an apostolic missionary doesn't come—they cannot even hear the gospel. Yes, our first responsibility is for "Jerusalem," but God loves the world.

GOD'S SCOUT

A large church contributed financial support toward 75 missionaries, including us. In fact, it was the second largest missions donor church in the nation, of any denomination. One day I walked down the long hallway in which photographs of the missionaries were displayed, studying the biographies of each. To my astonishment, not one of their missionaries was from that church! They gave lots of money to support other people's sons and daughters. A young businessman noticed the same phenomenon and decided to do something about it. Calling himself "God's scout," he volunteered to teach the college-and-career Sunday School class. Within 5 years 11 members of that church were on the mission field—all from that class! God hadn't called him to go as a missionary, but Frank heard the call to send.

⊚ **Do you know any boy, girl, or young adult about whom you think,** *That youngster would make a great missionary*? **They are spiritually alive, gifted, and active in service to God. Think over the young people in church you know and list any such possible candidates.**

_____

_____

⊚ **How could you become a "scout" used of God to encourage a potential missionary? Check off any strategy you think God wants you to use to help those you listed find God's purpose for their lives.**

❑ Pray for that person, especially that he will hear if God is calling.
❑ Talk with the person about her future ambitions.
❑ Seek opportunity to suggest the possibility of full-time ministry, even of missionary vocation.
❑ Find a task in the church for him in which his gifts will be challenged, developed, and used.
❑ Encourage her often.
❑ Like Frank, teach a class in which you seek to inspire members with a clear, strong vision of God's purposes in the world and their responsibility to participate with Him in achieving that purpose.

"HERE AM I, SEND ME"

In the past, only young people who had not yet launched into some other vocation were considered potential candidates for missionary service. Today many missionaries have joined the task force in mid-life, leaving other vocations. Most Americans change careers several times.

Perhaps God would give you the high privilege of being His ambassador to a people who have had no chance to hear the gospel. Why not begin today to ask the Holy Spirit to give you that gift?

When I was 18, I began to ask God for the gift of apostleship. I wanted my life to count to the maximum for God's purpose in this world. I found the same ambition Paul spoke of burning in my spirit—to proclaim Christ where He had never been named (Rom. 15:20).

We encountered many obstacles: I didn't think I had the gift of evangelism; I had an illness the doctors said was incurable; others said we shouldn't go because "God is blessing you where you are" (a strange logic); we had four children (several mission boards didn't like that); and finally, after we boarded ship for Japan, my daughter was injured and we had to disembark. But we kept on obeying the command to "desire earnestly"; we kept asking God to send us and use us. I'm so glad we did. Surely no joy is quite like living among people who have never heard the gospel and watching the Holy Spirit work in giving hope to the hopeless, healing broken lives, and forming a church where there was no witness before.

Perhaps God would give you that high privilege. Write out in your journal how you feel about the idea, or how you feel about being a sender. Then talk to Him about it.

DAY 4

THE MOST IMPORTANT TASK

A magnificent southern thunderstorm was entertaining me one evening. From my porch, I watched the display of cosmic fireworks when all of a sudden there was a mighty explosion right in our backyard–an extravaganza of sight and sound. Lightning had struck the transformer. In a moment, we lost all light and power–for days we were without power. Yet, just a half mile away, giant electrical towers trooped through the fields, bearing unlimited supplies of light and power. The situation reminded me of how many Christians live. Power flows all around them, but they aren't connected.

HOW THE POWER FLOWS

Holy Spirit power flows through prayer. Prayer forms the human conduit for divine energy. Since the Spirit acts in response to the believing prayer of an obedient people, prayer is the most important part of evangelism. As E.M. Bounds said, "much prayer, much power, little prayer, little power, no prayer, no power."

In his letter to the Colossians, Paul gives straight-forward instruction on prayer for missions. Underline the statement(s) in Paul's text that best match the conclusion about prayer I've given in the right column. Then draw a connecting line between the verse and the conclusion that best goes with it.

I want you to know how much I am struggling for you and for those at Laodicea, and for all who have not met me personally (Col. 2:1).

Continue earnestly in prayer, being vigilant in it with thanksgiving; meanwhile praying also for us, that God would open to us a door for the word, to speak the mystery of Christ, for which I am also in chains, that I may make it manifest, as I ought to speak (Col. 4:2-4, NKJV).

Epaphras, ... always labouring fervently for you in prayers, that ye may stand perfect and complete in all the will of God (Col. 4:12, KJV).

Prayer is not to be a sleepy routine but is spiritual warfare.

Prayer is not to be sporadic or occasional but regular and persistent.

Prayer is not only regular but also on "battle alert," on the lookout to pray for special needs as the Spirit alerts us.

Prayer should be so filled with faith that we can give thanks even before we see the answer.

Prayer is not only for those we are with but for those we may never have seen.

Pray for godliness of life.

Pray for the Holy Spirit to work in the ministry of the missionary.

If we pray for our missionaries at all, it may be a routine reading over some brief request. But the kind of prayer Paul describes is very different. In these verses he calls such prayer "struggling." He describes it with the words "earnestly," "always laboring fervently." It sounds like a spiritual battle in prayer against unseen enemies that fight to hold captive those we aim to release.

Notice that our prayer isn't to be occasional but continuing, regular—daily, at least. Furthermore, our fervent labor in prayer is not only the regular set times for prayer but in between times. We are to be sensitive to the Spirit's intimations of special need for special prayer.

When Paul says "with thanksgiving," he doesn't mean merely saying thank you when God answers, important as that is. We are to thank God for the answer even as we ask. In other words, faith-filled prayer.

Paul gives instruction on what we're to pray about: (1) the missionary's ministry and (2) the missionary's life. The Holy Spirit must empower both or nothing of eternal significance will be done. He said to pray that doors of opportunity would open up and that the missionary team would have the ability to make the mysterious gospel understandable. That's Spirit-energized ministry.

Paul recognized the need for the fruit of the Spirit as seen in his instruction to believers in that same passage: "Be wise in the way you act toward outsiders, make the most of every opportunity. Let your conversation be always full of grace, seasoned with salt, so that you may know how to answer everyone" (Col. 4:5-6). Furthermore, Paul tells the Ephesians in a similar passage (Eph. 6:19-20) to plead with God that he might have courage. Missionaries may have the most glorious good news; but if their lives don't demonstrate the beauty and strength of Christ, their proclamation will not be as effective as it could be. So we must pray for both the ministry and the life, the gifts of the Spirit and the fruit of the Spirit.

On home leave from service overseas, I had just completed my report on Japan and stood at the door of the church to greet the people. I felt a tug on my jacket. Looking around I saw a tiny, retired schoolteacher who said, "Robertson, I know you're busy, but please don't leave till I have a chance to talk with you for a minute."

"Why, Miss Ethelyn," I responded, "I'm not busy; let's talk right now." I knew she prayed for me continually and fervently, one who was combat-ready and fighting my spiritual wars with me. We went to a nearby stone wall, and no sooner had we sat than she began to pepper me with questions about my work. I soon realized she knew more about my work than my fellow missionaries. When she began to ask about the conference I had left in Japan just 48 hours earlier, I said, "Miss Ethelyn, how do you know all this stuff?"

"Why, Robertson," she remonstrated, "you're my missionary! I've been praying for you for 12 years. I should know something, shouldn't I?"

Pray also for me, that whenever I open my mouth, words may be given me so that I will fearlessly make known the mystery of the gospel, for which I am an ambassador in chains. Pray that I may declare it fearlessly, as I should.
—Ephesians 6:19-20

Choose some missionary you know about and write out a prayer for that missionary. In addition to what you know to be the missionary's need, be sure to include all the ideas Paul gave the Colossians on what to pray for the missionary and the missionary team.

_____

_____

_____

_____

Perhaps you had trouble with that assignment because you don't know any missionaries that well. You need to design a strategy to get involved in God's enterprise as an intercessory prayer warrior. Here are some ideas.

- Ask your pastor or your denominational headquarters to introduce you to a missionary who works in an area in which you may have an interest.
- Most missionaries send out regular reports with prayer requests. Ask the missionary (s) you choose to put you on their mailing list.
- When missionaries visit the church, invite them home for dinner. And don't spend the time reworking the Super Bowl! Pull their story out of them, learn what their prayer needs are. Then pray!

If you don't have a missionary you can call "my missionary," why not make a telephone call to the church office or write a letter right now? Get started!

DAY 5

MEASURING MATURITY

The Spirit has given, is giving, or will give you the ability to do an important job for Him (1 Cor. 12). He then wraps that gift in the package called you and gives you to the church (Eph. 4). We studied gifts in unit 10. In this unit we examined the special gift of evangelism including evangelism-at-a-distance or missionary evangelism.

"Apostles" are so important in God's program of reaching the world because they are the Spirit's point-men and women in His strategy. We've seen how all must witness, some must evangelize, and some of the evangelists must go to those out of reach of present gospel witness. We've seen how the "going" will be effective to the extent there is praying. But one more thing exists, and it is for everyone.

One of the greatest blockades on the road to victory for King Jesus is something very practical, quite earthy. That thing is money, or should I say the lack of it, for the missionary enterprise. We seem to have plenty for our own needs. We provide to one degree or another for the needs of the local church, but when it comes to sending out missionaries, money dries up. In fact, only four cents of each dollar given by evangelicals in the USA is used for world missions. Ninety-six percent of giving is spent at home, on ourselves. Thousands of young adults are fully prepared and ready to go, but the money isn't there. What's the problem?

Jesus said spiritual immaturity in God's family is the root problem. He talked more about money than about heaven and hell combined. In fact, He taught far more about our relationships to possessions than He did about prayer! Apparently, He considered our bank statement an accurate measure of our spiritual maturity.

In the following six stories and teachings, Jesus illustrates six attitudes about money. Read the passages from your Bible and match each reference with one of the following attitudes. Write the number of the attitude beside the appropriate story.

1. sacrificial love giving	*3. impulse giving*	*5. legalistic giving*
2. faith giving	*4. non-giving*	*6. honest management*

____ Luke 11:42	____ Luke 12:16-21	____ Luke 12:27-31
____ Luke 16:1-13	____ Luke 19:1-8	____ Luke 21:1-4

Here's how I read those stories and instructions about money.

LEGALISTIC GIVING

Jesus had problems with the Pharisees and their giving, but it wasn't with their legalistic measuring one out of every ten grains of "bird seed" for God. It's what they left undone—justice and mercy (Luke 11:42). But, Christ added, "don't leave off tithing!" Far better to give 10 percent legalistically than not to give it! Yet very few church members tithe. At a large church with a four million dollar budget the business manager told me they had done a demographic study of their membership. "If every member quit his job, went on unemployment and started to tithe," he said, "we could double our budget!" Studies show that most churches are like that.

NON-GIVING

The wealthy farmer in Luke 12:16-21 was a self-centered non-giver. He spent it all on food and fun. Christ called him a fool, a dead man. Yet studies consistently show that most church members give very, very little.

FAITH GIVING

"O you of little faith!" Jesus said to His worry-wart disciples (Luke 12:28). Living by faith is the only way to live, and faith giving is one of the clearest evidences of God-focused living. Without faith it's impossible to please God at all (Heb. 11:6). Giving in the confidence that God will take care of the outcome is the validation for every level of giving. For example, the widow living on Social Security must have faith that God will care for her on 90 percent of her income when she gives her tithe. But there seems also to be a special gift of faith (Rom. 12:3). George Mueller cared for thousands of orphans on God's daily miracle provision. In fact, his faith stretched beyond caring for the orphans as he was able to give millions to foreign missionary work around the world. That's faith giving!

HONEST MANAGEMENT

Luke 16:1-13 is a tough passage to understand until you look for the one point Jesus was making in His story about the cheating manager. That fellow was sharp because he used present resources to prepare for his future. God's people aren't very smart, Jesus said, because they use their money to live well now and don't send it on ahead, investing in the Bank of Heaven at incredible interest rates. Besides, Jesus says, it's not your money to begin with. I'm the owner and you're just an interim manager (16:12). The only question is, will you be an honest one? Or will you be a cheating manager, using the Owner's possessions for your own benefit?

As a young man, I was an avid getter and keeper. It may surprise you to hear that I was also a faithful tither—God got His 10 percent off the top. Then I had a traumatic encounter with Jesus in the Book of Luke. I saw I wasn't an owner at all, and I stood condemned an embezzler. I didn't want to accept this teaching about managership—it would clip my wings, cage me in. But when I finally gave up and accepted God's view of my possessions, the very opposite of what I feared took place. It was like the cage door swung open and I was free. My intensity about making money was gone, my grief over losses and ecstacy over gains, my apprehension about the future—they all took wings. I was at ease because the corporation of my life belonged to the Infinite One and He guaranteed my life (Luke 12:31). That's what happens when we get honest about who the owner is!

IMPULSE GIVING

In the next story we meet an IRS agent up a tree! (Luke 19:1-9). When Zacchaeus met Jesus, he was changed into a new man and impulsively gave away half

> "Will a man rob God? Yet you rob me. But you ask, 'How do we rob you?' In tithes and offerings. You are under a curse—the whole nation of you—because you are robbing me."
> —Malachi 3:8-9

> The angels from
> their home on high
> Look down on us
> with wondering eye;
> That where we are
> but passing guests
> We build such strong
> and solid nests;
> And where we hope
> to live for aye,
> We scarce take thought
> one stone to lay.
> —Anonymous

"Sell your possessions and give to the poor. Provide purses for yourselves that will not wear out, a treasure in heaven that will not be exhausted, where no thief comes near and no moth destroys. For where your treasure is, there your heart will be also."
—Luke 12:33-34

his estate (v. 8). One of the first signs of spiritual life is the desire to give. A person begins to get his kicks out of giving instead of getting. Impulse givers may not give systematically, but they can be very generous when presented with a great need. Most Christians, most of the time, give at the impulse level.

SACRIFICIAL LOVE GIVING

Next, we find ourselves in church with Jesus doing something your pastor has never done. If he did, that would no doubt be his last Sunday as your pastor! Jesus watched the offering plate and noted how much each one put in (Luke 21:1-4). No doubt He does so today as well. There He discovered a very beautiful woman. Thin, with hunger-pinched features, no doubt, and shabby in appearance, but how beautiful she was! Out of a heart of love she gave everything she had.

The young talk-show host was interviewing Mother Theresa. The host's eyes sparkled as she heard Mother Theresa brag about the generosity of Americans. Then Mother Theresa added, "But you give out of your muchness, no? You don't give till it hurts."

The young woman blurted out in astonishment, "Must it hurt?"

"Love," said Mother Theresa, "will hurt." She had discovered the basic spiritual truth that love can only be measured by the sacrifice it makes.

There you have five different attitudes toward giving and one of non-giving: legalistic giving, non-giving, faith giving, honest management, impulse giving, and sacrificial love giving. Now let's rank them in order of advancing spiritual maturity. I'll give each level a familiar name and you can put your own ranking above each of them, using the descriptive terms we used above. I'll put the lowest level, "non-giving," on the bottom step by way of example.

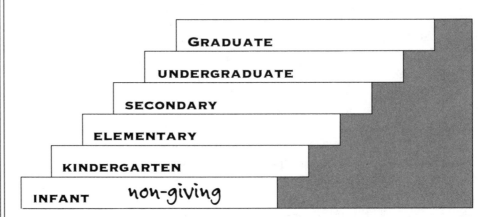

I ranked the levels beginning with non-giving for the infant. Did you ever see a generous infant? They're in the getting business. Every church has its quota. Next, I put impulse giving as a kindergarten Christian. True signs of life, to be sure, but little maturity. Then the basic, elementary level of tithing that graduates a believer into giving as a way of life.

Next, is the manager (secondary school) who has a different viewpoint from the tither. The tither says, "Here's this money; where shall I put it to honor God?" The manager says, "Look at this need! Look at this opportunity! How can I rearrange the resources under my control to meet that need?" Graduating beyond dutiful tithing to honest managership brings a change in lifestyle to advance the interests of God's business.

The next level is sacrificial giving (undergraduate). Any of us may sacrifice on occasion, but some disciples mature to a level of sacrifice as a way of life. They choose to live simply so that others may simply live. They exemplify the attitude of Jesus, who gave it all up to become one with a sin-impoverished world of dying people.

I put faith giving at the top level (graduate). Those with a special "gift of faith" give beyond sacrifice, trusting God for miracle provision.

The steps are not always clear-cut. Every level of giving must be validated by faith and motivated by love. But this set of goals is clear enough for me to evaluate my life. I know the painful—then liberating—move I made from tithing to managership. And I know very well, as I see the abject poverty of the world, that I don't live a sacrificial lifestyle. I may evidence spurts of sacrifice, but I fall far from Jesus' model of giving.

How about you? Honesty about our finances may be the hardest honesty of all. Review your giving for the past year. Check your records if you aren't sure. Now go back to the stair steps and put an asterisk (*) at the level you've been living. Are you pleased with that level? Is God pleased? What kind of lover does that show you to be? What kind of truster?

Remember God's style of giving. He created me, so I am His property. But I stole His creation and took possession of me. So, in the most astounding outpouring of love, He purchased me at terrible personal cost. Thank God for His incredible gift! (2 Cor. 9:15). Next, He guarantees my livelihood (Luke 12:31) and rewards me a hundred times over for any little thing I might give Him (Luke 18:29-30). Then, when I get to heaven He promises to reward me all over again! What a giver! What a lover!

In response to such love are you ready to move up one step in your stewardship? If you've never been a faithful tither, isn't it time to promise Him that 10 percent? Perhaps you've been a tither for years, but you did pretty much what you pleased with the other 90 percent. Isn't it time to become a manager? Whatever level of maturity you've achieved in your walk with God, don't you want to step up?

🌀 **Whatever your decision, tell Him about it and write it in your journal before finishing this lesson.**

We've listened to Jesus' teaching about giving at this point in our study because lack of giving is a major obstacle to world evangelism. Spiritually mature Christians give sacrificially.

Our relationship to things is a measure of our spiritual maturity. Spiritual maturity is the theme of our whole study. Giving ties together the fruit of the Spirit (character) with evangelism (purpose). Because the key to our response about money is love, this study sets the stage for our final unit. Next we will examine the ultimate goal of life: loving oneness with God.

---

[1] Estimate based on the national estimate of 20% evangelical Christian. Columbia, SC, may actually have 50% or more, rather than the conservative estimate here of 30%.

UNIT 12

A MARRIAGE MADE IN HEAVEN

Chapel seating was assigned, but I didn't mind. The girl I most wanted to be near was seated right in front of me every day! When she ran those lovely fingers through her thick, chestnut-colored hair, it drove me crazy. Finally, I got up enough courage to ask Muriel for a date. I was intoxicated with her infectious laughter, attractive face, delightful creativity, deep love for God, and her caring ways with people. And she was so much fun. Friendship soon blossomed into love and we talked of marriage. Would it be a marriage made in heaven?

By the time we were engaged, my mind was so consumed with Muriel I could think of nothing else. The wedding came, agonizingly slow, and then the ecstatic honeymoon for two innocents in Estes Park, Colorado. Could love ever be more intimate, more satisfying? We had a lot to learn.

Children bond a couple closer, but they can also test the bonds. Though it doesn't always happen that way, love deepened with every shared pain, heightened with every shared joy. Our hearts got so intertwined they seemed like one.

Now at the end of the road, when Muriel's mind barely functions at the borders of consciousness, deep into Alzheimer's, the love still grows. I like to think it's been a marriage made in heaven.

There's one marriage, however, I know was made in heaven. Did you know that the chief image of human relationship to God in the Old Testament was of Israel as the wife of God? A chief image in the New Testament is of the church as the bride of Christ. There's a marriage made in heaven!

Which is the real marriage and which the reflection? Did the Holy Spirit take the human institution of marriage and draw an analogy with God's relationship to people so we could understand the unseen world better? Or was it the other way around? Was the plan for the relationship between God and His beloved so intimate that it required a temporary earthly model for us to understand the ultimate, eternal relationship? If so, God made humans on a dual model–man and wife–to show us what His grand plan of union with Him was to be. Either way, that intimate identity with God in love is truly a marriage made in heaven! This incredible revelation of what God intended from the start is the theme of our final unit of study.

Unit Memory Verses

"I pray ... that they all may be one, as You, Father, are in Me,
and I in You: that they also may be one in Us ... I in them, and You in Me."
–John 17:21,23, NKJV

If the Spirit of him who raised Jesus from the dead is living in you,
he who raised Christ from the dead will also give life to your mortal bodies
through his Spirit, who lives in you.–Romans 8:11

DAY 1

WHERE ARE WE HEADED?

This week we come to the end of our study of the activities of the Holy Spirit and our responses to Him. What will be the final outcome of this relationship? Why did God create you? Why did He recreate you? Theologians write volumes to answer those questions; and each of us, no doubt, has our own opinion.

Check the answer closest to your own idea of God's ultimate purpose in creating and saving you.

❑ to become like Christ
❑ to be holy
❑ to glorify God
❑ to worship God
❑ to love God
❑ to experience loving oneness with God

Let's examine each of these possible responses by category.

CHRISTLIKENESS
Since we've been studying spiraling up into ever greater likeness to Christ for 12 weeks, to become like Christ would seem to be a good choice.

Go back now to the list of possible ultimate purposes; put an X beside any characteristic that does not describe Jesus.

That was an easy assignment! Jesus embodies all of them, so you could choose "become like Christ" as the comprehensive goal of human creation and redemption. If we were like Christ in all the ways in the list, we would certainly fulfill everything God purposed in our creation and redemption. But in thinking of Christlikeness, we must be careful to include the relationship that Jesus has with the Father. We often limit the idea of "Christlikeness" to having attitudes and behavior like Christ. We use Christlike as something like a synonym for holiness.

HOLINESS
Holiness is important because without it no one will see God (Heb. 12:14). But it's a limited goal. We often use holiness to describe growing away from sinful attitudes and actions. That is hardly the ultimate goal of life. Making holiness the primary goal creates another problem. Striving for holiness can become self-oriented and legalistic. Our ultimate purpose must be God-oriented, not self-oriented.

Look back to the list and put an asterisk (*) by those goals in the list that focus exclusively on God.

GLORY OF GOD
Focusing on God is certainly biblical and surely all we do should bring Him glory (1 Cor. 10:31). The problem with making the glory of God our ultimate goal is that, like Christlikeness, it isn't very specific. We're left with the task of spelling out in detail how we can best glorify Him.

WORSHIP

Some people seek to give a more specific focus to our purpose of glorifying God. Worship is a particular form of giving glory to God. Therefore, they make worship the goal of life.

Worship as a life purpose is another exclusively God-oriented choice. Indeed our whole lives should be worship, demonstrating His worth, but making worshiping Him the ultimate goal presents another problem: Why would a God of love be so self-centered as to demand worship as the whole purpose of making and saving His people? Is God selfish?

Five-year-old Kent was trying hard to get our guests to notice him and his talents. "Oh, Kent, quit showing off," I said.

He apparently devoted some deep thought to the subject, because early the next morning he had developed his response: "Daddy, why does God want us to brag on Him?"

> To understand why we worship, look at God's self-revelation in Scripture. What does He want above all else? In each of the couplets below check the one you think best describes what God thinks or feels.
>
> ❏ (1a) God feels fulfilled when we worship Him.
> ❏ (1b) God knows we can be fulfilled only as we relate to Him as the glorious God He is.
>
> ❏ (2a) God knows we'll destroy ourselves if we break with reality and take credit for what He does.
> ❏ (2b) God likes to take all the credit.
>
> ❏ (3a) God is jealous—it angers Him for anyone else to be honored.
> ❏ (3b) God is jealous—it hurts Him when we love others more than Him.

Many Bible students believe God desires that we conform to the reality of who He is for our own good. To get out of alignment with reality is self-destructive, allowing self to usurp the honor that belongs to God alone. God expects us to recognize who He is and behave accordingly because such recognition and behavior will result in our good. I chose (1b), (2a), (3b).

Did you have trouble with the last couplet? The term "jealous" applied to God may jar us, but the Bible repeatedly tells us He's a jealous God. Perhaps we get a clue of what God is teaching us by considering the fundamental command of both the Old and New Testaments: to love God.

When God came in person to reveal His heart purpose, He said, "'Love the Lord your God with all your heart and with all your soul and with all your mind.' This is the first and greatest commandment" (Matt. 22:37-38). "First and greatest" makes clear what God is concerned about.

Jesus quoted this commandment from the foundational revelation of God's will in the Old Testament, what the Jews call the *Shema* (Deut. 6:5). He then explained its importance. Everything else He said—everything taught in the Bible, "the law and prophets"—hangs on this command, along with the command to love one's neighbor (Matt. 22:40).

Perhaps we'd be safe to make loving God our chief end, except for one thing. Genuine love must be mutual. It's not so much that we love Him, but that He loves us! (1 John 4:10). So we must search for a more complete statement of God's purpose for us.

LOVING ONENESS WITH GOD

As we saw in unit 11, God is love in His nature (1 John 4:8,16). From all eternity the Father, Son, and Holy Spirit are bound together in bonds of eternal love. From the overflow of that love, He designed a creature to love Him back.

God's purpose all along has been to have a loving, mutual relationship with us. That's why He calls His relationship to us a marriage! When a man "knew" a woman in Bible times it meant they became one in intimate identity. That's why we say the goal of life is knowing God—an identity so close it could be likened to marriage. Closer than that—it could be likened to the unity the Father and Son have with one another. Now we see how being like Christ fits into the ultimate goal! We are intended to be like Him not only in character but in relationship.

Our memory verse is taken from a prayer of Jesus that speaks of our unity with one another (part of being like Jesus) intertwined with our unity with God. This also, we now see clearly, is part of our being like Jesus. Here's the whole passage, including both kinds of oneness—with God as a basis for unity with one another.

> *"My prayer is not for them alone. I pray also for those who will believe in me through their message, that all of them may be one, Father, just as you are in me and I am in you. May they also be in us so that the world may believe that you have sent me. I have given them the glory that you gave me, that they may be one as we are one: I in them and you in me. May they be brought to complete unity to let the world know that you sent me and have loved them even as you have loved me.*
>
> *"Father, I want those you have given me to be with me where I am, and to see my glory, the glory you have given me because you loved me before the creation of the world.*
>
> *"Righteous Father, though the world does not know you, I know you, and they know you have sent me. I have made you known to them, and will continue to make you known in order that the love you have for me may be in them and that I myself may be in them"* (John 17:20-26).

Astounding! The love relationship He planned for us is intimate, exclusive, and permanent. The only way to exhaust its meaning is to say it's like the Father's love for the Son and the Son's love for the Father! That's why the two of them made that greatest of all sacrifices—He died for us so that we, alive or dead, might live in union with Him (1 Thess. 5:10).

Jesus' prayer in John 17 speaks of two unities—among believers and with God.

- The unity among believers shows outsiders whose disciples we are. Such unity has often proved difficult to achieve. Unity with one another is indeed the mark of true discipleship.
- The basis for unity between believers is our oneness with the Father, the Son, and the Holy Spirit. This second unity is beyond comprehension. It's like trying to explain to a five-year-old the glories of married love.

A child doesn't have a clue. It's the same with us. If the unbeliever can't understand the glories of present unity with Christ, no more can we understand the ecstasies of our future union with Christ in heaven. We just don't have the capacity to grasp a whole new dimension of the human-divine relationship. We haven't matured yet. We've not undergone the final transformation into God-compatible beings. One day we will experience God in all His fullness.

At the beginning of this lesson we listed the purposes God had in mind for us. All are important, and we've looked at each of them briefly in an attempt to examine the many-faceted splendor of His plan for us. Let's have one more go at it.

⊚ Here are the purposes God had in creating and re-creating us. They were listed at the beginning of this lesson: to become like Christ, glorify God, be holy, love God, worship God, and experience loving oneness with God. On the building blocks below write each purpose in the order you think they build. Put the most foundational in the bottom block—without this one none of the others can happen. The purpose of this activity is not to get the "right" answer. The purpose is to see more clearly the inter-relatedness of all God's purposes for you. In fact, the more difficulty you have with the exercise the more you may be probing that inter-relatedness.

Whatever your order, isn't it glorious? These statements describe God's purpose for our relationship with Him. We've been studying the activities of the Spirit to better understand and cooperate with God in this project. "We know that we live in him and he in us, because he has given us of his Spirit" (1 John 4:13).

⊚ Pause now and thank God for all the glorious purposes He has in mind for you.

DAY 2

ALL GLORY, WORSHIP, AND HONOR

Loving oneness with God has two sides: God's love for you and your love for Him. In this lesson we'll think about your love for Him. Focusing on God is the true evidence of love, but it's not just proof of where your heart is. Focusing your attention on God is also how you express your love for Him, and how you can grow in it, too. To glorify and worship God, then, is an essential evidence and expression of love, as well as a way to deepen love.

Have you ever considered the differences between glorifying and worshiping God? The two actions overlap, but each word has a slightly different emphasis. When we honor and glorify God the focus is on how we show Him off to others. When we worship we direct our attention wholly to Him.

GLORIFYING GOD

🌀 List some of the ways you can put the spotlight on God—honor Him—causing others to see His majesty, beauty, wisdom, power, holiness, love, justice, and truth.

1. _____

2. _____

3. _____

4. _____

5. _____

I listed (1) living a life that authentically reflects His character, (2) praising Him to others in conversation and song, (3) winning others to faith so more people will honor Him, (4) always giving Him credit for the good that happens, and (5) defending Him against false accusation. The list goes on, but those are some important ways to put God's glories on display.

🌀 Review the lists—both yours and mine—and asterisk any you want to emphasize more in your own life.

Glorifying God doesn't have to be a "major production." Muriel was often an example to me of spontaneously giving God credit. In the grocery store check-out line I've heard her exclaim to the clerk, "Wow! Isn't God good! Look what He helped me find!" Her heart full of love was forever bubbling over.

WORSHIPING GOD

Many genuine Christians don't experience much worship in a "worship service"; they don't feel much warm devotion in their "devotional" time. Yet God longs for those who will worship Him in spirit and in truth (John 4:23). To get a running start on bringing to life your "worship service" next Sunday, let's worship Him now. We can do that in many ways—actually all of life should exalt His worth. Telling Him how greatly we value Him, exulting in His person, that is worship.

Worship with Scripture. Do you have a favorite Psalm of praise? If none comes immediately to mind, try Psalm 8 or 19. To "tune your heart to sing His praise" slowly read aloud the Psalm you chose, consciously speaking those words to God.

Worship in Song. Look at the topical index of your hymnal under "Worship," "Praise," and "Thanksgiving" and choose some of your favorite hymns of praise. Don't choose testimony songs that focus on your personal experiences. Choose those that speak to God and worship Him. If you don't have a hymnal, perhaps you can recall a favorite hymn or song of adoration. Or you could choose some of the all-time favorites printed below. Sing your heart out to the all glorious One!

"Holy, Holy, Holy"

Holy, holy, holy! Lord God almighty!
Early in the morning our song shall rise to thee;
Holy, holy, holy, merciful and mighty!
God in three Persons, blessed Trinity!

Holy, holy, holy! tho the darkness hide thee,
Tho the eye of sinful man thy glory may not see;
Only Thou art holy; there is none beside thee,
Perfect in pow'r, in love, and purity.

Holy, holy, holy! Lord God Almighty!
All thy woks shall praise thy name, in earth, and sky, and sea;
Holy, holy, holy; merciful and mighty!
God in three Persons, blessed Trinity!
—Reginald Heber

"Worthy of Worship"

Worthy of worship, worthy of praise,
worthy of honor and glory;
Worthy of all the glad songs we can sing,
worthy of all of the off'rings we bring.

You are worthy, Father, Creator.
You are worthy, Saviour, Sustainer.
You are worthy, worthy and wonderful;
Worthy of worship and praise.[1]
—Terry W. York

Worship in Your Own Words. Now that others have inspired you with their expressions of worship, we're ready to worship Him in our own words. Write out in your journal a prayer of worship. If you're courageous try putting it into verse—a hymn of worship! Write 3 stanzas:

1. First, tell God everything about His person you admire, His marvelous characteristics. (Hint: I listed many of them near the beginning of this lesson, just before the exercise on "Glorifying God"). That's worship.
2. Next, review the major activities of God since the start of time, His works of creation and redemption. Praise Him for each of those activities you admire or for which you are especially grateful. That's praise.
3. Finally, thank God for everything He has done for you personally. Be sure to include earthly blessings as well as the spiritual. That's thanksgiving.

Worship Him Forever. If I asked you to name the hymnbook of the Bible I'm sure you'd name the Book of Psalms. You'd be right—it's the hymnbook of God's people of all the ages. But a close second is found in the New Testament.

Do you have any idea which book would qualify? _____

John was overwhelmed with dreadful visions of future doom, but he constantly bursts into praise. He records some of the worship that will one day be offered to God on high in the last book of the Bible, Revelation. As he lets us in on that celestial worship, I think he's inviting us to join him in adoration. He gives us a preview of the glorious worship in which we will one day participate. Let's join him in that worship now ...

"Holy, holy, holy
is the Lord God Almighty,
who was, and is, and is to come.

You are worthy, our Lord and God,
to receive glory and honor and power,
for you created all things,
and by your will they were created
and have their being."
—Revelation 4:8,11

"Worthy is the Lamb, who was slain,
to receive power and wealth and wisdom and strength
and honor and glory and praise!…
To him who sits on the throne and to the Lamb
be praise and honor and glory and power,
for ever and ever!"
—Revelation 5:12-13

If you know a contemporary song that sets music to those words, don't hesitate to sing it now!

"Amen!
Praise and glory
and wisdom and thanks and honor
and power and strength
be to our God for ever and ever,
Amen!"
—Revelation 7:12

"Great and marvelous are your deeds,
*   Lord God Almighty.*
Just and true are your ways,
*   King of the ages.*
Who will not fear you, O Lord,
*   and bring glory to your name?*
For you alone are holy.
All nations will come
*   and worship before you,*
for your righteous acts have been revealed."
—Revelation 15:3-4

KING OF KINGS AND LORD OF LORDS
—Revelation 19:16

If you have a recording of the "Hallelujah Chorus" in Handel's *Messiah* this might be a great time to listen to it again. And sing along!

Perhaps, because of the pressures or griefs in your life or foreboding about an ominous future, you do not feel like joining John in such worship. Your heart is just too heavy to sing joyfully. How could John be so exuberant in his praise when throughout the book he so incessantly strikes the solemn gong of doom? The secret is found at the beginning of his book:

On the Lord's Day I was in the Spirit, and I heard behind me a loud voice like a trumpet (Rev. 1:10).

After this I looked, and there before me was a door standing open in heaven. And the voice I had first heard speaking to me like a trumpet said, "Come up here, and I will show you what must take place after this." At once I was in the Spirit (Rev. 4:1-2).

John the Seer was "in the Spirit." To be in the Spirit, no matter how threatening the circumstances, is to overflow with praise and worship to the mighty Victor. By the Spirit we can worship always. In fact, if we're filled with the Spirit, that's exactly what we'll do! Remember, the heavy heart lifts on the wings of praise.

To love God is to worship and adore Him and to tell others incessantly about His greatness. May your worship today be part of a life filled more and more with worship of the God who is worthy of all glory, honor, and praise!

DAY 3

BEST FRIENDS

I'm sure every one of the disciples would have said, "Jesus is my best friend." They walked the village streets and dusty country roads together and listened intently as He talked. But they didn't just listen—they talked, too, and without inhibition. Such an intimate companionship! Do you ever wish you could have been there?

Jesus anticipated our loneliness. He promised to send another Comforter who would not just walk with us but who would actually be in us (John 14:15-21). He was telling us, "I love you with an everlasting love. I won't leave you orphaned."

The God kind of love is more than my love for Him expressed in worship and praise. Much more. It's His love for me! As in marriage, love is the bridge that must reach out from both sides if ever there is to be a union.

LEVELS OF INTIMACY

Consider the following six levels of intimacy in a human relationship:

1. Muriel and I met and liked one another. We'd get together occasionally and talk about things of mutual interest.
2. Then love began to fill the relationship, so each of us began to move out of our comfort zones. Muriel tried to figure out football, and I dragged myself to art museums. But still we didn't touch certain topics.
3. Eventually we reached the stage of mutual trust and agreed that nothing is off-limits—we'll fully share our hearts, no secrets.
4. Then we were married and intimacy was complete, or was it? We hadn't been together long enough to have pain. But we did enjoy one another's companionship and moments of delight.
5. We hit the difficult times and ran to embrace one another in shared agony.
6. Finally, my life came to the place where fun wasn't all that fun if Muriel wasn't with me; heartache was almost unbearable if she didn't share it. It was as if the other was there even when she/he wasn't; and when we were apart, the desire to be together became a gnawing hunger. Outsiders couldn't disturb the freedom and comfort between us.

Reflect on your relationship to God and, in the list above, put a check by the level of human relationship that parallels most closely your present experience of God.

Actually, there's a seventh level, a closer intimacy than Muriel and I could ever experience, because we're finite humans. Such intimacy can be experienced only with God, as we shall see. Let's explore three levels of union with God.

THREE LEVELS OF UNION WITH GOD

Basic Friendship. Josh was furious about his Christmas gift. It wouldn't work right. Suddenly, he threw it across the room where it crashed through a valued lamp shade. In the following months, Josh tried–with varying degrees of success–to bridle his temper. Ours was an unlikely friendship. He was only three, and our conversations didn't rise to great heights.

Josh taught me something about God and me–another unlikely friendship. I certainly can't converse on God's level. Sometimes I get angry with a gift God gives me. I sometimes say a bad thing, do a foolish thing, or enjoy a sinful thing.

Through it all God continues to love me. Against the backdrop of this lopsided love affair, Jesus calls us friends (John 15:15). He doesn't call us slaves or even children, both of which we are, but friends!

Josh has been my friend now for several years. He's especially hard to resist when a smile breaks across that pixie face as he offers a gift of atonement (usually some well-loved toy), hugs me tight, and says, "Sorry, Pawpaw." Josh moved to a distant city and entered first grade. A few weeks later I received a letter, the first from my buddy: "I Luv Yoo Yoo Are The Bes Fred I everhad."

It's so good to be best friends with God! But there's a level of intimacy above basic friendship.

Daily Companionship. My youngest son Kent has always had a prayer life I envied–from his high school days on. But I wasn't prepared for what I discovered when he recently came to stay with me for six weeks. I hadn't finished cleaning the guest room when he arrived; so when he went out for an errand, I finished. As I picked up a scrap of paper from the floor, I noticed a cryptic message: "Get up at 3:00 a.m. every day and stay awake." Sure enough, every morning at 3:00 the light in the kitchen would go on and stay on. It was good for me to know what was happening; that way I wouldn't intrude on Kent's time with his beloved.

Jesus is his beloved. In reporting to the students and faculty of Columbia International University on his work among the slum dwellers of Calcutta, Kent reminisced about his student days. He told of how he decided not to get married, on the advice of the apostle Paul (1 Cor. 7), so he could serve God more fully. Then he said, "I was walking down the campus road toward the dining hall when I was met by a parade of dating couples, out for an evening stroll. They seemed so happy. Then the thought struck me, *They can't even imagine what a great time God and I are having.*"

Later I talked with him about his prayer life and how, in my judgment, he was jeopardizing his health with all his fasting and prayer. He seemed so God-intoxicated. "Dad," he said, "I think I have more fun with God than you do!" I'm afraid he does.

> **Have you thought about how God-intoxicated you are? Since beginning your study of *Life in the Spirit* has your daily time with God ...**

❑ increased in length
❑ stayed about the same
❑ decreased

215

⟳ **Has your sense of God's companionship in that daily time ...**

❑ grown closer, more real
❑ stayed about the same
❑ grown more distant and formal

Constant Awareness of His Presence. At age 20 I discovered the motto of Frederic Franson, the pioneer who founded 5 Scandinavian mission agencies at the close of the 19th century. Franson's life theme was *CCCC*–Constant Conscious Communion with Christ. The moment I heard it my heart leaped. "That's what I want, Lord!" I cried out. And God heard my prayer. For about 2 months that summer I was not only always conscious of the Lord's presence, I seemed to be constantly, consciously conversing with God. But then the feeling of closeness slipped away.

I pled for the return of that experience, but it never came back. I'm not sure why He gave me that foretaste of heaven nor why He withdrew it. Was it something like Paul's brief visit to "the third heaven," not intended to be permanent, not designed for daily human experience? Yet the mystics down the ages testify of a life-pattern of constant conscious communion with Christ. Perhaps God would give you that high level of intimacy if you sought it. Don't let my experience discourage you.

In the meantime, until that day when we all have such a life-filling experience in His presence, I can promise something very special: a constant relationship of intimacy, an uninterrupted awareness of the Spirit's presence.

⟳ **What is your level of intimacy with God today?**

❑ basic friendship
❑ a special time of intimate companionship every day
❑ constant awareness of His presence

Don't settle for "a superficial relationship with a friendly stranger," as someone has described it. Don't be afraid of intimacy. He won't reject you because you don't measure up. No one measures up. He loves you and longs for your companionship. Run and embrace Him–He's waiting, eagerly.

DAY 4

CONSUMMATION

We've considered several levels of intimacy, but the highest and best lies ahead. The grand climax will be all the Spirit's work in us consummated as we find ourselves "filled to all the fullness of God." That, too, will be the Spirit's work.

THE SPIRIT'S LAST GREAT ACTIVITY

⟳ **In the margin write Romans 8:11, one of this week's memory verses.**

Some understand this verse to refer to spiritual rather than physical resurrection. They understand the verse to say Holy Spirit power energizes the spiritually dead to make them alive in Christ. The immediate context of the passage does speak of that regenerating work of the Spirit, but Paul addresses Christians here, not the spiritually dead. He assures them that the Spirit will yet give life to their physical bodies.

I believe, therefore, that Paul speaks here of the final resurrection. A clear parallel and a connection does exist with the already-accomplished spiritual resurrection. But the final resurrection is a major theme of the last half of the eighth chapter of Romans. I believe Paul is inserting a preview of that in our memory verse. Our physical resurrection is the grand climax of all the Spirit's work in us. It is the consummation of all He intended from the start: God's image fully restored, and union with God fully consummated.

Here's John's beautiful description of that occasion:

> *Then I heard what sounded like a great multitude, like the roar of rushing waters and like loud peals of thunder, shouting:*
>
> *"Hallelujah!*
> *   For our Lord God Almighty reigns.*
> *Let us rejoice and be glad and give him glory!*
> *For the wedding of the Lamb has come,*
> *   and his bride has made herself ready.*
> *Fine linen, bright and clean,*
> *   was given her to wear."*
> *(Fine linen stands for the righteous acts of the saints.)*
>
> *Then the angel said to me, "Write: 'Blessed are those who are invited to the wedding supper of the Lamb!'" And he added, "These are the true words of God."*
> —Revelation 19:6-9

WHAT A DAY THAT WILL BE!

In a sense we're already married to God, united with Him forever. But in another sense, the consummation of that marriage is yet to be. You might call our present relationship an engagement and the Holy Spirit our engagement ring. God "set his seal of ownership on us, and put his Spirit in our hearts as a deposit, guaranteeing what is to come" (2 Cor. 1:22; see also 5:5 and Eph. 1:14). Exciting as the engagement has been, our present experience of God will fade into the dim recesses of memory when the marriage is consummated! The climax of all the Spirit's work is to usher us into the banquet hall to introduce us to our beloved where we shall meet Him "face to face" (1 Cor. 13:12). The Spirit's work will be complete when "we shall be like him, for we shall see him as he is" (1 John 3:2).

Many of God's promises about eternity will be fulfilled when we die and are instantly with Him. Others will be fulfilled when the bride, the church, is completed and Jesus returns to take her to the final celebration. Since the Bible doesn't explain all the delightful mystery of it, I'm not sure exactly what will happen when; no one knows. What a glorious anticipation! As I think about eternity, here are some of the things I look forward to:

• Jesus. Seeing Him, feeling His warm embrace, being united with Him in a union so intimate I don't have the capacity even to imagine.

• The Father. Seeing Him smile and hearing Him say, "Well done." I want to tell Him how grateful I am for His love for me, so great He let His own Son go for me. In fact, for the first time I'll be able to worship Him as I have always longed to, but never seemed able.

- The Spirit. I want to tell Him in detail how deeply I appreciate all He's done for me.
- Being reunited with my son Bob, my parents, and other loved ones who got there before me, and, especially, my precious Muriel fully restored.
- All sorrow, pain, sickness, weakness, sin, and failure gone forever.
- Jesus' smile when I give Him my wedding present—my life investment for Him.
- Being transformed into the likeness of Jesus, the spiral complete.

Do you resonate with any of those hopes? What do you most look forward to? Number my list in the order of your own priority, leaving out any you don't anticipate and adding any I haven't mentioned.

NOT EVERYONE WANTS TO DIE

Not everyone anticipates that day. One of my best friends, John, was dying an agonizing death of bone cancer. When I visited him in his home he said, "Robertson, you probably want to go to heaven, but I don't. I've got too many things planned to get done for God right here on earth." He declined rapidly, and soon I heard he had made his final trip to the hospital. I rushed to the hospital, and found his room. When I entered John said, "Robertson, I've got something to tell you about death. It takes too long." I reached his bedside and groped for words of comfort, but he continued: "I can't figure out the purpose of all this pain and suffering."

I responded, "I haven't got it all figured out either. But I do notice one thing it's done for you. A few weeks ago you didn't want to go to be with Jesus. Now you can hardly wait."

John grimaced. "You're right, pal." A few hours later he had his desire.

As you think about death or, better, about that grand celebration at the end of time, how do you feel about it? Check the one that is nearest to how you feel.

- ❏ I'm with John. I'm happy to contemplate that last great day and glad I'll be there, but I'm in no hurry; I've got too much important and fun things to do right here. I want to stay around as long as I can.
- ❏ I'm with Paul. I'm so excited I can hardly wait to be with Jesus. It's like my wedding day.
- ❏ I'm more than a little apprehensive about that day; I'm afraid my wedding gift to Jesus won't amount to much.
- ❏ I dread the day. What an embarrassment I'll be to Him and to myself.
- ❏ I wish it would go away; I'm not even sure I'll be there.
- ❏ other: _____

If you think the Spirit would be pleased if you felt differently from what you marked, what's gone wrong? We began our walk with the Spirit in eternity where He designed us to be God-compatible. We've kept "in step with the Spirit" (Gal. 5:25) through His work of transforming us, a spiral up from one degree of Christ's glorious likeness to another. We're headed toward the grand finale when the Spirit will complete His work. But somewhere we must have gotten out of step, because we don't rejoice with the Bridegroom in anticipating that glorious wedding day. If that's your situation, don't you want to get back in step with the Spirit?

To get back in step, turn to the table of contents of *Life in the Spirit* and see if you can identify the work of the Spirit you've missed out on. Circle the title of that unit or lesson and then re-read it. Is the Spirit gently nudging you to do something about it now in preparation for your wedding day? Do it now!

DAY 5

LIFE IN THE SPIRIT: SPIRALING UP

We've come to the conclusion of our study of *Life in the Spirit*. Perhaps for you it's not the end but a new beginning. It has been for me. As I walked through Scripture with you, I experienced many fresh encounters with the Spirit and His truth. I've been spiraling up.

As a farewell to your formal study see how many of the 10 activities of the Spirit you can recall:

_____   _____

_____   _____

_____   _____

_____   _____

_____   _____

Here they are in a scrambled list. Number them in the order we studied them.

_____ glorifying
_____ indwelling
_____ creating
_____ revealing (including both inspiration and illumination)
_____ filling
_____ redeeming
_____ transforming (sanctifying)
_____ gift-giving
_____ overcoming
_____ sending

LIFE IN THE SPIRIT: SUMMARY

We started in fellowship with God since the Spirit created us in God's very image. When we chose to abandon that love relationship and headed for hell, the Spirit gave us a great revelation of truth—of our true condition and God's salvation, so hope was born. Next the Spirit stopped our downward spiral by doing two or three things simultaneously. As we responded to His convicting work with repentance and faith, He regenerated us. He changed our very nature and came to live in us. On the course map I summarized those activities with the word *redeeming*. A part of the process of regeneration is indwelling; in some mysterious way He filled us with Himself. This began the great spiral up, the process of sanctification. Sanctification actually describes the entire process of spiraling into likeness to Christ, so on the course map I used the word *transforming*.

For most of us, however, the process of sanctification isn't an unbroken upward spiral. Through drift or rebellion we break fellowship. We grieve the Spirit. When we drift or rebel, we are no longer filled—He is no longer in full control, the dominant characteristic of our lives. Even in our rebellion God continues to offer grace and restoration; whenever we reenter the close relationship by yielding to His will and trusting Him, the process begins again.

As we trust and obey Him, the Spirit produces all kinds of Jesus fruit in us and custom designs a pattern of unique abilities so we can serve. We call that combination the fruit of the Spirit and the gifts of the Spirit. Isn't it marvelous? He provides everything to be what we were designed to be (fruit) and do what we were designed to do (gifts).

One of those gifts is the ability to win others to faith. Whether or not I have the gift of evangelism, though, the Spirit builds His church. He does it through that very church itself, body-life reproduction for world evangelization. Finally, He will one day raise our dead bodies just in time for the marriage celebration; unless we're still alive when the Bridegroom comes. But even then we'll not bypass the work of the Spirit; for we shall all be changed, in a moment, in the blink of an eye!

🌀 **Take time to read aloud or sing William Cowper's great hymn "O for a Closer Walk with God" that appears in the margin. Think deeply about the words of the hymn as you express them aloud to the Spirit.**

On the spiral below write in order from bottom to top the following characteristics in the order you have experienced spiritual growth: conscious companionship with God, obey, trust, yield, love God, become like Jesus, know God, perfect oneness with God.

Did you have difficulty? I did, because actually each of the responses reinforces the others. Anywhere you start, the others follow along. Except that "know," "yield," and "trust" must be at the beginning or none of the rest will follow. The knowing and trusting, however, will grow and so reappear in the spiral as a result of loving and companioning with God. Of course, the perfect oneness with God must come at the top of the spiral. Isn't it exciting? The Spirit transforms us as we respond and participate with Him. That's life in the Spirit!

O for a closer walk with God,
A calm and heav'nly frame,
A light to shine upon the road
That leads me to the Lamb!

Return, O holy Dove, return,
Sweet messenger of rest!
I hate the sins that made Thee
    mourn,
And drove Thee from my breast.

The dearest idol I have known,
What e'er that idol be,
Help me to tear it from Thy
    throne,
And worship only Thee.

So shall my walk be close with
    God,
Calm and serene my frame;
So purer light shall mark the road
That leads me to the Lamb.

—William Cowper, 1779

DON'T BE AFRAID!

When our children were small, I occasionally took speaking engagements away from our home base in Japan. The children developed a celebration response when I returned. One day when I came in the gate, our four-year-old Kent was playing in the back yard. He'd flooded it to make a gigantic mud pie and was thickly coated with sticky goo from head to toe. He sighted my entrance and sounded the alarm: "Daddy!" he shouted and ran to embrace me. Here I was, all dressed up in my one preacher-suit. What should I do? Oh, hug him good, of course.

His older brothers and sisters—all five of them—swarmed out to greet me. Then each dashed to prepare my welcome—one got a chair, another plugged in an electric fan. As if that weren't enough, another got a fistful of hand fans and began to vigorously churn the hot, humid air. Someone else took my mud-spattered jacket. Kent stood in the background and silently watched. Suddenly he disappeared. In the kitchen he pushed a chair over to the wall cabinet where the instant drink mix was stashed. He'd never done it before, but he poured an ample supply into a tall glass, filled it with water and anchored it with two chubby, muddy fingers grasping the rim on the inside.

What do you suppose I did? No, I couldn't pitch it out into the garden, for the little guy was watching me like a hawk.

"Did you make this all by yourself?" I asked. Standing first on one foot, then the other, twisting his grimy T-shirt up till his whole dirty midriff stuck out, he nodded two silent, quick jerks. Under his close surveillance, I took a sip of the gritty, brown drink.

Kent waited a moment and then, with eager anticipation, he asked, "Did you like it?" You think I lied, don't you? But I didn't. I told the very truth.

"Kent, I loved it!" Oh, I didn't love the gritty, brown water, but it was his love-gift to me. I loved it!

When the Lord returns and we gather to celebrate, the gift offered by the best among us will have in it a muddy finger or two. But if it's the gift of our true love, He'll be well-pleased. "I love it!" He'll say, and our joy will be complete. Our next stop on the spiral up is the marriage made in heaven. Rejoice! Don't be afraid.

Here's my journal entry for our final time together. I invite you to join me in prayer.

> **Holy Spirit of God, what a wonder You are! From beginning to end You made it all happen. And You not only do for me, You love me and want to be with me. That I can't understand, but I love You, too, and want to be Your intimate companion always. Hold me close and when I start to drift away, draw me back. I want to become all that a mortal can be, so here I am, Yours to do with as You will.**
>
> **Father and Dear Son, how can I ever express my gratitude for Your great gift at Calvary and Your great gift at Pentecost? I cannot, so I offer You all of me with the hope that it will bring You some small joy.**
>
> **On the authority of Jesus' name I come. Amen.**

LIFE IN THE SPIRIT

GROUP COVENANT

I, _____

covenant with my Life in the Spirit group to do the following:

1. Complete the study of the *Life in the Spirit* workbook each week before the group session.
2. Pray regularly for my fellow group members.
3. Participate in all group sessions unless urgent circumstances beyond my control prevent my attendance. When unable to attend, I will make up the session at the earliest possible time with the group leader or group member assigned.
4. Participate openly and honestly in the group sessions.
5. Keep confidential any personal matters shared by others in the group.
6. Be patient with my Christian brothers and sisters and my church as God works to make us what He wants us to be. I will trust God to convince others of His will. I will not try to manipulate or pressure others to do what I think is best. I will simply bear witness of what I sense God may be saying to us and watch to see how the Spirit uses that witness.
7. Pray at least weekly for my pastor and my church.

Others: _____

_____

_____

_____

_____

Signed: _____ Date: _____

Life in the Spirit Group Members:

_____   _____

_____   _____

_____   _____

_____   _____

_____   _____

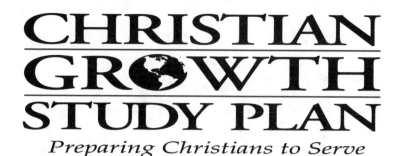

CHRISTIAN GROWTH STUDY PLAN

Preparing Christians to Serve

In the **Christian Growth Study Plan (formerly Church Study Course),** this book *Life in the Spirit* is a resource for course credit in the subject area Women's Enrichment of the Christian Growth category of diploma plans. To receive credit, read the book, complete the learning activities, show your work to your pastor, a staff member or church leader, then complete the following information. This page may be duplicated. Send the completed page to:

Christian Growth Study Plan
127 Ninth Avenue, North, MSN 117
Nashville, TN 37234-0117
FAX: (615)251-5067

For information about the Christian Growth Study Plan, refer to the current Christian Growth Study Plan Catalog. Your church office may have a copy. If not, request a free copy from the Christian Growth Study Plan office (615/251-2525).

Life in the Spirit
COURSE NUMBER: CG-0259

PARTICIPANT INFORMATION

Social Security Number (USA ONLY)

Personal CGSP Number*

Date of Birth (MONTH, DAY, YEAR)

Name (First, Middle, Last)

Home Phone

Address (Street, Route, or P.O. Box)

City, State, or Province

Zip/Postal Code

CHURCH INFORMATION

Church Name

Address (Street, Route, or P.O. Box)

City, State, or Province

Zip/Postal Code

CHANGE REQUEST ONLY

☐ Former Name

☐ Former Address

City, State, or Province

Zip/Postal Code

☐ Former Church

City, State, or Province

Zip/Postal Code

Signature of Pastor, Conference Leader, or Other Church Leader

Date

New participants are requested but not required to give SS# and date of birth. Existing participants, please give CGSP# when using SS# for the first time. Thereafter, only one ID# is required. **Mail to:** Christian Growth Study Plan, 127 Ninth Ave., North, Nashville, TN 37234-0117. Fax: (615)251-5067

Rev. 6-99

Learn the Secrets of Intimacy with God

You were created for fellowship with God. Through prayer you communicate with the Father and deepen your relationship with Him.

This classic, in-depth study will lead you to develop intimacy with God and effectiveness in your prayer life. As you examine biblical examples and apply biblical prayer principles, your relationship with God will grow fresher every day.

Disciple's Prayer Life will teach you how to—
- develop a richer prayer life;
- discover the unique way God relates to you;
- give thanks and worship God;
- use Scripture in prayer and make decisions based on biblical principles;
- pray with others;
- confess sin;
- apply principles of asking;
- deal with unanswered prayer and hindrances to prayer;
- pray for yourself, others, and missions;
- develop a prayer ministry;
- continue growing in fellowship with God.

No matter where you are in your walk with God, you can develop a deeper, more intimate relationship with Him. *Disciple's Prayer Life* will show you the way. (ISBN 0-7673-3494-9)

To obtain more information or to place an order, contact Customer Service Center, MSN 113; 127 Ninth Avenue, North; Nashville, TN 37234-0113; Phone (800) 458-2772; Fax (615) 251-5933; Email *customerservice@lifeway.com*; order online *www.lifeway.com*.